TWEETS AND THE STREETS

Social Media and Contemporary Activism

Paolo Gerbaudo

PlutoPress
www.plutobooks.com

First published 2012 by Pluto Press
345 Archway Road, London N6 5AA

www.plutobooks.com

Distributed in the United States of America exclusively by
Palgrave Macmillan, a division of St. Martin's Press LLC,
175 Fifth Avenue, New York, NY 10010

British Library Cataloguing in Publication Data
A catalogue record for this book is available from the British Library

ISBN   978 0 7453 3249 9   Hardback
ISBN   978 0 7453 3248 2   Paperback
ISBN   978 1 8496 4800 4   PDF eBook
ISBN   978 1 8496 4802 8   Kindle eBook
ISBN   978 1 8496 4801 1   EPUB eBook

Library of Congress Cataloging in Publication Data applied for

Designed and produced for Pluto Press by Chase Publishing Services Ltd
Typeset from disk by Stanford DTP Services, Northampton, England
Simultaneously printed digitally by CPI Antony Rowe, Chippenham, UK and
Edwards Bros in the United States of America

Contents

Acknowledgements

As happens with most academic books, this volume has been the result not only of a solitary work of writing up, but also of conversations with dozens of people with whom I have exchanged ideas, developed discussions, and constructed common understandings. I am deeply indebted to them all. First and foremost I have to acknowledge the availability and kindness of the 80 interviewees who offered their testimonies and whose names are recorded in the Appendix. These interviews were precious occasions for getting to know passionate people who have dedicated their energy to the fight for democracy, economic equality and social justice. I also want to thank all the people who kindly made themselves available to provide their comments and advice. Among them the biggest thanks goes to Alice Mattoni, Patrick McCurdy and Iman Hamam, who were veritable travel companions during the writing up and editing phase of the book and who were always ready to offer thoughtful comments and constructive criticisms.

I must also express my gratitude to Des Freedman, Samuel Toledano, Jo Littler, Alex Taylor, Nicola Montagna, Ben Little, Joseph Hill, and Emad el-Din Aysha for having provided comments on draft chapters. I would like to acknowledge the support and sympathy of my colleagues at Middlesex University during the early stages of developing the book, and in particular Andrew Goffey, Sarah Baker, Sophia Drakopoulos, Constantina Papoulias and Vivienne Francis. My thanks also go to my colleagues in the Sociology, Anthropology, Psychology and Egyptology (SAPE) Department at the American University in Cairo, in particular to Amy Holmes, Mohammed Tabishat, Ivan Panovic and Mona Abaza. Besides my colleagues Alex Foti and Shimri Zameret, and many other friends provided me with useful insights during the writing up. I would like to acknowledge the help given by some of my interviewees who were very generous in supplying me with further contacts. I am indebted to Sofia de Roa for many of the contacts in Spain, to Shane Gill for helping me secure interviews with Occupy organisers, and to Hannah el-Sissi for some of the interviews conducted in Egypt. I would also like to express my gratitude to Mariluz Congosto for making available a selection of tweets by the indignados movement, and to the Arab hacking group R-shief for sharing their dataset of tweets on Occupy and on the Arab Spring. My last and most important thanks go to my partner Lara Pelaez Madrid, for having accompanied me on the many research trips I undertook in preparation of this book, and for having supported me through the difficulties of the final editing stage.

The research was made possible by the Middlesex University Assistant Dean's fund to conduct research in Spain and in Egypt, and by a British Academy research grant for conducting research into new media and politics. Without the funds thus made available it would have been impossible to cover the substantial costs incurred in conducting the fieldwork which constituted the basis for this book.

Introduction

Ok so #Tahrir anyone?
@Sarahngb – 15 October 2011

On the 29th of July 2011, I happened to be witness to the brutal eviction of the protest camp at Tahrir square in central Cairo. Erected on the 8th of July, the camp was the third in a series of mass sit-ins that had re-occupied the square since the fall of Hosni Mubarak, each publicised by its own Twitter hashtag carrying the date of its beginning: #Apr8, #Jun28 and #Jul8. Observing the scene from behind one of the green metal fences encircling the square, I saw platoons of soldiers trashing the tents erected on the roundabout. A group of around 200 protesters re-gathered on the side of the square nearest to the Mogamma, the grey headquarters of Egyptian bureaucracy, their bodies densely packed on the asphalt. After a few minutes the troops advanced in square formation and made their way into the crowd, their wooden sticks swinging in the air. The protestors resisted the first onslaught. But then came a second, and a third. The crowd began dispersing, fleeing the soldiers alone or in small groups.

A few metres to my left I noticed a young Egyptian woman standing by the fence. She was in her early twenties, with long curly black hair and a pair of designer glasses. I guessed she was from an upper-class area of Cairo like Maadi, Mohandessin or Nasr City. She seemed as distressed as I was at witnessing the attack without being able (or daring enough) to raise a finger to stop it. Reaching into her bag she extracted what I immediately recognised as an HTC phone, the kind with a sliding keyboard, a sort of weird marriage between an iPhone and a Blackberry. She aimed the phone's camera at the square and snapped a picture of yet another violent arrest. Then she started tapping her fingers on the keyboard. She stared for a second at the screen before clicking the 'enter' button and then furtively put the phone away as though worried she might be noticed and targeted. At that point a group of protesters ran towards us, fleeing from a group of military policemen chasing them. We both vanished from the square, running in opposite directions.

While writing this book I have often thought back to this scene. It seems to encapsulate so much about the contemporary protest experience, with its intersection of 'tweets and the streets', of mediated communication and physical gatherings in public spaces. I never quite managed to track down the tweet the young Egyptian woman sent that day. So I was left wondering: What might she have written in her message? Was she simply reporting what was going in the square? Or was she inciting her 'tweep'[1] comrades to join in a counter-attack against the police? Or suggesting the best way to elude security when approaching the square? Or was she just recording a protest souvenir to show off to her friends? Who would be reading her tweet, and how would they be reacting? Would they be inspired to join the protests, or would they be scared away? Who was she anyway? Some kind of 'leader', or a 'follower'? And did all this tweeting and re-tweeting really matter when it came to influencing collective action, mobilising and coordinating people on the ground? Or was all this just an activist delusion: a way of feeling part of the action while in fact always standing on the sidelines?

These and similar questions have haunted me during the ethnographic fieldwork conducted in the course of researching this book. Visiting the places in which different social movements blossomed during 2011 – earning it the label 'year of the protester', as celebrated by *Time* magazine[2] – from Cairo, to Madrid, Barcelona and New York, I have witnessed manifold manifestations of activist's use of social media. Within these 'popular' movements – popular because they appeal to the 'people' (Laclau, 2005) as the majority of the population in their home countries – activists have made full use of that 'group of Internet-based applications ... that allow the creation and exchange of user-generated content' (Kaplan and Haenlein, 2010: 60). Where self-managed activist internet services like Indymedia and activist mailing lists were the media of choice of the anti-globalisation movement, contemporary activists are instead shamelessly appropriating corporate social networking sites like Facebook and Twitter.

Commenting on this enthusiastic adoption of social media, pundits and journalists have readily resorted to expressions like 'the Facebook revolution'[3] or 'the Twitter revolution'. Yet, this celebration of the emancipatory power of communication technologies has not been much help in understanding *how* exactly the use of these media reshapes the 'repertoire of communication' (Mattoni, 2012) of contemporary movements and affects the experience of participants. One danger when approaching the field of social media is the possibility of being overwhelmed by the sheer abundance and diversity of the communicative practices they channel. As we will see in the course of this book, uses of social media among activists are almost as diverse as their venues. They are often used as a means of representation, a tool of 'citizen journalism' employed to elicit 'external attention' (Aday et al., 2010), for example in the use of web live-stream services like Bambuser,[4] or YouTube videos documenting episodes of police brutality. Yet what is more interesting, and what has possibly brought them so much attention, is their 'internal' or 'local' use: their use as *means of organisation* of collective action, and more specifically as *means of mobilisation* in the crucial task of 'getting people on the streets' (Lievrouw, 2009: 154).

The mobilising role of social media, which constitutes the topic of this book, has already been duly noticed by a number of pundits and journalists commenting on the popular movements of 2011. Tweeting on the 27th of January about the Egyptian revolution, American author Jared Cohen cited one Egyptian activist summing up activist media use as follows: 'facebook used to set the date, twitter used to share logistics, youtube to show the world, all to connect people'. In his flamboyant account of what he calls the 'revolutions of 2009–2011', BBC journalist Paul Mason listed the functionalities of the 'full suite of information tools' used by contemporary activists:

> Facebook is used to form groups, covert and overt—in order to establish those strong but flexible connections. Twitter is used for real-time *organisation* and news dissemination, bypassing the cumbersome 'newsgathering' operations of the mainstream media. YouTube and the Twitter-linked photographic sites— Yfrog, Flickr and Twitpic—are used to provide instant evidence of the claims being made. Link-shorteners like bit.ly are used to disseminate key articles via Twitter. (Mason 2010: 75)

But what difference do social media really make to the ways in which participants are mobilised and protest is organised, besides trivial operations like 'fixing dates' and 'opening groups'? Is their importance merely 'technical', as quotations like this one seem to suggest?

To understand the social significance of media practices and of social media in particular it is helpful to historicise things, contrasting contemporary forms of communication with past ones. In a way, modern media have always constituted a channel through which social movements not only communicate but also organise their actions and mobilise their constituencies. One need only think here of Lenin's classic description of the Party newspaper as 'propagandist', 'agitator' and 'organiser' of collective action (Lenin 1902/1969: 156). Social media can be seen as the contemporary equivalent of what the newspaper, the poster, the leaflet or direct mail were for the labour movement. They are means not simply to convey abstract opinions, but also to give a shape to the way in which people come together and act together, or, to use the metaphorical language that will be adopted in this book, to *choreograph* collective action. With its hierarchical and centralised structure the Party newspaper appeared a perfect reflection of the Leninist vanguard Party. So what do social media like Twitter and Facebook, with their constitutive evanescence and multiplicity, tell us about the movements that have adopted them as key means of communication? How do the communicative practices constructed through them reflect the forms of organisation of contemporary social movements?

To explore these questions, I will undertake a qualitative analysis of activist use of social media in the popular movements of 2011, focusing on their role as means of mobilisation of collective action. The volume proceeds chronologically, beginning with the Arab Spring and the use of social media during the Egyptian uprising, and looking in particular at the role played by the cosmopolitan 'Facebook youth' as the leading force in the mobilisation. It then goes on to discuss the adaptation and transformation of the 'Tahrir model' in the context of the 'indignados' in Spain, documenting the way in which organisers used social media before and after the watershed protests of the 15th of May (15-M). Finally, I will discuss the use of social media in the mobilisation of the Occupy movement in the US, and the tortuous interaction between online communication and on-the-ground organising which characterised the emergence of this movement. These different social movements are analysed diachronically, tracing the different stages of their development, reconstructing the role played by social media in each of them, and looking at their interaction with other forms of communication.

Empirically, I draw on a body of ethnographic research comprising 80 interviews with activists and many observations of public gatherings mainly conducted in Egypt, Spain and the US. This methodology allows an appreciation of the use of social media, not from the 'God's-eye view' offered by quantitative research with its surveys of participants' media use and its info-visualisations of Twitter traffic, but from the 'ground-level' view of the activists and participants using these tools. The book was initially set to incorporate case studies from Greece, Tunisia and the UK, where I have also conducted fieldwork. I eventually decided for reasons of space to drop these additional case studies. However, the interviews conducted in these countries have been used as background data to verify the general applicability of the claims I am developing, and I will refer directly to some of them in the comparative Chapter 5.

Here in the introduction I will explain the gist of my approach to the study of social media and activism – an approach developed in opposition not only to the unbounded techno-optimism of social media theorists such as Clay Shirky, but also to the techno-pessimism of commentators like Evgeniy Morozov and Malcom Gladwell. I argue that both positions are characterised by an essentialist vision of social media as being automatically either suitable or unsuitable as means of mobilisation. These approaches tend to look at social media in the abstract, without due attention to their intervention in specific local geographies of action or to their embeddedness in the culture of the social movements adopting them. I propose that the crucial element in understanding the role of social media in contemporary social movements is their interaction with and mediation of emerging forms of public gatherings and in particular the mass sit-ins which have become the hallmark of contemporary popular movements. My claim is that social media have been chiefly responsible for the construction of a *choreography of assembly* as a process of symbolic construction of public space which facilitates and guides the physical *assembling* of a highly dispersed and individualised constituency. Together with the stress on the imbrication between media and locality which animates this book, my key contention is that the introduction of social media in social movements does not simply result in a situation of absolute spontaneity and unrestrained participation. On the contrary, influential Facebook admins and activist tweeps become 'soft leaders' or choreographers, involved in setting the scene, and constructing an emotional space within which collective action can unfold.

BEYOND TWITTER FETISHISM

During the clashes between protesters and police in central Cairo in December 2011, not far from where I witnessed the first scene portrayed in this book, I noticed some graffiti in which the Twitter blue bird was overlaid by a red back-lashed circle. Below it figured the script 'the revolution will not be tweeted', a pun on Gil Scott-Heron's famous song-title 'The Revolution Will Not be Televised', the last verse of which proclaims that instead 'it will be live'. It is not hard to understand why many activists in Egypt and beyond feel the need to reiterate this opinion regarding tweeting (first uttered by techno-pessimist Malcom Gladwell [2010]), given the extent to which the Egyptian revolution has been banalised as a 'social media revolution' by news media obsessed with the latest technology fad.

At least since the anti-globalisation movement's adoption of the internet as a major tool, news media have constantly approached the emergence of any new movement in terms of the technology defining it. This discourse reached a climax with the blossoming of the Arab Spring in 2011. From CNN to the BBC, 'Facebook protest' or 'Twitter protest' became obsessively repeated catch-phrases during the 18-day revolution that brought down Mubarak. After Mubarak fell, Egyptian bloggers and tweeps like Gigi Ibrahim and Sandmonkey were instantly cast as the celebrities, or 'micro-celeb-rities', of an otherwise supposedly 'leaderless' social movement, while new shows like Al-Jazeera English's *The Stream* were created to applaud the emancipatory power of social media.

The celebration of the social media revolution also reached the higher echelons of politics. The long-awaited and duly prophesised emergence of a 'Facebook revolution' was read as a confirmation of the good work done by the US State department and its 'internet freedom' agenda. Topping the wave of self-congratulation in June 2011, Alec Ross, Hillary Clinton's senior adviser, called the internet the 'Che Guevara of the twenty-first century'. Thanks to the rise of new media, 'hierarchies are being levelled', he declared, in a tone that would not have been out of place coming from an anarchist. 'People at the top of those hierarchies are finding themselves on much shakier ground.'[5] The message was clear: the revolution had been made in Cairo, but it would not have taken place without the latest technologies engineered in Silicon Valley. Mark Zuckerberg (Facebook CEO) and Jack Dorsey (Twitter CEO) may not themselves have been on the barricades, but they were operative in the virtual supply lines, as it were.

No one has contributed more to this techno-celebratory discourse within academia than NYU professor Clay Shirky. Reading his books *Here Comes Everybody* (2008) and *Cognitive Surplus* (2010), one is drawn into a passionate apology for everything technological. Shirky argues that social media are *new* tools enabling *new* forms of group formation. These new tools are making our lives easier; making our communication faster and faster, that is, invariably better: 'as more people adopt simple social tools, and as those tools allow increasingly rapid communication, the speed of group actions also increases' (Shirky, 2008: 161). In Shirky's world, transaction costs are lowered, obstacles to collective action removed, new more efficient forms of coordination created. Now that, thanks to these new tools, 'group-forming has gone from hard to ridiculously easy, we are seeing an explosion of experiments with new groups and new kinds of groups' (Shirky, 2008: 54).

Commenting on the events in Tunisia and Egypt, Shirky has further emphasised the almighty power of social media as a means of collective action. In an article published in *Foreign Affairs*, he affirmed that 'as the communication landscape gets denser, more complex, more participatory, the networked population is gaining greater access to information, more opportunities to engage in public speech, and an enhanced ability to undertake collective action' (Shirky, 2011). Here, more information is seen as automatically entailing more possibilities for collective action. This view is also exemplified in Paul Mason's account of contemporary activism: 'one fact is clear: people know more than they used to ... they have greater and more instant access to knowledge, and reliable ways of counteracting disinformation'. 'Why should a revolution in knowledge and technology not be producing an equally dramatic – albeit diametrically opposite – change in human behaviour?' Mason asks (2012: 147).

Not everyone agrees with this seamlessly optimistic vision of the influence of social media on contemporary social movements, according to which more information automatically translates into more collective action. If Shirky is king of the techno-optimists, Belarusan scholar Evgenyi Morozov is the prince of techno-pessimists. Morozov, who had himself initially contributed to the celebratory discourse on social media, has more recently vigorously denounced the risks of 'slacktivism', or activism for slackers. For Morozov slacktivisim is 'feel good activism that has zero political or social impact' but creates 'an illusion of having a meaningful impact on the world without demanding anything more than joining a Facebook group'.[6]

In his book *The Net Delusion* (2011), Morozov has further attacked the idea that the diffusion of communication technology made in the United States will automatically bring democracy to each and every corner of the world. He criticises techno-optimistic visions holding that 'technology empowers the people who, oppressed by years of authoritarian rule, will inevitably rebel mobilising themselves through text messages, Facebook, Twitter, and whatever tool comes along each year' (Morozov, 2011: xii). As Morozov notes, social media like Twitter and Facebook are mostly used for entertainment purposes, for sharing one's own daily doings rather than for political organising. Moreover, he rightly alerts us to the fact that social media can create serious risks for activists, given the increased possibilities for monitoring by state security apparatus.

This kind of critical analysis of the impact of social media on activism has also been taken up by the *New Yorker* writer and best-selling author Malcom Gladwell, whose argument may be summed up in the Cairo graffiti formula 'the revolution will not be tweeted'. Radical political actions, Gladwell argues, require strong ties, like those identified by Stanford sociologist Doug McAdam among participants in the Freedom Summer of the 1960s in the Jim Crow South, where many were killed by segregationists (McAdam, 1988). Social media at best provides weak ties and is therefore unsuitable for revolutionary action, Gladwell argues. His position has been ridiculed by many theorists after the evidence of the role played by social media in the Arab Spring. However, at least he and Morozov have had the courage to go against the tide of boundless optimism spawned by the likes of Shirky.

In and of itself there is nothing wrong in asserting the importance of communication technologies in social movements. Scholars of the calibre of Sidney Tarrow (1994) and Benedict Anderson (1991) have eloquently discussed the influence of print technology on the rise of modern social movements. In fact, it would be hard to talk about such movements without mentioning all the technologies involved in publicising and organising their actions: flyers, posters, megaphones, banners, television, newspapers and the like. Furthermore in a society that has turned technology and science into a sort of secular religion (Ellul, 1964), it is hardly surprising that social movements are eager to experiment with the latest electronic gadget and to cast themselves as drivers of innovation.

The problem comes though, when social media are turned into a 'fetish' of collective action; in other words, when such media are endowed with mystical qualities that only obscure the work of the groups and organisers using them. When this happens, the techno-visionary discourse on social media appears as the reflection of a neoliberal ideology, incapable of understanding collective action except as the result of some sort of technological miracle fleetingly binding together egotistical individuals. Morozov and Gladwell are right to be suspicious of the excessive optimism of Shirky and his acolytes, and of the neoliberal politics which underlies it. Yet they risk committing the opposite error, assuming that a certain technology is inherently unsuited for becoming a channel of mobilisation. In so doing, they disregard the fact that the process of mobilisation cannot be reduced to the material affordances of the technologies it adopts but also involves the construction of shared meanings, identities and narratives (Johnston and Klandermans, 1995).

To elucidate these aspects of the problem, in this book I propose a cultural and phenomenological interpretation of the role of social media as means of mobilisation. Rather than being concerned merely with the efficiency or otherwise of different communication technologies, I pay attention to what activists actually do with them, to the concrete and local 'media practices' (Couldry, 2004) activists develop in their use. This approach to the study of social media allows us to recuperate so much of what gets lost in contemporary techno-deterministic accounts. In particular, I devote much attention to the role played by identity and emotions in the process of mobilisation, and their contribution in the symbolic construction of a sense of togetherness among activists. The role of emotions has been a highly neglected topic in social movement studies (Goodwin, Jasper, Polletta, 2001) and in new media studies alike (Ben-Ze'ev, 2004). Nevertheless, as I will show, this aspect is crucial to an understanding of the way in which social media contribute to the process of mobilisation in contemporary popular movements, as a reflection of their 'personal' orientation, and of the importance of sustaining an imaginary of 'friendship' and 'sharing' in their use.

SOCIAL MEDIA AND OCCUPIED SQUARES

In order to overcome the abstraction and essentialism underlying the contemporary debate about social media, we need to leave these 'new tools' aside for a moment and foreground the larger picture. It is impossible to understand the role of these media as means for mobilisation without an appreciation of the ways in which they intervene on specific social movements and of the way in which their use among activists reflects and enacts the values, identities and narratives which typify these movements. For this purpose we need to develop a situated analysis of social media practices paying attention to their interaction with other forms of communication and with the particular physical geography of those cities within which social movements have manifested themselves.

The social movements analysed in this book – the Egyptian uprising, the Spanish indignados and Occupy – are marked by a huge diversity in terms of culture, social composition and the nature of the political system in which they operate. It is evident for one thing that given the level of repression encountered by participants and the intensity of the mobilisation, the Egyptian revolution has little in common with the movements that tried to imitate it in the West. Likewise, between the indignados and Occupy the differences are huge, despite the fact that both movements target the economic crisis and the politics of austerity and have adopted similar tactics and organisational forms. Given the extent to which these movements are more national than global, they necessarily reflect the specificity of their national cultures. Notwithstanding these differences, however, there are also remarkable elements of commonality, which will allow us to see them as part of a common protest wave, sharing similar cultural traits.

First and foremost, all three social movements considered in this book are 'popular' movements: movements which appeal to the 'people' (Laclau, 2005) as the majority of the population. This feature is perfectly condensed in the Occupy slogan 'we are the 99%', but is also well represented in the Egyptian uprising with its slogan 'we are one hand', and in the indignados claim to represent 'normal' Spaniards. This majoritarian character has been clearly reflected not only in the discourse and imaginary of each movement, but also in the diversity of its constituency, encompassing many people outside of the metropolitan and idealist middle-class youth who in recent years have constituted the 'mobilisation potential' of so-called 'new social movements' (Kriesi et al., 1995). The majoritarian character of contemporary movements registers a clear difference from the anti-globalisation movement. The latter was marked by a self-conscious minoritarian identity famously expressed in Zapatista Subcomandante Marcos' statement: 'Marcos is all the exploited, marginalised, oppressed *minorities* resisting and saying "Enough".'[7] This minoritarian orientation of the anti-globalisation movement, with its emphasis on diversity and autonomy, has also had a strong influence on the scholarly analyses of new media practices in social movements, which have seen the internet as a means of producing autonomy and diversity. Arguably, however, we need to question many of the concepts developed in these analyses of the anti-globalisation movement's use of the internet, since they can be shown to have little purchase on contemporary popular movements. In fact, as we will see in the course of this book, in contrast to the 'logics of networking' (Juris, 2008) of the anti-globalisation movement, contemporary popular movements are marked by a stress on unity and the adoption of practices of 'centring' which strongly resonate with Laclau's description of 'populism' (Laclau, 2005).

The most evident manifestation of this stress on unity has been the tactic of the mass sit-in, the physical occupation of public space which often evolves into a semi-permanent protest camp. This has led some to refer to the contemporary forms of protest as 'take the squares movements'[8] or 'occupy movements'.[9] These movements have all been involved in a struggle for the 'appropriation of public space' (Lefebvre, 1974/1991), reclaiming streets and squares for public use and political organising. If Egyptian activists managed to capture the attention both of their fellow citizens and of the world at large, it was thanks less to their Facebook pages and tweets than to their physical occupation of Tahrir square in central Cairo. Inspired by that example, on the 15 May 2011, Spanish activists angered at the 'politicos y banqueros' managed to earn the respect of the majority of Spaniards, and to trigger the euphoria of thousands of 'indignants', by peacefully occupying Puerta del Sol in Central Madrid, holding it for one month, and inspiring hundreds of other occupations across the country. After the 'Arab Spring' and the 'European Summer', the 'American Autumn' has also seen a revival of the importance of public space, through the actions of the Occupy movement, whose very name carries an incitement to take back the streets from which people had been kept away during the long years of the neoliberal consensus. These occupations can be understood as *rituals of popular reunion* in which individuals are 'fused' (Alexander et al., 2006: 38) into a collective subject going under the name of the 'people' (Laclau, 2005).

The importance of the struggle for public space in contemporary social movements invites us to rethink the way in which we understand the role of new media and social media in particular. For a long time theoretical analysis has located these forms of communication in another space, a 'cyberspace' or online space as opposed to offline space. This perspective is well exemplified by Manuel Castells description of the internet as a 'network of brains' (Castells 2009), which will be fully examined in the next chapter. Counter to this disembodied view we need to understand media in general and social media in particular as processes responsible for 're-cast[ing] the organisation of the spatial and temporal scenes of social life' (Barnett in Couldry and McCarthy, 2004: 59) rather than as involved in the construction of another 'virtual' space bereft of physical geography.

It is evident that at this level there is a deep contradiction between the spatial relationships intrinsic to the two practices which have become the trademarks of contemporary protest culture: social media and protest camps. Social media like Twitter and Facebook are means of facilitating interpersonal connections across a distance. They appear as a perfect reflection of the condition of individualisation (Bauman, 2001; Beck and Beck-Gernsheim, 2002) of contemporary societies, allowing us to deal with others while not having to engage fully with them. From a spatial perspective, the experience of the protest camp, with its density of bodies in close physical proximity, appears as precisely the opposite of the kind of 'virtual proximity' (Bauman, 2003) facilitated by social media. Protest camps are sites of an intense communitarianism, as seen in the context of assemblies, and the day-to-day experience of collective eating, sleeping, cleaning and defending the space, which at first sight seems to have little in common with the experience generated by social media. What are the practices involved in connecting these two contradictory poles of contemporary collective action? How are Facebook users and tweeps transformed into 'occupiers'?

AN EMOTIONAL CHOREOGRAPHY

In this book I argue that social media have indeed had an important impact on the social movements of 2011, but that this impact is far more complex and ambiguous than gurus like Shirky would allow for. Their main contribution, among the different roles that have been assigned to them, has been at the level of the creation of what in this book I call a *choreography of assembly*. This has to be understood as a process of symbolic construction of public space, which revolves around an emotional 'scene-setting' and 'scripting' (Alexander et al., 2006: 36) of participants' physical assembling. This practice is made visible in the use of social media in directing people towards specific protest events, in providing participants with suggestions and instructions about how to act, and in the construction of an emotional narration to sustain their coming together in public space. Thus, contrary to those authors who see social media and new media generally as creating an alternative virtual- or cyber-space (for example McCaughey and

Ayers, 2003), I stress how social media use must be understood as complementing existing forms of face-to-face gatherings (rather than substituting for them), but also as a vehicle for the creation of new forms of proximity and face-to-face interaction. Countering the spatial dispersion of contemporary societies, Facebook messages and activist tweets have contributed in constructing a new sense of social centrality, focused around 'occupied squares', which are thereby transformed into *trending places*, or venues of *magnetic gatherings*, with a great power of emotional attraction.

At the same time, I also highlight the risk of seclusion that the use of social media can create, when their use is not accompanied by street-work and interaction with those on the other side of the digital divide, who, to use a recurrent activist expression, 'do not have a Facebook account'.

The adoption of the term 'choreography' crucially serves to indicate that the process of the symbolic construction of public space, for all the participatory character and techno-libertarian claims of protest culture, has not been entirely 'spontaneous' or 'leaderless' – as many pundits, journalists, activists and academics alike have suggested.[10] In a theoretical frame, my main target throughout the book is the discourse of 'horizontalism' (Juris, 2008) informed by notions like 'networks' (Castells, 1996, 2009) and 'swarms' (Negri, Hardt, 2000, 2005), which will be discussed and criticised in the following chapter. I argue that far from inaugurating a situation of absolute 'leaderlessness', social media have in fact facilitated the rise of complex and 'liquid' (Bauman, 2000) or 'soft' forms of leadership which exploit the interactive and participatory character of the new communication technologies. Influential Facebook admins and activist tweeps have played a crucial role in setting the scene for the movements' gatherings in public space, by constructing common identifications and accumulating or triggering an emotional impulse towards public assembly. Just like conventional choreographers in the field of dance, these core organisers are for the most part invisible on the stage itself. They are reluctant leaders or 'anti-leaders': leaders who, subscribing to the ideology of horizontalism, do not want to be seen as leaders in the first place but whose scene-setting and scripting work has been decisive in bringing a degree of coherence to people's spontaneous and creative participation in the protest movements.

As I will show in the course of the book, this choreographing role of social media cannot be reduced to a purely *instrumental* activity, as a quasi-military form of tactical coordination (Arquilla and Ronfeldt, 2001; Rheingold, 2003) allowing activists to become 'as free as dancers, as quick-witted as football players, as surprising as guerrillas' (as prophesied by Magnus Enzensberger in Hands, 2011: 50). Instead, and crucially, it entails the *symbolic* construction of a *sense of togetherness* and the fuelling of an *emotional tension* extending from distant mediated connections to the 'effervescence' of physical proximity (Durkheim, 1912/1965: 162). The form of 'soft' leadership conjured up by the notion of choreography is one which exploits the personal character of social media and their everyday use as a means of maintaining diffuse spheres of friendship and intimacy characterised by a vibrant emotionality. Facebook messages, tweets and blog posts have constituted not simply channels of information but also crucial *emotional conduits* through which organisers have condensed individual sentiments of indignation, anger, pride and a sense of shared victimhood and transformed them into political passions driving the process of mobilisation. These and other social media have been used to create a sense of commonality among participants essential for the mobilisation of a spatially dispersed and socially diverse constituency.

This emotional character of the choreography of assembly fundamentally reflects not simply the nature of the media used but also the popular character of these movements. Contemporary protest culture is sustained by a narrative of *popular reunion*, which revolves around a re-composition or 'fusion' of individuals in a collective subject with majoritarian ambitions. In this context, social media have acted as a means of collective aggregation, facilitating the convergence of disparate individuals around common symbols and places, signifying their unity *despite* diversity. Naturally, the downside of this construction of unity against a corrupt and brutal system is a tendency to elide the differences among participants. This is an issue which has understandably troubled some anti-authoritarian activists, especially those who 'grew up' during the years of the anti-globalisation protests around the turn of the millennium.

Having teased out the general argument to be put forward in what follows, it is worth making explicit an important political *caveat*. This book is written from a perspective highly sympathetic to the social movements under discussion. Nonetheless, one of my key concerns is to avoid becoming merely an apologist for their actions. This is in my view an error often made by activist researchers, who risk turning academic work into a celebratory homage to collective action, which neither adds a great deal to our understanding nor serves as effective movement propaganda. To the contrary, throughout the volume I am constantly concerned with identifying the contradictions, obstacles, and risks faced in the development of collective action and in the use of social media. This critical approach derives from my conviction that only by unearthing such negative elements can we hope to gain a better understanding of contemporary protest culture and thereby to aid activists in their development of new forms of communication and organisation.

CHAPTER SUMMARY

Chapter 1 develops a theoretical framework within which to analyse the significance of social media practices for contemporary popular movements. It begins by critically assessing dominant understandings of collective action, and in particular the concepts of 'swarms' and 'networks' advanced by authors such as Manuel Castells and Antonio Negri and Michael Hardt. I argue that by putting the emphasis on spontaneity and irreducible multiplicity these notions tend to obscure the lines of force inherent in the process of mobilisation, and to neglect the fact that it involves the creation of a sense of togetherness and a common identity. This is particularly relevant in the case of contemporary popular movements, as spectacularly illustrated by their creation of physical centres in public space. Counter to Castells and Hardt and Negri, I rescue the importance of the construction of a sense of unity at the core of the process of mobilisation. I propose to look at mobilisation as a process of symbolic and material gathering or assembling, staged against the situation of spatial dispersion which characterises post-industrial societies. This process is not only physical, but also involves complex forms of mediation, which I endeavour to capture through the idea of a *choreography of assembly*.

Chapter 2 discusses the role of social media in the 2011 revolution against Mubarak in Egypt. The Egyptian revolution was characterised by the protagonism of the cosmopolitan internet-connected youth, the so-called *shabab-al-Facebook* (Facebook youth). Social media, and in particular Facebook pages like Kullena Khaled Said (We are all Khaled Said) were instrumental in instigating the coming together of the movement in public space by facilitating an emotional condensation of people's anger at the regime, and acting as a springboard for street-level agitation. Once the movement hit the streets, however, these media became less important than face-to-face communication. Tahrir square, with the bodily density it attracted, came to constitute a physical beacon for the coordination of the movement, which was why the communication blackout imposed by the Mubarak regime had only a limited effect. Apart from the *shabab-al-Facebook*, I also discuss the role of another section of the movement, the activist elite of the so-called 'Twitter pashas', highlighting the risk of isolation from mainstream society entailed in their obsessive engagement with the micro-blogging site.

Chapter 3 discusses the use of social media in the indignados protest in Spain in 2011. I show how organisers used the participatory imaginary of social media and the internet to 'harvest' the individual frustration of many Spaniards who did not feel represented by any organisation, and to transform that frustration into a collective political passion made visible in public space. In the second part of the chapter I turn to the use made of social media in the attempt to sustain the protest. I argue that the occupation of Puerta del Sol, and the social media messaging radiating out of it, created a symbolic centre and focal point for maintaining a diffuse sense of participation. Twitter feeds and live-streaming video in particular generated an attraction to the square, facilitating the mobilisation of supporters and sympathisers towards this symbolic centre.

Chapter 4 analyses the use of social media as means of mobilisation in the Occupy Wall Street movement in the US. It argues that here, in contrast to the protests in Egypt and Spain, the use of social media initially failed as a rallying point for *emotional condensation* and as a symbolic springboard towards participation. The original call launched by *Adbusters* failed to secure the mobilisation of a large number of participants, and it needed a long and laborious phase of organising on the ground before the movement found some degree of coherence and a common identity. Only once activists had occupied Zuccotti Park did websites like the 'We are the 99%' Tumblr blog contribute to the construction of a popular identification and the gathering of a diverse constituency beyond the activist community. In the case of Occupy Wall Street, social media for the most part featured as an extension of the actions which were taking place on the ground. Using Twitter, activists entered into emotional conversations with sympathisers, sustaining a diffuse sense of solidarity. Only a few of these sympathisers actually joined the occupation, however, testifying to the difficulties involved in turning sympathy into actual participation.

Chapter 5 develops a comparative analysis of the use of social media as means of mobilisation and their role in the construction of a *choreography of assembly*. It highlights the fact that social media are used as the conduits for liquid organisational practices developed against the negative backdrop of bureaucratic organisations. However, this liquid and informal character of contemporary movements does not mean that they are leaderless as they often claim to be. In fact, the use of social media is paralleled by the emergence of new forms of indirect or 'choreographic' leadership, making use of the interactive and personal character of social media. In this framework, Facebook and Twitter are assigned different roles. While Facebook is used as a recruitment platform to bring new people in, Twitter is mainly employed as a means of internal coordination within the activist community. The role of both websites as organisational means is further elucidated by looking at the way in which they are used in constructing an emotional tension, creating an impetus towards and attraction to places of gathering.

The Conclusion draws together the findings emerging from the previous chapters and discusses their implications. It highlights how within contemporary social movements social media have been employed to generate a new experience of public space, staged against the background of a society of dispersion. Here I look at some of the more problematic questions emerging from the preceding discussion, including the tensions between the tactical and emotional uses of social media, between organisation and spontaneity, and between evanescence and continuity, and the question of the sustainability of contemporary social movements in their current forms.

Finally, in the Appendix, the reader will find a list of the 80 interviewees whose testimonies have been used in the book, alongside a description of the sampling and interviewing methods adopted in the course of the empirical investigation. All unattributed quotations in the text are drawn from these interviews.

1
'Friendly' Reunions: Social Media and the Choreography of Assembly

In late December 2010, a few weeks after the UK student movement had been defeated by the parliamentary approval of the proposed university reforms, the *Guardian* website became the venue for a curious war of words between young activist 'tweep' and *New Statesman* columnist Laurie Penny, and Alex Callinicos, the chair of the Trotskyist Socialist Workers Party (SWP). The exchange began on December 24th with a 'Comment is Free' column entitled 'Out with the Old Politics', in which Penny criticised the SWP and its forms of engagement with protesters:

> It is highly likely that even after a nuclear attack the only remaining life-forms will be cockroaches and sour-faced vendors of the Socialist Worker. Stunningly, the paper is still being peddled at every demonstration to young *cyber-activists* for whom the very concept of a newspaper is almost as outdated as the notion of ideological *unity* as a basis for action.[1]

In the article, Penny contrasted the young, leaderless, 'multi-headed hydra' student movement, whose favourite media were Twitter and Facebook, with the bureaucratic, centralist and sluggish Old Left, perfectly condensed in the outdated form of the newspaper and in the invasiveness of its street vendors. In his scathing reply, Callinicos criticised Penny's 'delusion of absolute novelty':

> The student protests have in many ways been highly traditional forms of collective action. True, the internet and in particular Facebook and other social media have emerged as very powerful means of communication and mobilisation. But what they have helped to deliver were demonstrations that have confronted both the forces and the symbols of the British state, not in cyberspace, but on the streets.[2]

The argument between Penny and Callinicos is illustrative of much of the public debate about the impact of social media on contemporary social movements. In Penny's interventions we encounter a series of key ideas which have come to characterise the way in which contemporary activists understand the shift from 'old' to 'new' forms of collective action facilitated by technological innovation. Because of the availability of contemporary social media, activists like Penny argue, social movements can finally become leaderless, horizontal, and spontaneous. They no longer have to face the question of *unity* so obsessively important for dinosaurs like the Socialist Workers Party, which seems to be stuck in the era of Gutenberg. Much of the scholarship produced in the last few years about the impact of new media on contemporary society, and on activism in particular, has followed a similar line of reasoning. It asserts that the internet allows for more flexible relationships, enabling individuals to interact without the need for central coordination or a sense of unity in the display of collective action. This narrative is also exemplified by Paul Mason's account of contemporary protest movements in which he describes them as 'networked' and activists as 'horizontalists'. In his book *Why It's Kicking Off Everywhere* (2012), there are 118 instances of the words 'network' or 'networked'. There is little doubt that the idea of networked protest is reaching its climax in the debate about contemporary activism. But is this really the best image with which to capture the dynamics of the mobilisation of contemporary social movements and the role played by social media in this process?

As someone who considers himself a leftist libertarian and who has participated in direct action campaigns, I have little doubt over whom to sympathise with between Penny and Mason or Callinicos. Yet, after years of hearing the terms 'horizontal', 'open' and 'networked' floated around in activist circles, I have grown increasingly suspicious not only of them but of the whole ideology of 'horizontalism' (Juris, 2008). I am convinced that this idea tends to obscure the forms of organising underlying contemporary collective action and the forms of hierarchy, or the 'hierarchy of engagement' (Haunss and Leach, 2009), which continue to exist also within informal organisations like contemporary social movements (Freeman, 1972). The ideology of horizontalism obscures the fact that the process of mobilisation is constitutively ridden with imbalances and asymmetrical relationships between those who mobilise and those mobilised, between those *leading* the process and those following (Melucci, 1996a: 345). Moreover, this idea returns to an image of collective action as a static process, and thus overlooks the dynamic character which we associate with the concept of social movements, the fact that they are 'things that move', as evident in the etymology of this sociological notion across a number of languages from Arabic to German and English.

But there is a more fundamental critique which needs to be directed at the imaginary of horizontalism with its emphasis on de-centralisation and irreducible multiplicity. The critique turns on the fact that the process of mobilisation chiefly involves a process of *gathering* or *assembling* of individuals and groups around something they share in common. While this feature is arguably common to all social movements, it is particularly important in the case of popular movements, given their attempt to mobilise a diverse and dispersed constituency under the name of the 'people'. This aspect has been spectacularly illustrated by the movements of 2011, which have constructed long-term mass sit-ins resembling rituals of popular reunion, in which a dispersed constituency is 'fused' (Alexander et al., 2006) into a collective actor. While emphasising multiplicity, network theorists have neglected the continuing importance of the question of unity and togetherness among participants. It is my contention that this question continues to be as relevant as ever in the era of social media. If anything, the multiplication of communicative channels and the individualisation of our mediated interactions, epitomised by the popularity of social media, make this question all the more urgent.

In this chapter I want to engage critically with this libertarian discourse of 'horizontalism', while developing a conceptual framework for analysing the role of social media in the process of mobilisation. The starting point is a discussion of the two main concepts which have informed this discourse: the metaphors of 'network' and 'swarm', as employed by, respectively, Manuel Castells (1996, 2009) and Hardt and Negri (2000, 2004, 2009). These authors correctly identify a condition of dispersion as the fundamental feature of spatial experience in post-industrial societies. They are opposed to the industrial imaginary of the mass and the crowd, and aim at advancing new subjectivities which escape the *reduction ad unum*: the fusion of individuals into a collective actor. The limit of this theoretical lineage is that it accepts dispersion and individualism as constitutive dimensions of contemporary society, rather than as the point of departure in the process of construction of collective action. The risks we face in a society of network and multitudes are made visible by the dispersion and seclusion which dominates the urban landscape, and by the danger of isolation inherent in social media, with their tendency to exacerbate the dynamics of social fragmentation. In and of themselves social media do not automatically allow for collective action to unfold without becoming channels for the construction of common identities and thick networks of solidarity and trust.

Building on the work of an array of authors including Zygmunt Bauman (2000, 2001), Hannah Arendt (1958), Alberto Melucci (1996), Ernesto Laclau and Chantal Mouffe (Laclau, 1996, 2005; Laclau and Mouffe, 1985), I develop an alternative understanding of the process of mobilisation, based on the notion of 'assembling' or 'gathering' rather than 'networking'. Nevertheless, the spatial dispersion which characterises contemporary social space with its 'fear of crowds' (Davis, 1992a) makes this process of gathering particularly problematic and requires complex practices of symbolic and technological mediation. In conceptualising this process of mediation of physical assembling through the notion of a *choreography of assembly*, I put forward the hypothesis that collective action is never completely spontaneous given that pure spontaneity does not exist (Gramsci, 1971: 196). Rather, in the absence of a formal organisational structure, collective action is always structured by the forms of communication responsible for 'setting the scene' for its display.

NETWORKS WITHOUT CENTRES

When contemporary activists like Laurie Penny describe social movements as leaderless, horizontal aggregates, they often do so by resorting to the language of networks. No concept has been as influential in capturing the impact of new media on activism, as testified by the sheer number of instances of the term in contemporary activist discourse. The concept in itself is not all that new. At least since the times of the French philosopher de Saint Simon, fantasising about networks of canals uniting the whole of Europe, it has been used to invoke an imaginary of modernisation and social connection (Mattelart, 1996: 85). Moreover, since the 1960s the term has been used in sociology in relation to the dynamics of groupings of friends, relatives, colleagues, and comrades. But it was the Catalan sociologist Manuel Castells who popularised the term among contemporary activists, transforming it from an analytic, almost technical, category into an overarching spatial metaphor for describing the 'morphology' of post-industrial societies. Used to express the idea of increasing flexibility and de-centralisation, the concept quickly became a standard reference point for many authors studying the impact of new media on contemporary activism (see for example, de Donk et al., 2004; McCaughey and Ayers, 2003).

In essence, the thesis proposed by Castells asserts an historical shift from the pyramidal structures characteristic of bureaucratic organisations – the company, the party, the state – to networks. For Castells the 'solid' and 'rigid' economic, social and political institutions of mass society, well described by Max Weber, have given way to more flexible and adaptable structures. This is first and foremost the consequence of technological innovation. The revolution in micro-electronics, beginning in the 1960s, created the necessary conditions for new forms of communication and cooperation which no longer required central *coordination* (Castells, 2000). Such societal shifts invest different social activities: from the economy, to social movements, to drug trafficking, the whole of society is restructured after the model of networks (Castells, 1996, 2000).

This account of the development of network technologies also has a bearing on the working of the so-called web 2.0. Social media in particular are characterised by a high degree of interactivity, and by a focus on user-generated content. Practically speaking, this means that users are also to a great extent 'producers' in communicative interactions. Social media typify the nature of the 'participatory culture' Henry Jenkins suggests is an underlying feature of the contemporary media landscape, in which people are no longer simply positioned at the receiving end of processes of communication (Jenkins, 2006). Castells has described this media landscape as dominated by a paradigm of 'self mass-communication' in which individuals and groups can broadcast their messages to large audiences (Castells, 2009: 416). For Castells, the advent of mass self-communication carries the promise of autonomy from bureaucratic structures and increasing scope for political and social engagement from below.

This evolutionary narrative is evidently coloured by an anti-authoritarian spirit. Castells' discussion resonates deeply with the emphasis on self-determination and self-management put forward by the cultural movements of the 1960s and '70s. Castells himself notes that, apart from the rise of new technologies, the 'networking paradigm' was informed by the libertarian and participatory culture inaugurated by new social movements such as environmentalism, feminism, and the student movement (Castells, 2004). Crucial in this context is the emphasis on horizontality and decentralisation, since 'by definition a network has no center' (Castells, 2000: 15).

For Castells, these new forms of networked cooperation emancipate social groups from the top-down logic of command and from the need for leaders.

Given this anti-authoritarian twist, it is not surprising that the language of networks came to be enthusiastically adopted by activist groups within the emerging anti-globalisation (or more positively 'alter-globalisation') movement. David Graeber was probably right when he observed that even though many in the movement would not have defined themselves as anarchists, nevertheless 'anarchism is the heart of the movement, its soul; the source of most of what's new and hopeful about it' (Graeber, 2002: 2). Since its inception with the protests in Seattle in 1999, the anti-globalisation movement was marked by a libertarian emphasis on self-organisation and direct action. For these activists, the imaginary of networks came to provide a useful term of reference for defining flexible and anti-hierarchical forms of organisation, at a time marked by the diffusion of the internet as a major platform for protest communications.

Emails, listservs, Indymedia websites, and web-forums became the communicative toolkit of a 'new way of doing politics', whose fundamental logic was 'networking' (Juris, 2008). In a 2002 article published in the *New Left Review*, the Canadian campaigning journalist Naomi Klein described the relationship between the movement and the internet in the following terms:

> Rather than a single movement, what is emerging is thousands of movements intricately linked to one another, much as 'hotlinks' connect their websites on the Internet. This analogy is more than coincidental and is in fact key to understanding the changing nature of political organising. Although many have observed that the recent mass protests would have been impossible without the Internet, what has been overlooked is how the communication technology that facilitates these campaigns is shaping the movement in its own image. Thanks to the Net, mobilisations are able to unfold with sparse bureaucracy and minimal hierarchy; forced consensus and laboured manifestos are fading into the background, replaced instead by a culture of constant, loosely structured and sometimes compulsive information-swapping. (Klein, 2002: 4)

The anti-globalisation movement came to be seen (and to see itself) as a reflection of its communicative structure. What in previous movements would have been called groups, associations or collectives, now often took the name of networks so as to express their adherence to this new model of organising.

The level of popularity of the network paradigm within the anti-globalisation movement can be appreciated by reading the ethnographic account produced by Jeffrey Juris, himself a student of Manuel Castells. Developing his analysis from the standpoint of activist groups in Barcelona, and analysing the protests in Prague and Genoa, Juris affirms the 'networking logic' at the core of the politics of these new movements, who practice a leaderless politics based on consensual decision-making and participation. Crucial for sustaining these values is an investment in the production and circulation of information, as testified by practices such as 'Indymedia, culture jamming, guerrilla communication, and electronic civil disobedience' (Juris, 2008: 284). For Juris, 'expanding and diversifying networks is more than a concrete organisational objective; it is also a highly valued political goal'. Networks are 'an emerging ideal', the pre-figuration of a society which is 'self-produced, self-developed, and self-managed', a model for re-organising society in the direction of an 'informational utopics' (Juris, 2008: 15).

The problem with this analysis is that while being a faithful reflection of activist discourse it risks accepting the latter at face-value as an empirical description of what happens 'on the ground'. The space of participation of the anti-globalisation movement, or at least of those groups which Juris calls 'networked movements', is described as an 'open' and 'horizontal' one. Juris himself admits that everything is not as smooth and friction-less as these terms might suggest, and that there are always obstacles which limit radical possibilities (Juris, 2008: 9). Yet he seems to overlook the fact that the continuing presence of hierarchies is less an isolated anomaly to be superseded with perseverance and good will than an ineliminable element of the kind of informal politics nurtured by direct action groups.

We know from activist scholars like the feminist writer Jo Freeman that the informal types of organisation which have dominated the so-called 'new social movements' since the 1960s, and of which contemporary 'networked movements' can be considered the inheritors, develop their own kinds of informal hierarchies. Despite the refusal to have formal leaders and clear organisational structures they nevertheless often come to be dominated by narrow and exclusive cliques formed around friendship networks. Structureless-ness, understood as a healthy reaction to 'overstructured societies', becomes a 'goddess' in its own right (Freeman, 1972: 2). In the absence of formal organisational structures, exclusive friendship networks become channels of coordination within social movements, breeding 'new informal elites' (Freeman, 1972: 3). The ideology of structurelessness thus becomes an astute way of side-stepping the question of leadership, and allows the de facto leaders to remain unaccountable because invisible. While I sympathise with Juris' critique of Leninist politics, I am convinced that his reliance on almost metaphysical concepts such as 'openness' and 'horizontality' constitutes an ideological obstacle for understanding the dynamics of the contemporary space of participation.

This intellectual impasse is to a great extent the result of that abstraction from material and local contexts of interaction which the language of networks carries with itself. As Kevin McDonald rightly notes, this discourse 'expels the body and the senses', neglecting the constitutive immersion of individuals in a physical environment. For him, 'networks appear disembodied and too located in a culture of simultaneity', and convey a static image of social movements insofar as 'typically researchers attempt to "map" networks in a way that disembodies them, and locates them in a one-dimensional time' (McDonald, 2006: 37). The accusation to be levelled at Castells is that he is, fundamentally, a cognitivist: one who, along with Descartes, sees the mind as detached from the body. This is particularly evident in his recent book *Communication Power* (2009), in which he draws on several insights from neuroscience to define contemporary society as informed by an all encompassing 'network of brains' or 'neural network of brains'. His discussion of communication resembles the abstraction of Habermas' idea of the public sphere, which interestingly Habermas has himself re-defined as a 'network for communicating information and points of view' (Habermas, 1996: 360). What is missing in his treatment is the corporeal character of contemporary activism, whose importance is testified to by the array of physical occupations of sites in Cairo, Madrid, New York and hundreds of other cities.

Besides the bodily character of collective action, its emplaced nature is also overlooked. Following a thread which goes back to Debord's analysis of the society of the spectacle, Baudrillard's notion of hyper-reality (Baudrillard and Poster, 1988: 166–84), and Augé's concept of non-places (1995), Castells is convinced that modern technologies of communication entail a withering away of the logics of place. In his treatment of the network society, the 'space of flows' of the internet overtakes the 'space of places', marginalising local interactions and the identities constructed therein (Castells, 1996:

429). But how are we to understand the Arab Spring, the indignados, or Occupy, if we do not retain a sense of the importance of place in contemporary societies? Castells' definition of these movements as 'wiki-revolutions', 'self-generating and self-organising', seems to add little to the journalistic cliché of the 'Facebook (or Twitter) revolution'. 'Fearful around the world, but *united* on the *Web*'[3] read the title of a lecture Castells delivered at Berkeley about the Spanish indignados movement. This techno-visionary attitude does not seem able to provide us with a vocabulary and imaginary that would capture the gist of contemporary forms of collective action.

SWARMS WITHOUT HIVES

A network with wings: thus one could jokingly condense the similarities and differences between Castells' and Hardt's and Negri's pet concepts. The venerable Italian post-operaismo thinker and Duke's maverick professor employ the notion of swarms as part of their ambitious project of defining a new social class: the multitude (Hardt and Negri, 2000, 2004, 2009). The multitude is for them what the proletariat was for Marx: the revolutionary subject. Yet differently from the working class, the multitude, as its name suggests, is characterised by an irreducible multiplicity. Hardt and Negri contrast the multitude with industrial society's imaginary of the crowd and the people. As the anthropologist William Mazzarella, himself a Marxist autonomist, observes, 'It would not be an exaggeration to say that the coherence of the figure of the multitude, in the writings of Hardt and Negri, *depends* on its opposition to the figure of the crowd' (Mazzarella, 2010: 71).

Hardt and Negri see the emergence of this actor as a consequence of the shift in the productive system from material to immaterial production, where communication, the construction of social relations, and affectivity become the central terrain of capitalist accumulation. In *Empire*, they describe the multitude as rising in opposition to the force of global capitalism, as 'a force that sustains Empire and at the same time the force that calls for and makes necessary its destruction'. They describe the multitude as characterised by 'nomadism' and 'deterritorialising power', building on the Deleuzian contrast between the State, with its territoriality and fixity, and the War Machine, with its smooth space continuously traversed by flows (Hardt and Negri, 2000: 61). The concept of the swarm comes to represent this nomadic corporeality, this 'body without organs' (Deleuze and Guattari, 1987: 40), a multitude which can act together without being reduced to one identity or one place.

Communicative processes are crucial in the coordination of swarms. Thanks to the availability of complex technical linkages the swarm comes to establish and maintain a particular form of general intellect, what Hardt and Negri call the 'swarm intelligence', without the need for a central structure:

> recent researchers in artificial intelligence and computational methods use the term swarm intelligence to name collective and distributed techniques of problem solving without centralized control or provision of a global model ... the intelligence of the swarm is based fundamentally on communication ... the members of the multitude do not have to become the *same* or renounce their creativity in order to communicate and cooperate with each other. They remain different in terms of race, sex, sexuality and so forth. What we need to understand, then, is the collective intelligence that can emerge from the communication and cooperation of such a varied multiplicity. (Hardt and Negri, 2004: 91–2)

The resonance between the concept of the swarm and the social phenomenon of 'flash-mobs' is apparent. Flash-mobs emerged in 2003, after a social experiment conducted by *Wired!* journalist Bill Wasik, who circulated an email inviting people to gather in front of a jewellery shop and then disperse, as a form of extravagant artistic performance. The idea was quickly taken up around the US to organise festive events, ranging from pillow fights to collective mockeries. But it was soon also adopted by activists as a way to exploit the potential of flexible coordination offered by the internet and mobile media. With their rapid assembly and sudden dispersion, flash-mobs came to capture the sense of a liquid sociality, made up of transient ad-hoc gatherings facilitated by modern technologies of communication. Californian techno-visionary Howard Rheingold talked of these groups as 'smart mobs', social aggregates 'which cooperate in ways never before possible because they carry devices that possess both communication and computing capabilities' (Rheingold, 2003: 12).

If Castells – who began publishing his path-breaking trilogy *The Information Age: Economy, Society and Culture* back in 1996 – was the social theorist of the rise of the World Wide Web, Hardt's and Negri's joint work, which came at a later stage, bears the stamp of the era of mobile media and the new forms of collective action their diffusion inspired. Compared to Castells' discussion of networks, Hardt and Negri do recuperate an appreciation of the role of the body and of its mobility, by way of that vitalistic stream of thought which runs from Spinoza to Deleuze. Yet they too fail to take into account the emplaced character of collective action, the fact that it requires physical locations as stages for its performances. They see the multitude as the reflection of a de-centred Empire, which 'establishes no territorial center of power and does not rely on fixed boundaries or barriers' (Hardt and Negri, 2000: xii, xiii). Within this framework they discount the 'politics of place' proposed by a number of radical thinkers and geographers. They distrust attempts 'to recompose sites of resistance that are founded on the identities of the social subjects or national and regional groups, often grounding political analysis in the localization of struggle' (Hardt and Negri, 2000: 40).

The place of the multitude, Hardt and Negri suggest, is a 'non-place' (Hardt and Negri, 2000: 40). In a global world, appealing to a logic of place is not an option. This theme also appears in writings by Negri's comrade, Paolo Virno, who, in the concise and punchy *Grammar of the Multitude*, interestingly contrasts two derivations of the Greek word 'topos': a place, as in 'topology'; or a figure of language as in the English 'topic'. The multitude, Virno argues, has no place, which means that its members are all bound to an experience of 'Unheimlichkeit' or foreignness (Virno, 2004: 58). What binds them together is instead the presence of a common language. Virno is more pessimistic than Hardt and Negri in making this assertion, and sees more clearly the risks of isolation and solitude which underlie contemporary social experience. But equally he evades the question of how it is possible to construct a political project without at the same time constructing places and constructing territories.

Playing with the metaphor of 'swarm' as used by Hardt and Negri, one could say that what they are describing is in fact 'swarms without hives'. We know from biology that while honey-bees fly across great distances they also need a fixed place to return to, and some comrade bees to remain there to keep the hive in place. But there is little sense of the importance of such local geographies in Hardt and Hegri's account, framed as it is within the nomadic and fluid space of globalisation. In sum, both Castells and Hardt and Negri's work can be seen as attempts to rethink new forms of collective action beyond the imaginary of industrial society and its social formations and to make sense of the impact of new media on contemporary collective action. Hardt and Negri repeat several times that the multitude, unlike the crowd, goes beyond the reduction of plurality to a singularity – the so-called *reduction ad unum*. Similarly Castells defines the network in opposition to the mass and mass society, constantly represented as authoritarian and undemocratic. This rejection of the imaginary of the crowd or the mass interestingly also brings about a disregard for the importance of places as sites for the display of collective action – which clearly leaves little room for an understanding of the 'take the square movements' of 2011, and the importance that the occupation of public spaces has acquired in their unfolding.

A LANDSCAPE OF DISPERSION

Despite the criticisms made of both Castells' and Hardt and Negri's analysis, there is no denying that they correctly identify a situation of radical heterogeneity and multiplicity at the root of contemporary society. They are right in asserting that the post-industrial age is characterised by a social complexity which largely escapes the 'capture' of traditional bureaucratic organisations like parties and trade unions. The problem, however, is that they accept this condition of multiplicity as also automatically defining collective action, rather than as the point of departure for a complex process of social re-composition and symbolic articulation, facilitating the 'fusion' of individuals into a new collective agent. While celebrating the anti-authoritarian nature of contemporary social formations, they seem unconcerned about the challenges this situation of radical multiplicity poses, and the obstacles to mobilisation it raises.

The phenomena captured by terms like 'swarm' and 'network' can, from a critical perspective, be seen as fundamentally involving an experience of individualisation, perfectly epitomised by the type of interactions channelled through social media. Since the 1990s theorists like Zygmunt Bauman, Ulrich Beck and Alberto Melucci have noted how post-industrial societies are invested by a process of restructuring in which individuals become the 'fundamental units of the social system', as described by Melucci (1996a: 91). In this context, individuals are to a great extent disembedded from pre-established and stable collective identities. They are faced with a situation Bauman describes as one of 'liquidity' – as opposed to the 'solidity' of industrial societies – in which social relationships are characterised by uncertainty and have an 'until-further-notice' character. Deprived of strong collective identifications, individuals are compelled to seek 'biographical solutions to systemic contradictions' (Beck, 1992: 137).

It is evident that this trend towards individualisation creates obstacles for the development of collective action. Traditionally, social movement theorists have seen the existence of a strong identity and a sense of collective solidarity as crucial pre-conditions for collective action. This idea is encapsulated in the notion of 'cat-net' (a portmanteau of category and network) adopted by social movement historian Charles Tilly. On the one hand social movements require a common identity among participants as members of a collective category, distinct from other categories (for example, workers as distinct from students or the unemployed). On the other hand they rely on the presence of dense social networks based on strong ties (Tilly, 1978: 62–4). The condition of social individualisation described by Bauman and Beck is to some extent precisely the opposite of the circumstances Tilly would envisage as facilitating collective action. In contemporary society strong collective identities appear the exception rather than the norm, and social networks are dominated by 'weak ties' (Granovetter, 1974) rather than strong ones.

Social movements have traditionally relied on the existence of local face-to-face networks, which have been considered almost unanimously by scholars as the most important channel for mobilisation (see for example Melucci, 1996a: 292). Throughout modern history, social movement organisers have regularly tapped into the energy of urban centres and their 'public geography' (Sennett, 1977: 41), encompassing the places in which people rub shoulders with one another and construct lasting relationships of solidarity. This phenomenon is well testified by Georges Rudé's description of the French Revolution as a drama unfolding between key sites in Paris such as the Île de la Cité, Les Tuileries, the Cornmarket, and the Faubourg St. Antoine, 'soon to be distinguished as the most revolutionary of all the faubourgs' (Rudé, 1964: 97). Charles Tilly notes that from the eighteenth century onwards London 'was segregated into small subcommunities', wherein protest actions 'capitalized on authorized public gatherings such as markets, hangings, and ceremonies' (Tilly, 1981: 47). Finally, for Marx, the industrial factory introduced a condition of spatial concentration in which workers were isolated from broader society but shared a common everyday experience which came to form the basis for their political organisation (Kohn, 2003: 46).

This kind of spatial concentration in the workplace described by Marx, or in city space as described by Tilly and Rudé, is, however, precisely what appears to be mostly missing in the social space of contemporary post-industrial societies. The dispersed spatial arrangement we face today is well captured by the Marxist Autonomist theory of the 'social factory', that is (as Negri puts it) a 'factory without walls' in which the entire urban fabric is the terrain of capitalist accumulation but at the same time also a stage for resistance (Negri, 1989: 97). While for some people, including Negri himself, this situation allows for the development of new forms of resistance (such as the so-called 'metropolitan strike', aimed at blocking the city as a whole rather than a specific economic activity), for others it constitutes a serious obstacle to the emergence of collective action. Bauman in particular offers a pessimistic diagnosis of contemporary social space by affirming that 'contemporary hardships and sufferings are *dispersed* and *scattered*; and so is the dissent which they spawn'. In this context, 'the *dispersion* of dissent, the impossibility of *condensing* it and *anchoring* it in a common cause and unloading it against a common culprit only makes the pain yet more bitter' (Bauman, 2000: 54).

The dispersion Bauman talks about here is first and foremost a physical one, inscribed in an urban space shaped by the emergence of sprawls, new towns and gated communities, which shift populations away from the crime and dangers (real or supposed) of inner city areas. From the US to Egypt, urban development has followed this pattern, creating a space conforming to the individualist ideology of a globally dominant neoliberalism. The model for this reshaping of space has been Los Angeles, with the development of the city as a sprawl, a physical network without centres, much like the communication networks described by Castells. Socialist writer Mike Davis has been a trenchant critic of this development (1992a, 1992b, 1998). For him, the contemporary policies of urban management perfectly mirrors the contradictions of global capitalism. The upper middle classes, who own a disproportionate amount of society's wealth, escape into gated communities, while the slums expand ever further. The desire for a privatised intimacy and a sense of security which fuels the advance of the diffused space of suburbia is underscored for Davis by a strategy of segregation: the neoliberal elite's modern adaptation of the old adage 'divide and rule' (Davis, 1992a).

The rise of sprawls is accompanied by a 'privatization of the physical public sphere' whose consequence is 'the destruction of any truly democratic space' whereby constitutional rights to public assembly are *de facto* curtailed and social encounter is frowned upon (Davis, 1992a: 155). For Davis, at its core, the spatial logic of contemporary capitalism is driven by a 'fear of crowds' (1992a: 178–9) in which public gatherings are criminalised. The sprawling neoliberal city described by Davis appears to mark a new stage in that process of the 'fall of the public man' described by Richard Sennett, as the city withers away as 'a milieu where strangers are likely to meet' (Sennett, 1977: 48). Gathering places are carefully regimented and encounters between different classes or ethnic groups are frowned upon. Public spaces are deprived of their life, only to be later simulated in a corporate form inside shopping malls and plazas. These sanitised public spaces, Bauman reflects, are 'inhospitable', conducive neither to social encounter nor to political organisation: 'public space is increasingly empty of public issues. It fails to perform its past role of a meeting-and-dialogue place for private troubles and public issues' (Bauman, 2000: 40). The condition of spatial dispersion which affects contemporary societies has thus to be seen as the very material enactment of individuali-sation, whereby in the absence of stable and intense face-to-face contacts, people resort to transient mediated connections or 'transactions' (Bauman, 2001: 73).

It is important to note that spatial dispersion and the crisis of public space are not just Western phenomena; just as neoliberalism has spread well beyond Europe and the US and been adopted as the economic and social policy of authoritarian regimes like Mubarak's Egypt. In recent decades Cairo has witnessed a decline of the city centre locally known as 'Downtown', accompanied by the creation of new peripheral neighbourhoods for the rising middle classes. Since the 1990s huge shopping malls have mushroomed in the city's suburbs, catering for middle-class consumption, next to which extends the *ashwaa'iyyat*, the slums wherein reside those who provide labour for the needs of the middle classes (builders, cleaners, gardeners and the like) (see for example Singerman and Amar, 2006; Singerman, 2009). Egyptian sociologist Mona Abaza describes how these 'new cities in the desert mainly consist of walled, gated communities, landscaped compounds and condominiums, connected by highways that are easily accessible to "Carrefour" mega stores' (Abaza, 2011). The rise of these gated communities has been accompanied by a sanitisation of the 'popular life' which used to thrive in the city centre around Tahrir square, which was to become the hotspot of the 2011 Egyptian revolution.

PROMISES OF CONNECTION, THREATS OF ISOLATION

It is remarkable how in the face of this situation of spatial dispersion and individualisation contemporary technologies of communication constantly offer us a redemptive promise of 'connection'. As Bauman observes, mobile phones and internet websites offer a 'virtual proximity' which 'no longer requires physical closeness' (Bauman, 2003: 62), a closeness so hard to find in contemporary social space. Following a similar line of reasoning, theorist Mark Poster argues that media has been substituted for place as a means of aggregation in contemporary society:

> Contemporary social relations seem to be devoid of a basic level of interactive practices that, in the past, was the matrix of democratising politics: loci such as the agora, the New England Town Hall, the village church, the coffee house, the tavern, the public square, a convenient barn, a union hall, a park, a factory lunchroom, and even a street corner. Many of these places remain but no longer serve as organising centres for political discussion and action. It appears that the media and especially television have become the animating source for political discussion and action. (Poster, 2001: 178)

If, for Poster, television and more recently the internet have come to make up for the decline of places as sites of social and political aggregation, the irony is that while they 'aggregate' people around common symbols, these media also contribute to the tendency towards dispersion and fragmentation inherent in contemporary urban space. While enabling connection at a distance and establishing 'virtual proximity', contemporary media interactions also run the risk of isolating us from our local community, enclosing us in a mediated 'capsule' (Cauter, 2004).

The fragmenting and 'encapsulating' dynamics of communication technologies are well illustrated by the use of mobile media and the way in which they create barriers between different social groupings. Norwegian media researcher Richard Ling has examined how the diffusion of mobile phones has heavily reshaped the 'microco-ordination' of everyday life – the ways in which we arrange our social interactions with others. This 'can be seen in the iterative agreement as to when and where to meet friends' and 'in the ability to call ahead when we are late to an appointment' (Ling, 2004: 70). Thanks to these affordances, mobile media eliminate the need to rely on specific meeting points – i.e., places where one might also unexpectedly bump into others – thus potentially secluding people within very specific social circles. According to Ling, the mobile phone 'sets up a barrier between ourselves and our physical situation' and thus 'supports the development of cliques', or what he calls 'virtual walled communities' (Ling, 2004: 190). While mobile media do indeed 'bring us together', at the same time they also 'tear us apart' (Ling and Campbell, 2009). The trade-off for the extensive connections they offer is a numbing of our experience of locality and a reduction in our contacts with people outside of our mediated social circles.

Similar observations can be made with respect to social media, insofar as they are effecting an increasing 'mediatisation' of interpersonal communication (Konijn, 2008). As the very adjective 'social' in 'social media' suggests, they are means through which people mediate and manage their connections to extensive social networks of friends and acquaintances from a distance. These services have become particularly useful precisely because of the spatial dispersion characteristic of post-industrial society. The problem is that by encouraging us to focus on our extended but nevertheless still exclusive circles of mediated friendship and acquaintanceship, social media run the risk of exacerbating our 'elective affinities' (Bourdieu, 1984: 241), that is, our tendency to relate with those who are similar to us, regardless of where they are located. Todd Gitlin has rightly argued that the internet has tended 'to reproduce the dynamics of secession, exclusion and segmentation' of contemporary societies and exacerbated the separation between the 'information-rich' and the 'information-poor' (Gitlin, 1998: 172). Instead of one unitary public sphere *à la* Habermas, the internet has produced many 'sphericules'.

If the city of sprawls is the spatial embodiment of a situation of individualisation, electronic communication points to what American sociologist Barry Wellman has called a 'networked individualism' – a situation in which the person rather than a specific place becomes the 'portal'.

Because connections are to people and not to places, the technology affords shifting of work and community ties from linking people-in-places to linking people at any place. Computer-supported communication is every*where*, but it is situated no*where*. It is

I-alone that is reachable wherever I am: at a home, hotel, office, highway, or shopping centre. (Wellman, 2003: 17)

Social media allow to construct connections with distant others. However, these connections run the risk of taking energy and time away from interactions based on physical proximity. This tendency of new media to engender dynamics of seclusion from local communities and the thickness of face-to-face networks is an aspect overlooked by both Castells and Hardt and Negri, who, while celebrating the new possibilities of cooperation these technologies offer, tend to ignore their negative side-effects.

To sum up, the contemporary situation of spatial dispersion and communicative fragmentation does not seem to bode well for facilitating a process of mass mobilisation. This issue is well illustrated in a thought experiment proposed by Gerald Marwell, Pamela E. Oliver and Ralph Prahl in their attempt to theorise the 'critical mass' factor in social movements. They ask us to consider the condition of workers living in two ideal-typical cities: Alpha (characterised by spatial and communicative density), and Beta (characterised by dispersion):

> Alpha is fairly isolated, and most of its affected employees live in a single suburb, Centauri. They attend Centauri's churches; their children attend Centauri's public schools; they belong to Centauri chapters of social and service clubs; they all are served by the same local telephone exchange. In contrast, Beta is part of an ethnically diverse two-state megalopolis, and its affected employees are *scattered* across a dozen different suburbs in two states and four counties. Thus, they rarely see one another after work. They go to different churches, send their children to different schools, read four or five different newspapers, and pay toll charges for telephone calls between many of the suburbs. (Marwell et al., 1988: 505)

'We would find virtual unanimity among sociologists in predicting that the employees in Alpha are more likely than those in Beta to act collectively', the researchers conclude. They affirm that the spatial and communicative structure of Alpha is more conducive to sustaining a sense of unity among individuals. In the same way, they suggest that there would also be 'universal unanimity' among sociologists that the type of space and media system we are dealing with today resembles Beta rather than Alpha.

THE PERFORMATIVITY OF ASSEMBLING

As we have seen, the dispersed and individualised nature of contemporary social experience raises irksome questions about the possibility of collective action. And yet the 2011 wave of social movements offered the most blatant empirical demonstration that mass protest is still possible even in the fragmented conditions of contemporary society. But how did these movements manage to coalesce despite the dispersion? How was a 'critical mass' achieved in a context which seemed ill-suited to its formation?

To understand contemporary social movements we need to depart from the classical literature for which a strong common identity and thick networks invariably have to *pre-exist* collective action (e.g., Tilly, 1978). At the same time, however, we also need to be suspicious of interpretations (such as those offered by Hardt and Negri and Castells) that view collective action as springing forth spontaneously, without the need for organisational mediation or symbolic articulation to shape and guide it. Counter to both these positions, and following Ernesto Laclau, I am convinced that the 'proliferation of points of ruptures' which characterises contemporary social experience, and is epitomised by the forms of interaction underlying social media, 'makes necessary political forms of social aggregation' (Laclau, 2005: 230). In the absence of embedded identities and thick social networks to sustain collective action, these elements need to be created pro-actively and ad-hoc in the course of the process of mobilisation.

The renewed importance of the question of unity in the context of contemporary popular movements has also recently been recognised by network theorists like Jeffrey Juris. Analysing the Occupy movement in the US, Juris has argued that it is underscored precisely by 'logics of aggregation' in contrast to the 'logics of networking' he had earlier identified as the trait of the anti-globalisation movement (Juris, 2012). He describes these logics of aggregation as involving the 'assembling of masses of individuals from diverse backgrounds within physical spaces', arguing that 'whereas the use of listservs and websites in the movements for global justice during the late 1990s and 2000s helped to generate and diffuse distributed networking logics, in the #Occupy movements social media have contributed to powerful logics of aggregation' (Juris, 2012: 260–1).

The risk in Juris' description is to see this shift from networking to aggregation as simply a consequence of the different technical tools employed, rather than as a reflection of the specific culture of the new movements and of their 'popular' character and majoritarian ambitions. Moreover, Juris appears somewhat suspicious of these 'logics of aggregation' and is reassured by the fact that the 'logic of networking', with its emphasis on diversity, continues to survive.

If the practices of contemporary popular movements pose serious theoretical and analytical problems for network theorists like Juris, this is because the forms of *assembly* or *gathering* in public space they involve are to a great extent at odds with the vision of society as a network without centres, as proposed by Castells, but also with the image of a constantly moving swarm without a hive, as portrayed by Hardt and Negri. As we will see in later chapters, the protest camps of the indignados, of the Egyptian revolution, of Occupy Wall Street, are marked by a striving for the construction of a sense of centrality and spatial fixity which is in effect precisely the reverse of the constitutive diffuseness of networks, and of the nomadism of swarms. The emergence of these new forms of popular assembly raises questions not only about their internal working and the type of communities constituted within them (see for example, Feigenbaum, Frenzel, and McCurdy, forthcoming), but also about the processes through which these assemblies come into being, or in other words about the nature of mobilisation as a process (rather than a state) of spatial *assembling*, with its own specific choreography.

The problem of mobilisation as deployed in social movement theory is precisely the question of how people are *assembled*, starting from a situation of varying spatial dispersion. As in the military sense of the term, mobilisation involves a *physical concentration of participants in space and time*, which precedes the phase of combat (Clausewitz, 2004). For Melucci, mobilisation is 'the process by which a social movement is created and begins to take action'. It is the operation 'by which a collective actor *gathers* and organises its resources for the pursuit of a shared objective against the resistance of groups opposing that objective' (Melucci, 1996a: 288). Similarly for Anthony Oberschall, mobilisation is 'the process whereby activists build loyalty and commitment for their cause and *assemble* followers, funds and resources, all of which increase their capacity to act collectively' (Oberschall, 1973: 384).

It is evident that within each specific social movement this process of assembling acquires very different dynamics depending on the degree of spatial dispersion of the constituency being mobilised. There is a huge difference between mobilising a constituency which is in some ways already partly *assembled* around common workplaces, neighbourhoods, social and subcultural scenes, and mobilising a constituency which is by and large deprived of these common poles of aggregation. For example, the anti-globalisation movement relied on the presence of local activist scenes like the one described by Haunss and Leach (2009) in order to hold itself together between phases of mobilisation. The situation is very different with contemporary popular movements, for which there is no social scene capable of encompassing the diverse constituency they aim to mobilise, and where the ad-hoc creation and maintenance of spaces of gathering thus acquires a fundamental importance. This process of assembling in public space thus come to require a great deal of attention, proportional precisely to the degree of spatial dispersion and social fragmentation they are attempting to recompose.

Hannah Arendt's reflections on political action and public space offer some useful insights for making sense of the process of mobilisation as the re-composition of a prior situation of spatial dispersion. For Arendt, action (by which she exclusively means political action, as opposed to 'work' and 'labour') never happens in isolation. It always requires the construction of a sense of 'togetherness' among those involved, manifest in what Arendt calls a 'space of appearance':

> The space of appearance comes into being wherever men are together in the manner of speech and action ... Its peculiarity is that, unlike the spaces which are the work of our hands, it does not survive the actuality of the movement which brought it into being, but disappears not only with the dispersal of men— as in the case of great catastrophes when the body politic of a people is destroyed—but with the disappearance or arrest of the activities themselves. Wherever people *gather together*, it is potentially there, but only potentially, not necessarily and not forever. (Arendt, 1958: 199)

Arendt suggests that public space is not a datum or a material architecture acting as a venue, but rather a form of experience resulting from the process of gathering and its re-composition of a prior situation of dispersion. Public space, in other words, needs to be performatively constructed and re-constructed through the act of gathering of otherwise dispersed individuals.

Arendt's analysis of togetherness and assembly resonates deeply with Emile Durkheim's description of the gatherings of Australian tribes:

The life of Australian societies alternates between two different phases. At times the population is scattered in small groups that go about their business independently. Each family lives by itself, hunting and fishing – in short striving by all possible means to provide for its needs. At other times, by contrast, the population is concentrated and condensed in particular places for a period varying from several days to several months. This *concentration* takes place when a clan or tribal group is summoned to meet, and on this occasion they hold either a religious ceremony or what ethnographers call a corroboree. (Durkheim, 1912/1965: 162)

Durkheim famously describes the gathering as a moment of 'collective effervescence' in which emotions are stirred up. He observes that 'the very fact of *assembling* is an exceptionally powerful stimulant. Once the individuals are assembled, their proximity generates a kind of electricity that quickly transports them to an extraordinary degree of exaltation' (Durkheim, 1912/1965: 162).

Drawing on these insights from both Arendt and Durkheim, we can offer a provisional definition of the process of mobilisation as *a performative act of gathering or assembling which spatially re-composes together in a temporary unity what was previously torn apart, and which in so doing creates public space as a form of collective and emplaced experience.* In the remainder of this chapter, I conceptualise the forms of symbolic and organisational mediation which intervene in this process, by coining the notion of 'choreography of assembly'. Working through this term, I discuss how processes of identity-building and emotional motivation are involved in giving a coherence to the spontaneity of protest participation

CHOREOGRAPHING PROTEST

The act of bodily assembling, which in general terms constitutes the spatial logic of the process of social movement mobilisation, revolves around the construction of a situation of bodily density dominated by face-to-face communication. Yet in turn, in the context of a 'mediatised society' (Thompson, 1995), the physical coming together of a previously dispersed group of people could hardly take place without a complex process of technical and symbolic mediation involved in summoning from a distance dispersed individuals. The act of assembling comes to be underscored by complex communicative and organisational practices, allowing for groups which are spatially dispersed but united by the same interests or convictions to act together. Within the field of social media, the most obvious examples of such a process come from websites like MeetUp,[4] informing users about 'offline' meetings they might be interested in; Doodle,[5] a web-polling application used to schedule meetings and other appointments; and of course the popular Facebook event function, used to invite people to various activities. These services are testament to the extent to which the assembling of social groupings in our fragmented and dispersed societies relies on a complex process of symbolic and technical mediation, or what I will refer to here as a 'choreography of assembly'. As I will argue in the course of the book, contemporary forms of protest communication, including activist tweets, Facebook pages, mobile phone apps and text messages revolve to a great extent precisely around acts of choreographing: *the mediated 'scene-setting' and 'scripting' of people's physical assembling in public space.*

Interestingly, in recent years the term 'choreography' has been widely used by anti-globalisation activists – including John Jordan, the initiator of the anti-road movement Reclaim the Streets – to refer to the process of protest organising. Dance historian Susan Leigh Foster (2003) has coined the term 'choreography of protest' to describe how a number of forms of protest – from the anti-HIV activism of ACT UP and the Seattle anti-WTO protests – were marked by a 'physicality' similar to that of dance (Foster, 2003). Taking a cue from Jeffrey Alexander's discussion of 'social performances' (Alexander, 2006: 36–9), my emphasis in adopting of the notion of choreography is not simply on the bodily and emplaced nature of collective action, but also crucially on its symbolic and mediated character, on the fact that media practices intervene in preparing the terrain, or setting the scene, for people coming together in public space.

Deriving etymologically from the Greek words for 'dance' and 'writing', the term choreography incorporates the idea of a symbolic mediation of bodily action. It can thus be used to describe how contemporary popular movements, despite their anti-authoritarian stress on improvisation and creative participation, nevertheless rely on a 'writing of movement', or in more general terms a 'writing of action', mostly hidden to external observers, but nevertheless highly effective in structuring the way in which people come together and act together in public space.

The choreographing of public gatherings in which social media are involved cannot be reduced to the circulation of practical information, or the logistics of organising protest events. The choreography of assembly of contemporary movements has its own cultural narrative, and it chiefly requires the construction of common collective identifications among participants, without which such practical information would fall on deaf ears. Throughout the history of social movements, media like newspapers, radio and TV have contributed in condensing *symbolic assemblages* which can later materialise into *bodily assemblies*. A number of theorists from Melucci to Laclau have remarked on the importance of identity-building in facilitating the coming together of social movements in public space. For Melucci the construction of a collective identity is one of the first tasks to be dealt with during the process of mobilisation, alongside 'the identification of an enemy, the definition of a purpose and an object at stake in the conflict' (Melucci, 1996a: 292). These different phases entail the progressive 'fusion' of participants into a common social body since, as Melucci suggests, through the process of mobilisation 'the different fragments joining together to form a movement are integrated into a new system of relations in which the original elements change their meanings' (Melucci 1996a: 292). Thus through the construction of common identities a dispersed constituency is *condensed* into a common subjectivity with the capacity 'to act as a *unified* and *delimited* subject and to retain control over their own action' (Melucci, 1996a: 72).

This process of condensation around a common identity cannot be reduced to the simple sharing of information, since it crucially involves an 'emotional investment' on the part of participants. For Melucci, 'passions and feelings, love and hate, faith and fear are all part of a body acting collectively'. He criticises those authors who see these aspects of collective action as 'irrational', insisting that 'there is no cognition without feeling and no meaning without emotion' (Melucci, 1996a: 72). Goodwin, Jasper and Polletta (2001) have likewise reasserted the importance of emotions in collective action. Jasper in his later work has highlighted the importance of an 'emotional energy', defined as 'a mood of excitement and enthusiasm' around a common identity, which constitutes a fundamental resource for protest participation (Jasper, 2011: 297).

Valuable insights for understanding collective identification in contemporary social movements can be drawn from Laclau's discussion of 'populism' as a process of the construction of the people, as developed in his *Populist Reason* (2005). For Laclau, the 'people' is a subject which does not pre-exist as an actor but needs to be pro-actively created through specific discursive operations. The creation of the people as a subject is for Laclau the task of 'populism' – a notion to which he does not attach the usual negative connotations. Populism is here simply a type of politics which differs from 'democratic' politics with its emphasis on difference and single issues, and which cuts the political space in two, pitting the people against corrupt institutions, incapable of responding to widespread social grievances.

The *emotional condensation* of the people around a common identity requires the presence of what Laclau calls an 'empty signifier': a leader, an image, a collective name or possibly also a place around which the unity of the people can be performatively created (Laclau, 1996: 36; 2005: 69). The empty signifier is a 'signifier without a signified', that is, a symbol which has been deprived of its particularistic content and can thus create a 'chain of equivalence' (Laclau, 2005: 93) between different groups of people with their respective grievances. Against the emphasis on multiplicity of authors like Castells and Hardt and Negri, Laclau thus suggests that the process of mobilisation entails to a great extent a *reductio ad unum*, a reduction of the 'complexity of the social' (Laclau, 2005: 94).

The choreography of assembly also crucially encompasses a process of *material precipitation* from symbolic assemblages to bodily assembly in public space. The nature of this process can be gleaned by looking at Frantz Fanon's discussion of the role played by the radio stations of the Front de Libération Nationale (FLN) in organising the struggle against the French colonizers in Algeria (1959–67). The FLN radio station Voice of Fighting Algeria was, Fanon says, 'of capital importance in consolidating and unifying the people'. Through its coverage,

> the fragments and splinters of acts gleaned by the correspondent of a newspaper more or less attached to the colonial domination, or communicated by the opposing military authorities lost their anarchic character and became organised into a national and Algerian political idea, assuming their place in an overall strategy of the reconquest of people's sovereignty. The *scattered* acts fitted into a vast epic. (Fanon, 1967: 84)

Fanon reflects at length on how listening to the radio created a new sense of mediated community among the people which sustained the mobilisation of the national liberation movement. While previously possessing a radio had been considered a sign of complicity with the colonial regime, with the inception of the Voice of Fighting Algeria the 'radio receiver lost its identity as an enemy. The radio set was no longer part of the occupier's arsenal of cultural oppression'. On the contrary, for Algerians, having a radio now 'meant paying one's taxes to the nation, buying the right of entry into the struggle of an *assembled* people' (Fanon, 1967: 84).

What is crucial, however, is that the role of radio did not stop at the level of creating a symbolic community, but also facilitated the physical gathering of people in public space. The assemblage described by Fanon was not only symbolic but also physical, since, given the scarcity of radios, people would crowd around one set in order to listen together. This coming together of the disparate constituted a fundamental threat for the French coloniser. The spread of these intimate gatherings in fact constituted the initial *nuclei* around which a process of mobilisation would form, in a world already 'cut in two' along a 'dividing line ... shown by barracks and police stations' (Fanon, 1965: 34). The radio thus facilitated the material precipitation of the movement, and the transformation of dissenting publics into protesting crowds.

The notion of a choreography of assembly is employed not simply to highlight the deeply mediated character of the process of physical assembling well represented in Fanon's example. It also crucially refers to the fact that such process of mediation express the nature of contemporary forms of indirect, emotional or 'choreographic' leadership which revolve around setting the general scene for participation, leaving participants to creatively 'navigate' the space thus created. Leadership here needs to be understood in general terms as a relatively centralised form of influence over the course a collective action will take. It is evident that if one looks within contemporary movements for a charismatic leader acting as 'figurehead' – a Gandhi or a Martin Luther King – one will find no such singular person. But leadership does not necessarily need to take such a form, and can acquire more discreet and diffuse manifestations.

As we know from the work of scholars such as Jo Freeman, also within anti-authoritarian, social movements there often tends to be an activist elite which exercise an elusive influence on internal organising. The kind of soft and invisible leadership proper to informal organisations can be understood as a form a 'dialogical relationship' which 'seeks understanding and agreement' (Barker et al., 2001: 18). This form of choreographic leadership works through a logic of consensus rather than a logic of command, in which leaders instead of giving orders are involved in 'proposing to these differentiated entities [that social movements are] how they should and can *identify* themselves and act together' by proposing 'collective *images*' and 'forms of action, and organisation' (Barker et al., 2001: 18) – or in terms of the metaphor of choreography, 'scripts', which participants are invited to perform. Rejecting the absolute spontaneity propounded by Castells and Hardt and Negri, the notion of choreography emphasises the importance of leaders and leading groups in giving a *coherence* – a common sense of unity, of place and of direction – to collective action.

The utility of the notion can be appreciated at three different levels: First, it allows us to analyse the *organisational* dynamics of the process of mobilisation and to ask *who* are the 'choreographers' of public gatherings, the people initiating and guiding them. Second, the utility of the term revolves around its capacity to capture the *temporal* character of the process of mobilisation. We know from social movement literature that mobilisation is a dynamic process involving different stages, in particular a phase of *initiation* and a phase of *sustainment*, the latter being particularly important in the case of long-term mass sit-ins. Likewise, we can see the choreography of assembly as fundamentally involving two different moments: the symbolic *condensation* of people around a common identity and their material *precipitation* in public space. Last but not least, the notion of choreography allows us to analyse the *spatial* character of the process of mobilisation and the way in which it connects dispersed participants with specific places of gathering. We can see this process as involving the weaving together of a spatial 'texture' (Lefebvre, 1974/1991: 222), a symbolic overlaying of physical space with cultural meanings and narratives. This in turn can be broken down into two separate moments of emotional tension: an *impetus* towards public gatherings during the phase of initiation, and an *attraction* to those gatherings during the phase of sustainment.

The ways in which social media may be utilised in the construction of a choreography of assembly will now be analysed in detail in the remaining chapters, looking at the different popular movements of 2011, from Egypt, to Spain, to the United States. For the reader's convenience in the next section I have included an overview of the cases studies covered in the book and a timeline of relevant events.

OVERVIEW OF THE CASE STUDIES

The 2011 Egyptian revolution

A few days after the successful overthrow of Tunisian president Ben Ali, on the 25th of January 2011, thousands of Egyptians took to the streets to protest against the dictatorship of Hosni Mubarak. After an uprising lasting for 18 days, which had its centre-point in Tahrir square in central Cairo, Mubarak relinquished his post, and a military council took power. The protests were celebrated as a demonstration of the power of social media as a vehicle of mobilisation. But how were social media actually concretely used by activists? And how did they interact with other forms of street level of communication in the process of gathering in public space?

The indignados movement in Spain

The 15th of May 2011 marked the day of beginning of a movement which drew inspiration and borrowed tactics from the Egyptian uprising. The 'indignados' or indignants as they came to be called took to the streets to voice their outrage against the politics of austerity and economic crisis which had put almost half of young people out of work. In imitation of Tahrir square they occupied Puerta del Sol in central Madrid for a month, after a demonstration which similarly to the Egyptian uprising had been called for on Facebook by a group of young activists with little prior political experience. The movement established a series of local assemblies, and organised marches throughout the country to collect people's demands. What was the role of social media in the process of mobilisation? How did the organisers use social media to harvest a common feeling of indignation?

Occupy Wall Street in the US

After the call launched by the countercultural magazine *Adbusters* on the 17th of September 2011, 300 people occupied a small park in central Manhattan. After a couple of weeks, they finally managed to attract news media's attention and to capture the imagination of US citizens. They appealed to the 99% of the population, all those fallen victim to the financial crisis. The movement soon spread to hundreds of locations across the US and beyond, while the 'meme' of Occupy came to be applied to different campaigns and actions. How were social media used in the process of participants' mobilisation in the case of Occupy Wall Street? And how does their use differ from that which characterised Egypt and Spain?

TIMELINE

Date	Event	Location
06/06/10	Khaled Said, a 28-year-old blogger and entrepreneur, is brutally killed by secret police in Alexandria after having posted on the internet a video documenting police corruption. Two days later, Google executive Wael Ghonim opens a Facebook page called Kullena Khaled Said (We are all Khaled Said).	Alexandria
17/12/10	Mohammed Bouazizi a 26-year-old street vendor, sets himself on fire in the small town of Sidi Bouzid in South Tunisia after having been harassed by a police officer. His suicide sparks demonstrations against President Ben Ali's regime.	Sidi Bouzid
14/01/11	Ben Ali flees Tunisia after several days of unrest in the country, putting an end to his 23 years in power.	Tunis
25/01/11	An estimated 50,000 people take to the streets of Cairo on Police Day, to protest against the 30-year regime of Hosni Mubarak. In the night they were violently dislodged from Tahrir square. But protests continued in the following days.	Cairo
28/01/11	Up to a million people take to the streets of Cairo on the 'Friday of Rage' demonstrations. After a long battle with police forces they occupy Tahrir square. In the evening army tanks move into the city. In the early morning the Mubarak regime shuts down all electronic communications, in what came to be known as the 'kill switch'.	Cairo
02/02/11	Day of the 'battle of the camel'. Demonstrators successfully defend Tahrir square against the attacks of pro-Mubarak thugs and plain-clothes policemen.	Cairo
11/02/11	Mubarak resigns after 18 days of uprising, leaving the country in the hands of the Supreme Council of Armed Forces (SCAF).	Cairo
08/03/11	Democracia Real Ya (Real Democracy Now) sets up its Facebook page which will serve as an organisational platform for the 'indignados' (outraged) movement.	Spain

Date	Event	Location
15/05/11	Hundreds of thousands of Spaniards take part in the demonstrations against austerity and corruption called by Democracia Real Ya. On the evening of the 15th, 50 people decide to occupy Puerta del Sol in central Madrid.	Madrid and 57 other cities in Spain
17/05/11	After the eviction of the encampment in the early morning, thousands of citizens converge on Puerta del Sol and set up a protest camp that will last for one month. Soon other acampadas spread across the country.	Madrid
25/05/11	Thousands of citizens flood Syntagma square in Athens, in imitation of the Spanish indignados movement, during a phase of rising social opposition against austerity measures put forward by Papandreou's government.	Athens
19/06/11	A huge demonstration in Madrid and several cities across Spain, a few days after the main occupations are voluntarily lifted by activists. In the summer the indignados organise a series of marches throughout the country, and set up neighbourhood assemblies.	Madrid
12/07/11	The Canadian countercultural magazine *Adbusters* launches on its website the first call to Occupy Wall Street.	Vancouver
02/08/11	First General Assembly of Occupy Wall Street, in Bowling Green next to the Wall Street bull statue. Sparks fly between socialist and anarchist activists.	New York
17/09/11	Protesters occupy Zuccotti Park in Downton Manhattan, near to the New York Stock Exchange in Wall Street.	New York
01/10/11	The mass arrest (700+ people) of Occupy protesters on Brooklyn Bridge draws the attention of mainstream media.	New York
15/10/11	'15O' global day of action for global change. Called by the Spanish indignados, and enacted worldwide in 950 cities in 82 countries. In New York activists occupy Times Square. In London activists set up a camp at the steps of St Paul's cathedral, which they will hold until February 2012.	Global
15/11/11	The Occupy Wall Street protest camp in Zuccotti Park is evicted by the NYPD. Two days later, 30,000 people take part in a protest against the financial system in the streets of Manhattan.	New York

2
'We are not guys of comment and like': The Revolutionary Coalescence of *Shabab-al-Facebook*

All we do is post on Facebook. We are the Facebook generation. Period.
Comment by a user on the Kullena Khaled Said page (quoted in Ghonim, 2012: 135)

During the sit-in held in July 2011 against the continuation of military rule, behind one of the green fences surrounding Tahrir square, a street vendor was busy selling revolutionary souvenirs. Among them was a T-shirt carrying the script '25th of January Revolution', next to which were two words: 'freedom' and 'Facebook'. Nearby, in Talaat Harb street, a graffiti painting reproduced the blue and white logo of Zuckerberg's social networking website. A little further on, one could still make out scanty painted letters composing the word 'Twitter' on a shop shutter.

These scripts looked quite awkward to Western eyes, used to seeing website logos like those of Facebook and Twitter flickering on a computer screen rather than daubed on the streets, and even less so as the content of political graffiti. But it is precisely this awkwardness that reveals something important about the dynamics of the Egyptian revolution as a process driven by an internet-savvy youth, the *shabab-al-Facebook* (Facebook youth). As I will explain in this chapter, in the course of the Egyptian revolution, social media became the means of a choreography of assembly, facilitating the coalescence of this cosmopolitan Facebook youth around a common identity, and its material precipitation into a 'street youth'. Derided for years by the state-owned media as 'guys of comment and like', the internet generation became infused with a missionary spirit of national salvation, incited by Facebook pages, blog posts, and tweets.

Social media and in particular Facebook functioned as a training ground for this politically inexperienced but media-savvy youth, and as a launching pad for the protests. The *shabab-al-Facebook* thus became street agitators of the *shaabi*, the lower classes which make up the great majority of Egyptian society. It was through

48

this interaction with groups separated by the digital divide that the *shabab-al-Facebook* successfully turned into the catalyst of a process of mass mobilisation. If social media played only a limited and very specific role in that process, it was nonetheless crucial in the coalescence of the initial revolutionary nucleus around which a number of 'rings' of participants would progressively cluster.

As we have seen, the uprisings in Egypt and before it in Tunisia have been celebrated in the media as 'Facebook revolutions', 'Twitter revolutions', or 'wiki-revolutions'. These labels rightly highlight the important role played by the internet and social media as platforms for protest communications. However, they overlook the fact that only a limited constituency was actually mobilised by such media, simply as a consequence of low levels of internet connection. In 2011 only 25 per cent of Egyptian households were connected to the internet, only 4 per cent of Egyptian adults were members of Facebook, and only a miniscule 0.15 per cent of them had a Twitter account (Dubai School of Government, 2011b). As the 'Tahrir media project', which surveyed the media uses of over 1,000 (mostly middle-class) protesters, shows, only a fraction of those who took to the streets were mobilised by Facebook and an even smaller number by Twitter. Only 16 per cent of the protesters interviewed in Cairo used Twitter, while 42 per cent of them used Facebook, despite the fact that, as Dunn and Wilson put it, they were part of a 'highly wired sample' (Wilson and Dunn, 2011). For the great mass of participants in the Egyptian uprising, mobilisation worked through more traditional channels such as oral communication and the mass media.

This evidence clearly urges us to be aware of the limited impact of social media as a means of mobilisation during the Egyptian revolution. More positively, it also invites us to ascertain the specific contribution to the process of mobilisation of that specific group for which the internet was indeed, alongside oral communication, the main medium of mobilisation: the so-called Facebook youth. It is this section of the movement whose experience and media-use I will focus on in here. As a consequence, the account proposed in this chapter is admittedly limited in its coverage and scope. First and foremost, it focuses on the 18 days of the uprising against Hosni Mubarak, rather than on the later protest waves, and specifically on the preparation of the protests and the first days of the uprising. I do not consider the communication strategies of the Muslim Brotherhood or of the trade unions, however much both groups may have been decisive in the success of the revolution. Finally, I do not discuss the role played by mass media, and in particular by Al-Jazeera, despite the fact that they played an important part in mobilising large sectors of the population beyond the young internet-connected middle class (Cottle, 2011).

The chapter begins by looking at how the Mubarak regime's tight control on public space prior to the revolution obliged activists to turn to the internet to share their dissent. Among the several activist blogs and websites, a leading role was played by the Kullena Khaled Said Facebook page, which acted as a site of *emotional condensation* for a largely un-politicised Facebook youth prior to the protests. Moreover, it served as a launch pad to create a *sense of anticipation* and an *impetus* prior to the *material precipitation* of the movement. This early online organising was soon paralleled by an intense ground-level effort to agitate the 'shaabi': the popular classes. From the very first days of the uprising, face-to-face communication overtook social media as medium of choice for the movement. In the last section of the chapter I turn to the role played by Twitter in the uprising. I argue that compared to Facebook, Twitter had a more limited impact. It was mostly geared at eliciting external attention, while also playing a role as a channel for tactical communication within the activist elite. Nevertheless, this medium has been seen by some activists as carrying the risk of isolation from mainstream Egyptian society, taking time away from street campaigning and more accessible forms of internet communication.

DESERT IN THE STREETS, OASIS ON THE INTERNET

Analyses of the role of the internet in the Egyptian revolution often overlook the fact that its popularity as a vehicle for protest organisation was a consequence of the strict policing of public space under Mubarak. Naturally the authoritarianism of the regime affected all basic civil and political rights. But of the three fundamental liberal-democratic freedoms – freedom of expression, of association, and of assembly – possibly the most repressed was the latter (Osman, 2010). In fact, under Mubarak a handful of opposition parties were allowed to exist, including the liberal el-Wafd, the social-democratic Tagamma, and the Nasserist el-Karama, though they acted for the most part as window-dressing for the regime, given that elections were systematically rigged. Also some opposition papers including *Masry Al-Youm* and *el-Shorouq* were formally permitted to operate, even though they were the target of constant legal harassment, and their editors were subject to intimidations.

The regime half-heartedly tolerated their existence given that they reached only limited sections of the Egyptian population, and thus did not endanger its maintenance of consensus. What the regime could in no way tolerate were public demonstrations in the streets, which could create a dangerous interaction between the activist community and the lower classes.

State of emergency laws maintained almost without interruption during Mubarak's tenure in power especially targeted the right of assembly in public space. The secret police, the notorious 'mukhabarat', was an infamous presence whose phantom-like existence acted as a powerful deterrent for all those harbouring aversion towards the regime (Bradley, 2008). The use of torture, violence, kidnappings and sometimes arbitrary killings of political opponents was common knowledge among the populace. The presence of police informants bred a common feeling of distrust even among relatives and friends – a common experience under a totalitarian regime. Yet for all the regime's attempt to silence dissent in public space, the thriving street life and thick social networks of Egyptian cities (Bayat, 2010) offered some room for the cultivation of defiance towards the regime. The tens of thousands of ''ahwa' coffee shops in Cairo, Alexandria and other major cities provided a highly diffuse infrastructure for the nurturing of dissent at street-level. It was not uncommon to hear people insulting Mubarak in private conversations. But the fear of police reprisals limited dissent to very specific private or semi-public locations and circles. Open dissent in the form of public demonstrations was restricted to a small community of activists, bloggers, opposition politicians and NGO workers with limited connection with the broader populace.

The average demonstration during the Mubarak years would number a few hundred people. A typical venue might be the stairs at the entrance of the journalists' syndicate, and other progressive syndicates acting as protest sanctuaries. People would gather for few minutes, unfold a banner, shout some slogans to a small audience of passers-by, before the police arrived to squeeze people in a tight containment cordon. 'We were looked at as crazy people' – recounts Sally Zohney, a 27-year-old political science graduate from Cairo University who regularly attended such demonstrations. 'People weren't really understanding why we were doing that. They weren't believing that it was possible to do away with the regime anyway.' The only major exception during the 2000s was the demonstration against the Iraq war in February 2003. Around 40,000 people, according to optimistic calculations, converged to Tahrir square but were soon dispersed by police charges and tear gas. It was only in the mid to late 2000s that a series of strikes and labour protests including sit-ins in front of parliament would set the basis for a popular 'repertoire of contention' (Tilly, 2003) which deeply informed the 2011 revolution.

Bearing in mind this 'inhospitability' of public space under Mubarak, we can better understand the reasons why the internet and Facebook in particular came to constitute such a popular platform for encouraging dissent against the regime. Using an admittedly stereotypical but nonetheless apt image, one could say that if Egyptian public space had become a desert for dissenting groups, where they could easily be identified and targeted, the internet came to constitute something like a diffuse oasis where oppositional identities could develop without being immediately crushed by the state.

In the 2000s the ICT sector experienced a momentous growth in Egypt (Abdulla, 2007). Cairo witnessed a rise of web start-ups and the development of local telephone companies including Etisalat and Mobinil. One man became the face of this 'Egypt 2.0' with its promise of political liberalisation. Ahmed Nazif, prime minister from 2004 until the revolution, and formerly minister of communication, put much effort into improving internet connectivity. Between 2005 and 2010 the internet penetration rate went up from 9 per cent to 24 per cent of household, still quite low given that the United States had by 2010 reached almost 80 per cent, but also underrated given Egyptians' intense use of internet cafés.[1] Realising that it could not effectively censor the internet without unleashing an avalanche of disapproval from its Western allies, the Mubarak regime presented the relative degree of online freedom enjoyed by Egyptians as proof of its agenda of political liberalisation (Hofheinz, 2005).

By leaving the internet relatively open, the regime also hoped to maintain the support of the young middle-class, that new generation of Egyptians which came to be known as the *shabab-al-Facebook* (Peterson, 2011). The regime's relative lenience towards internet access was not without its risks though. The expansion in ICT trained a workforce in the use of communication technologies which could, and did, become a dangerous weapon in the hands of the enemies of the regime. Moreover, blogs and Facebook groups became sites that were to breed a culture of irreverence and anti-authoritarianism, all the more explosive under the pressure of the authoritarian or 'pharaonic' system of government of Egypt.[2] In the late 2000s bloggers like Hossam al-Hamalawy (also known as Arabawy) and Alaa Abdel Fattah began drawing a significant following with their caustic commentaries on Egyptian politics. These and other bloggers were often arrested and harassed by the police, and the National Democratic Party of Mubarak even created a specific 'Electronic Commitee' to counter internet activists, while other bloggers and Facebook users were paid to post pro-regime messages (Ghonim, 2012: 69–70). Despite the repression of digital activism, Nazif often vaunted the opening of limited spaces of dissent on the internet as a consequence of his own policies. When heckled in January 2009 by a group of activists at Cairo University, the prime minister scathingly replied that the protesters were 'the same young people who used the Internet to express their opinions!'[3]

Figure 2.1   The Facebook logo turned into a graffiti in Talaat Harb, Cairo.
(Author: Paolo Gerbaudo)

The Cairo activists were part of the '6th of April' group which led the experimentations in the use of the internet as a platform for protest mobilisation. The group was mostly composed of young middle-class Cairenes and Alexandrians led by a young civil engineer Ahmed Maher. Many of them had joined the group out of disillusion with Kifaya ('Enough'), a movement formed in 2005 to demand an end to Mubarak's regime, but which displayed a disregard for economic problems closer to the heart of the majority of the population. To address this issue, the new 6th of April movement tried to build contacts with the labour movement. The group took its name from the date of a strike by textile workers in Mahalla el-Kobra, an industrial town in the Nile Delta, with which it expressed solidarity, calling for a national general strike on 6 April 2008.[4] The event was publicised on the 6th of April Facebook page and organised as a flash-mob. Supporters were invited to wear black clothes and line the public streets with their backs to the traffic to express their indignation at the regime.

The strike in Mahalla el-Kobra was brutally repressed by the police, with one dead and hundreds wounded, while the supporting demonstration in Cairo had a limited degree of success. But the regime this time took notice and arrested Israa Abdel Fattah, the admin of 6th of April Facebook page, who came to be known in the Egyptian media as 'Facebook girl'. The event added to a repertoire of protest practices which were progressively clustering around a common revolutionary identity, as summed up by Noor Ayman Noor, the activist son of prominent opposition figure, and former presidential candidate, Ayman Noor:

> The 6th of April set foundations for the fact that you can organise big protests online. Kifaya set foundations for the fact that you can go down on the streets and say 'kifaya Mubarak' [enough of Mubarak]. 25th of January didn't happen overnight. It was years of things building up, of people setting things in stone. And the best example of this is that on the 25th of January many of the chants that we were chanting were chants that we had been chanting in earlier demonstrations. Everything is a build-up, nothing happens overnight.

It was on this established 'repertoire of contention' (Tilly, 2003), not simply on the availability of powerful technologies of communication, that the conditions for the Egyptian revolution were set.

KHALED SAID: A COLLECTIVE PROFILE PICTURE

> It was summer 2010 and I wasn't really into politics. I was reading the news, sometimes I would write something on Facebook. But that was it. I wasn't really caring much about politics. Then Khaled Said's page began, and it spread very fast. A friend sent

me an invitation ... and I started looking at the news and really caring about what is happening to my country. And I watched the pictures which were brutal. And the guy did nothing but ask why are you searching me. A lot of people like me started really caring about this after they saw the photo of Khaled Said's face, which was very brutal, and I really thought sometimes that this could happen to me.

For many young middle-class Egyptians like Mustafa Shamaa, a 20-year-old student at Cairo Nile University, joining the Kullena Khaled Said Facebook page was akin to a ritual of political initiation which facilitated their participation in the revolutionary movement. 'That page is what got me into politics' says Mustafa. The Kullena Khaled Said and other Egyptian opposition Facebook pages contributed to motivating and uniting a constituency of young people otherwise lacking in strong political identifications.

The page was created to protest against the death of Khaled Said, a 28-year-old middle-class Alexandrian with a passion for blogging who had completed part of his studies in the US. On the 6th of June 2010, Said had been picked up at an internet café by two secret-police officers and beaten to death on the street allegedly for having posted online a video which documented the implication of members of the police force in a drug deal. The image of his face completely devastated by blows began circulating on the internet, awaking many to the brutal reality of Mubarak's Egypt. In reaction blog posts were written, videos published, and Facebook pages opened. The Kullena Khaled Said page duly became an emotional rallying point for the Facebook youth, who not only felt compassion for Khaled Said but also identified with him, thinking, as Mustafa himself did, 'that this could happen to me'.

Conspiracy theories continue to abound about the creation of the Khaled Said page and who was behind it. The 'official' version is that it was created by Wael Ghonim, a 30-year-old Egyptian working in Dubai as the Google marketing executive for the Middle East. The mystery surrounding the page was increased by the fact that Ghonim, in order to protect his identity, decided to use a fake account with the name 'elshaheed' ('the martyr' as Said was considered to be), and used the Tor software[5] to guarantee his online anonymity. Ghonim was a young liberal Egyptian and a devoted Muslim. He came from the Egyptian middle class and studied for an MBA at the elite American University in Cairo, as did many other digital activists. However, compared to many, Ghonim arguably had a more direct understanding of the condition and experience of the lower classes in Egypt, having studied at the state-run and overcrowded Orman high school in Cairo. An 'internet fanatic' since an early age, Ghonim did not have the typical skills and charisma of a revolutionary leader. As he himself admitted he found it easier to relate with people online rather than face-to-face (Ghonim, 2012: 13). But he was not completely new to activism either. In 2009 he had set up a Facebook page to support the presidential campaign of the former chief of the International Atomic Energy Agency (IAEA) Mohammed el-Baradei, who he had also met in person at his mansion in Cairo.

The response to the opening of the Kullena Khaled Said page was impressive. A whopping 36,000 users joined the page on the first day, quickly helping it to become the most popular anti-regime Facebook page. The massive participation registered by the page was testament to the degree of indignation many Egyptians felt, and indicative of the extent to which Facebook pages were one of the very few places through which it could be channelled. However, the popularity of the page was also the result of Wael Ghonim's marketing skills and particularly of his ability to construct a compelling emotional conversation with the page's users. Ghonim exploited the techniques he had learned during his MBA and perfected through his management of a number of successful Arabic websites before joining Google. His model in planning the campaign was the classic three-step 'sales tunnel':

> The first phase was to convince people to join the page and read its posts. The second was to convince them to start interacting with the content by 'liking' and 'commenting' on it. The third was to get them to participate in the page's online campaign and to contribute to its content themselves. The fourth and final phase would occur when people decided to take the activism onto the streets. This was my ultimate aspiration. (Ghonim, 2012: 67–8)

The success of the page rested on its ability to attract a diverse public of users, beyond those who were already politicised. For this purpose Ghonim used the Egyptian dialect Ammeya rather than the high-brow standard Arabic, and employed abundant visual material, videos, pictures and the like capable of attracting people with low literacy skills. Moreover, he carefully avoided the kind of confrontational language used on other Egyptian anti-regime Facebook pages, which he thought could discourage unpoliticised users. Finally, Ghonim tried to make users feel that they were not just 'liking' a page but were actually engaging in a conversation. To this end, he spent much time and effort answering user comments.

Figure 2.2   We Are All Khaled Said cartoon. (Courtesy: Carlos Latuff)

Through his posts – written in the first person, as if he were himself Khaled Said speaking from the tomb – Ghonim catalysed a process of emotional identification on the part of young middle-class Egyptians with someone with whom they had much to share. Exemplary of this process of collective identification was the fact that many users adopted the photo of Said as their own Facebook profile picture. In anticipation of the 25th of January demonstration, the Brazilian radical cartoonist Carlos Latuff, at the request of Egyptian activists, represented Said in a youthful grey jumper, holding a mouse-sized and scared-looking Hosni Mubarak. Said's profile as a blogger and the story of his 'martyrdom' made him a perfect hero for the *shabab-al-Facebook*: a dead leader that young middle-class people could rally around in the absence of living heroes. In this sense, Said was quite a different figure from Mohammed Bouazizi, the Tunisian street vendor from the small town of Sidi Bouzid who by setting himself on fire on the 17th of December 2010 in protest against an episode of police repression would light the fuse of the Tunisian revolution, and thereby of the Arab Spring as a whole. In a heavily class-ridden society like Egypt, Said's middle-class background played an important role in politicising that part of the population which had been the most reluctant to voice its discontent at the regime. As Mustafa Shamaa suggests, the main users of the page were those 'who had access to good food, access to the Internet ... who had been educated abroad, who went to international schools, who had been outside of Egypt, and had more awareness [but] who wouldn't care about the problems'.

In the words of Ahmed Sabry, a 48-year-old architect involved in the revolution, Facebook was for many a sort of 'training ground', which prepared the *shabab-al-Facebook* psychologically for the tough challenges that awaited them in the streets. It allowed them to build up a confidence in their own abilities from the relatively safe cover of a computer screen. Activist Nora Shalaby observes that the Facebook page 'showed that there were many people thinking the same, and wanted the torture to stop and wanted to see a regime change'. The mere existence of opposition Facebook pages was for many politically inexperienced young people proof of the fact that Mubarak's regime was less powerful than it pretended to be. Mustafa Shamaa recounts how 'the first time I watched the Khaled Said's page I got a bit scared. But then I saw that they didn't arrest the admin. And I realised that there was some safety and that we could write whatever we wanted to.'

If the figure of Khaled Said allowed this unpoliticised Egyptian middle-class youth to identify *with* one hero, it also allowed them to identify *against* a common enemy – not just the regime as a whole but more specifically the police. 'Ours was first and foremost a hate for police', explains Sally Zohney. 'The police represented everything that was wrong with Egyptian society.' Different categories of people had different reasons for harbouring this anger. Football 'ultras' – fans of popular clubs like Zamalek and el-Ahly – hated the police because of the frequent clashes after matches.[6] Microbus drivers hated them for being constantly targeted with arbitrary road fines, with which officers were topping up their miserly salaries. Young people resented them because of random searches and harassment.

The Kullena Khaled Said page became a stage for collecting and cataloguing the extent of the baseness of the regime, gathering all the evidence in one place and thus creating a 'chain of equivalence'

(Laclau, 2005: 94) between the grievances of different groups of people. As Sally Zohney reports:

> Everybody started posting videos of police brutality. Things people were shooting with their mobile phones: how they would rape prisoners, how they would electrify them etcetera ... It's overwhelming you know when you enter the page, and you see ten videos, and you see it is not one case or two cases, it is something very common ... You see police laughing while slapping people, and cursing them, and making them run naked on the floor.

The call for a demonstration on the 25th of January, 'Police Day', would provide this convergence of popular sentiment against the security forces which had coalesced on Facebook with a date on which to materialise.

RSVPING TO THE REVOLUTION

The organisational challenge faced by the admins of prominent anti-regime Facebook pages was how to transform the vocal publics gathered online into protesting crowds. While this was a daunting task given the widespread fear of police repression, it is remarkable how many users of these pages were impatient to move from Facebook to the streets. Nora Rafea, a 26-year-old activist, describes her feelings on using the Kullena Khaled Said page:

> Facebook for me was like oooh! We really need to stop this virtual world. If we really want to do something we really need to stop this. We have to go down. This was my idea. It's too comfortable, and you feel that you are just shouting words but you didn't actually do anything. For me it was like we need to get out of our circles. I say things and the people who like, like, like. They come from the same background and the same perspective, somehow unrelated from the ground, from reality, from the real people on the streets.

The fear of endangering users initially led Ghonim and the other admin of the page, Abdel Rahman Mansour, to 'focus on online activities that we could promote, to instil a sense of optimism and confidence that we could make a difference, even if only in the virtual world for the time being' (Ghonim, 2012: 67). However, just a few days after its opening, the page was already publicising street demonstrations.

At the suggestion of an Alexandrian user, a series of 'silent stands' were organised and publicised on the Facebook page (Ghonim, 2012: 70). The idea of the silent stands followed the format of the flash-mob, like those organised in previous years by the 6th of April group through its own Facebook page. People were asked to convene in a central area of the city at a given time to perform a small collective action. They would stand in silence in a public area, some of them reading the Koran or the Bible, as a way of expressing peacefully their indignation at the regime. In the first of these events, held on the 19th of June 2010, only a few hundred joined the gatherings in Cairo and Alexandria, a fraction of the thousands who had answered positively to the invitation on Facebook. This was just proof of the fact that Facebook RSVPs only rarely translate into actual attendance – a phenomenon we will see again in the different movements discussed in this book. Despite the relatively low turnout, the event was considered a moderate success by Ghonim, and a confirmation of the possibility of transforming Facebook publics into protesting crowds. In the following months, a number of other 'silent stands' were publicised on the page, even though after a while the format seemed to be wearing out through force of repetition.

Compared to the 'silent stands' of 2010, the call launched by the page for a mass demonstration on the 25th of January 2011 was understandably a much more daring act. In his autobiographical book, Ghonim explains the fixing of the date as a decision taken alone in a rush, on the evening of the 29th of December. He had just been discussing the options with Ahmed Maher, the leader of the 6th of April movement, on an internet chat. But Maher had asked for time to consider the date, and did not seem too enthusiastic, given that his group wanted to concentrate all its effort on the 6th of April. Ghonim however could not resist his own drive and posted the message 'January 25th is Police Day and it's a national holiday ... I think the police have done enough this year to deserve a special celebration ... What do you think?' (Ghonim, 2012: 121). With 471 likes, and 119 comments, the users' response was positive but not enthusiastic. A couple of days later, the Islamist bombing of a Coptic Church in Alexandria on the 1st of January, which killed 21 people, shifted attention away from the idea. It wasn't until the 14th of January, the day Ben Ali escaped from Tunisia, that Ghonim floated again the idea of an action on the 25th. This time the message attracted 3,022 likes and 1,748 comments, giving a clear sign that users enthused by the events in Tunisia were ready for action.

It is evident that the organisation of the 25th of January demonstration, which was to mark the beginning of the 18-day revolution, was not undertaken on the internet alone. It required a complex and laborious groundwork to sort out the logistics and publicise the protests among the populace. Seeing the event as a 'political opportunity' (Tarrow, 1994: 17–18) not to be missed, a 'Revolutionary Youth Coalition' formed on the ground, encompassing 6th of April activists, revolutionary socialists, members of el-Baradei's group the National Association for Change, and young dissidents from the Muslim Brotherhood. As Ahmed Sabry puts it, the demonstration 'was much more organised than people in the West think. There were several meeting places and phone numbers and mobile numbers for the lawyers.' The 6th of April Youth Movement played a particularly important role in coordinating events on the ground. They set up a 'war-room' in an office nearby Tahrir square from which they would coordinate on the phone activists in the different marches. Moreover, in anticipation of the 25th, they organised a series of rehearsal demonstrations in popular neighbourhoods to experiment with different tactics and test the reaction of the people on the streets. Activists also tried to convince established opposition groups to join them. While the Muslim Brotherhood and all other opposition parties initially turned down the invitation, key figures in the ultras pledged their support.

The Kullena Khaled Said Facebook page progressively came to function as a sort of megaphone through which, from its safe base in Dubai, Ghonim would relay to a broad and diffuse public the decisions taken by activists on the ground in Cairo and Alexandria. The Facebook page became a platform from which to share and streamline information, but more importantly to create a sense of anticipation about the upcoming event. A Facebook event was created titled 'January 25: Revolution against Torture, Poverty, Corruption and Unemployement'. On Friday the 21st, four days before the first protest, the page counted 100,000 confirmed attendees and many others would join in the following days.

But would all those appearing under the 'attending' list actually turn out? Or would the Facebook youth remain just a Facebook youth? These were the questions many people asked themselves on the eve of the demonstration, in a testament to the difficulty of constructing a sense of trust online (Tarrow, 1998). Previous protest events had already acquainted participants with the gulf between a Facebook count of attendees and the actual street count. Scepticism was thus unsurprisingly rife: 'I saw that people were saying they would take part in the protests but I didn't believe they would', recounts Reda a photographer and member of the ultras of el-Ahly who took to the streets on the 25th. Sally Zohney came to realise that many of her friends who had confirmed their attendance were not actually intending to participate:

> Before the 25th we had the event on Facebook of the 25th of January revolution, and you have many people saying attending, attending, attending and you say: 'alright, whatever'. And you see how many of those you know and you ask them are you guys really going? And they would say: no! Then why are you saying that you are going to attend on Facebook? Because we are supportive! And then you start realising that only one or two are actually going out of twenty people who said yes!

Fear of police repression, and mutual distrust among Facebook users, constituted two formidable obstacles on the way to achieving a good turnout on the day. Ghonim was aware of the risk. During the final days before the demonstration he put much effort into countering the defeatism reflected in some of the comments posted on the page, as epitomised by the following message: 'no one will do anything and you'll see. All we do is post on Facebook. We are the Facebook generation. Period' (Ghonim, 2012: 135). To dispel this impression, Ghonim focused on positive messages emphasising the people's determination to take to the streets, exemplified by the statement: 'we won't stand and watch other people on Facebook'. The motivational work done by Ghonim in preparation for the protests is exemplified by a message published on the 24th, which appealed to people's sense of pride:

> A person decided not to participate tomorrow, he is sitting in front of his computer and writes comments on Facebook saying: the people are cowards and nobody is really going to participate ... like I said before there is a phenomenon in psychology called projection ... you have a certain problem, in order to avoid pangs of your conscience you are saying to yourself that all the people are cowards ... Unfortunately my friend ... I am not a coward, I am demonstrating on the 25th Jan.

The same urge to dispel people's fear and uncertainty underscored the action of young activist Asmaa Mafhouz, who in anticipation of the protest posted a now-famous YouTube video in which she incited people to join the protests:

> If you think yourself a man, come with me on 25 January. Whoever says women shouldn't go to protests because they will get beaten, let him have some honor and manhood and come with me on 25 January. Whoever says it is not worth it because there will only be a handful of people, I want to tell him, 'You are the reason behind this, and you are a traitor, just like the president or any security cop who beats us in the streets.'[7]

This call to heroism cleverly used the machismo prevalent in Egyptian society as an expedient through which to mobilise young men, who would fear being ridiculed for having been surpassed in bravery by a young girl. On the eve of the protest similar videos and status messages confirmed the impression that 'it was going to be big' – as Ahmed Sharqaui, an Egyptian activist from the town of Zagazig, reflects. The last status message published on the Kullena Khaled Said page on the morning of the 25th, a few hours before the time set for the public gathering, took the tone of a generational challenge: 'today we are going to prove that we are not guys of "Comment and like" as they claim. We are REALITY on Earth we are demanding our rights and we are all participating.'

'OUR PEOPLE COME DOWN!'

If on the eve of the revolution Facebook groups played a crucial role in organising dissent against the regime, as soon as the movement 'landed' on the streets its communications shifted drastically. As Osama Hoon, a 6th of April activist, sums it up: 'before the 25th of January it was 80% Facebook, 20% face-to-face. After the 25th of January it was 20% Facebook, 80% face-to-face.' For all the sophistication achieved by the revolutionary movement on the internet in the preparation phase, it is remarkable how far the mobilising effort relied on a creative reinvention of the ancient art of face-to-face agitation. Facebook had proven a useful rallying point precisely because of the obstacles to communication imposed by the authoritarian regime on the streets. But for the revolution to gain sufficient support a direct interaction with the lower classes at street level was imperative, especially given the huge digital divide in Egyptian society where three quarters of the population have no internet access.

As Ghonim himself affirmed in a message on the Facebook page: 'reaching working class Egyptians is not going to happen through the Internet and Facebook'. In the status updates he posted in the days before the 25th, Ghonim put great emphasis on the need for people to 'get out', to 'spread out to streets, factories, mosques, and churches' (Ghonim, 2012: 143). A message posted on the 21st read: 'we have to guarantee that our messages are widespread especially in poor areas ... We all should move to the streets now and lessen the usage of Facebook.' On the 23rd, the admin appealed again to its users to speak to the Egypt that was not part of the *shabab-el-internet*: 'We have *gathered* on Facebook and our voice is very high now and can be heard clearly ... On Tuesday we have to be many on the streets ... we have to reach the other 60 million people who don't have [access to the] Internet.' Reaching out to those people was coming to be seen as the most important aim of the demonstrations.

The incitements launched by Ghonim through the Khaled Said Facebook page were matched by an intense effort to spread the message locally. Young 'internet people' thus turned into street agitators trying to persuade others among their network of friends and acquaintances to join the protests. 'We, the people of the Internet made ordinary people know that something is going to happen. That was the important thing for the 25th' – reflects Abdallah, a member of the ultras of el-Ahly. 'The people of the Internet and the Facebook activists, they went to speak with the normal people who are without Internet.' Ahmed Sabry recounts how 'before the 25th we were leafleting, and distributing flyers and talking to people. Myself I went to have a haircut and I convinced everyone in the barber shop that we are going on the 25th.' When the day came, the physical passage of marchers across different areas of Cairo provided the movement with an opportunity for agitating among the *shaabi*, many of whom resented the regime for the economic hardships they were suffering. Taking to the streets was the only way for the movement to break the double barrier of the digital divide and the censorship of the state-owned news media.

In order to maximise the movement's visibility on the streets and the possibility of contact with the local population, activists resorted to the tactic of 'feeder marches'. Instead of assembling directly in Tahrir square, protesters were invited to join up at four separate meeting points in different areas of Cairo, including the working-class neighbourhoods of Shubra and Imbaba. The exact locations were announced on the Kullena Khaled Said Facebook page only three days before the protests, in order to give the police little time to prepare. Before heading towards Tahrir, the marchers would make several turns in small residential streets in the neighbourhoods close to their initial assembly point, so as to gather more people along the way. The tactic was concisely explained in a small booklet distributed online in advance of the protests on Friday the 28th:

1) Assemble with your friends and neighbours in residential streets away from where security forces are.
2) Shout slogans in the name of Egypt and the people's freedom (positive slogans).
3) Encourage other residents to join (again with positive language).
4) Go out into the major streets in very large numbers in order to form the biggest possible assembly.
5) Head towards important government buildings while shouting positive slogans, to take them over.[8]

'The idea was that the demonstration was like a bus and everybody was riding it', explains Ahmed Sabry. 'The bigger the march became, the more people get confidence and want to join it.' The marching protesters thus formed not simply a 'contentious gathering'[9] (Tilly, 1978: 115), but also a contagious one: a gathering which would in turn gather more people on its passage through the streets. As Nora Shalaby explains: 'We always made sure we were going through small streets, where there are residential areas, not the big streets, where there are no residential buildings ... because that way you encourage people to come down and see the stuff.'

Using this tactic, the marchers managed to gather great numbers of people on the way, fuelling enthusiasm among those who participated and generating the confidence that they could prevail over the police forces. Abdallah recounts the itinerary of the march he joined on the 25th from Giza on the western bank of the Nile:

On the 25th I went to Mustafa Mahmud square in Giza. We were about 700 people, very few, in fact. Yes we were so stupid all of them Facebook activists, and like that, only coming there from the Internet. We moved there and it was about 11am in the morning ... We met and we went to Tahrir by foot ... When we reached the square we were 50,000 people. Yes many people came. They don't know anything. But when they hear what we are saying and when they saw us they joined us. They came from everywhere: from the shops, from the streets, from their homes, from everywhere.

To invite people to join the demonstrations, the marchers continuously repeated 'positive slogans' like 'aysh, hurreya, wa adala egtimaya' (bread, freedom and dignity), and the more famous 'el-shaab ureed iskat el-nisam' (the people want the fall of the regime). These were slogans many Egyptians could easily identify with. They avoided ideological language and instead concentrated on simple political and social demands particularly targeted at the plight of working-class people and the poor. The slogans were accompanied by direct exhortations to join the protests, like 'inzil, inzil, inzil' (come down! come down! come down!) and 'ya ahlina andamulina' (our families join us), addressed to bystanders on the streets and people watching the marchers go by from their windows and balconies. With these forms of street-level communication, the Facebook youth created a face-to-face contact with 'those Egyptians who don't have the internet', to use Ghonim's words. This involved a learning process, since for many people like Mohammed Saidi, a 22-year-old political science graduate, 'it was the first time that I'd done this, talking politics with strangers on the streets'.

On the 26th and 27th the movement continued to make itself visible in Cairo and Alexandria, while fighting between demonstrators and police raged in Suez. All the attention was now focused on preparation for the 28th: the 'Friday of Anger'. Meeting points for the feeder marches were once again publicised on the Kullena Khaled Said Facebook page. However, by this point the website had become just one among many poles of mobilisation and coordination, among which featured established organisations like the Muslim Brotherhood which had eventually pledged its support. On the day, the format of the feeder marches was intensified by using mosques as gathering points, and the noon Friday prayers as the pre-established gathering time. Nora Shalaby describing one march leaving from the *shaabi* area of Dar-el-Salam:

We waited until the prayer was over. And then a small protest came out of the mosque and we joined and we started walking. And then all of a sudden out of nowhere ... thugs started appearing ... We separated very quickly. We were not used to being attacked by thugs ... So we got kind of worried and we hid. And then we decided to go to Old Cairo to see whether we could find another march and we saw people just standing, waiting for more people to join until they started walking. And we joined them and we were calling to people on the balconies: 'Join us! Join us!'

If on the 25th the crowd was composed of '70% to 80% middle class people', as activist Hannah el-Sissi put it, on the 28th 'everybody joined', including the *shaabi*. An anecdote recounted by Marwa Hussein, a journalist on the *el-Ahram* newspaper, testifies to the diversity of the crowd: 'On the 28th I met one guy who was very confused about all this Facebook hype, who didn't know at all what this Facebook thing was and in the middle of the demo I had to explain it to him.' On the day, hundreds of thousands of people took to the streets in Cairo, Alexandria, Suez and other Egyptian cities. Many police stations across the capital, and the HQ of Mubarak's National Democratic Party (NDP), were set ablaze. After several hours of battling with the police, during which hundreds of protestors lost their lives, the marchers finally occupied Tahrir square, which they would defend from the attacks of thugs and plain-clothes policemen for 15 more days until the resignation of Hosni Mubarak.

NEVER MIND THE KILL SWITCH

Overnight on the 27th, in anticipation of the 'Friday of Rage', the Egyptian government had taken the unprecedented step of switching off all internet and mobile phone communications in the country (Dunn, 2011). Just after midnight, all major internet service providers such as Telecom Egypt, Link, Etisalat, and others were shut down in a matter of minutes. The government exploited the presence of a series of infrastructural bottlenecks in the Egyptian network. Only one ISP, Noor Data Networks, which serves the Egyptian stock exchange, was unaffected by the attack. In the early hours of the 28th, mobile phone services (Vodafone, Mobinil and Etisalat) were also shut down in most areas of the country.

The regime clearly hoped that the move would disrupt the activists' capacity for coordination and scare most people off the streets. And indeed, my interviewees concur in describing the sense of disorientation which the unavailability of internet and (more importantly) of mobile phones caused on that day. But the shutdown did not prove a fatal blow for the movement. In fact, on the day, many more people took to the streets than they had done on the 25th. The fact is that the government's move was 'too little too late', as Ahmed Sabry puts it. Once the revolutionary process had been set in motion, a spatial automatism was established: 'people simply knew they needed to go to Tahrir', says Mohammed el-Agati of the NGO Arab Forum for Alternatives. The square rather than the internet became the main coordination platform of the revolutionary movement. In response to police repression and the communication shutdown, people established a permanent sit-in in Tahrir. As the blogger Mahmoud Salem explained in an interview with American broadcaster PBS: 'when they shut down the internet they brought back the people together in a way they never even imagined'.[10] The 'thickness' of Egyptian face-to-face social networks provided an effective and ready-made substitute for Facebook and Twitter.

Not only did the kill switch fail to disrupt the internal coordination of the movement, it also proved to be a formidable mobilising factor by revealing the wickedness of the regime and thus motivating many who were still undecided. Nora Rafea tells the story of her cousin, for whom the kill switch was a moment of conversion to the movement:

> My cousin was very sceptical of the revolution. Before the 28th he really criticised us and wrote on his status: 'are you guys joking? A revolution through Facebook? What the hell! There is no hope...' And then the moment they shut down the communications this person turned 180 degrees and said 'OK, this is too much, I am going to take to the streets.' It was a changing point for him ... he found that action ridiculous ... and he joined the streets. In the morning I saw his wife and she told me that he had gone to the demonstrations. And I couldn't believe it.

The decision taken by the government also revealed the distance between the regime's official version of events on the state-owned media and the reality on the streets. 'This made a lot of people very angry', explains Mustafa Shamaa. 'How come you are doing this? On state TV you are saying that there is no protest and you are switching off the internet and mobile phones?' For Noor Ayman Noor, the government's decision was perceived as a betrayal by the middle-class youth:

> Over the last several years the former regime had gotten us so addicted to our mobile phones, so addicted to our computers, and to the internet and so many things ... and suddenly we wake up one morning and we have nothing ... Many people including

those who were not planning on going down, when they saw the police doing what they did, they said no we have to go down.

If some people took to the streets out of rage at the government's actions, others did so mainly for practical reasons: to look for their friends and relatives they could not otherwise get in contact with because of the communications shut-down. As discussed in Chapter 1, mobile phones have introduced forms of microcoordination (Ling, 2004: 70) which have reshaped our everyday social interactions. When the mobile services were switched off, the capacity for micro-coordination was severely disrupted, obliging people to take to the streets if they wanted to get in contact with their peers. Mustafa Shamaa illustrates this point in his testimony:

> Some of my friends they ran into the protests because the phone was off and they couldn't get in touch with their brothers and sisters. So they went to the protests to look for them and they made the numbers increase. I know a lot of people who did that ... my cousin for example came to the protests looking for me. And this actually made the difference.

The internet shut-down made it impossible to maintain a safe distance by following events on the internet or talking on the phone to one's friends on the streets. The government's decision thus eliminated the possibility of a passive though sympathetic spectatorship. To get even a glimpse of what was going on, one had to take to the streets. The kill switch thus demonstrated the ambiguous role of modern communication technologies in the process of mobilisation, and the extent to which they can also simply be used to maintain a virtual connection with activism without ever joining them physically.

With the communications shut-down the occupation in Tahrir square became an immersive face-to-face communicative event. 'We had no idea that the world was following us, we had no idea of what the media was saying, what the TV was saying, what Al-Jazeera was reporting, what the people in the streets were doing' recalls Sally Zohney, 'we were living in another dimension'. Many of my interviewees recounted with melancholy the experience of national and cross-class brotherliness in the square, and the encounters they had with people they would never have got to know otherwise. As Nora Shalaby recounts, the square gathered 'people of different backgrounds, of different classes, just sitting together talking.' For some activists like Sally Zohney it was even frustrating when the government reversed the kill switch after five days:

> I really regret that they brought the internet back during the revolution ... It divided people ... Protesting you think that everyone is with you ... And even if you don't see them you just think that everyone is in the same spirit, and everyone is as supportive and as excited ... But then they brought back Facebook and you saw people writing 'enough with the criminals in the streets' ... and you begin having an argument on Facebook with them and tell them 'I am not a criminal, why do you call me a criminal' and them answering 'yes you are a criminal if you do this'... and people accusing each other over who is really patriotic who is not, who is with what and blablabla ... and it created more divisions ... And at some point I didn't want to use the internet anymore except for information: 'OK tomorrow we are going that way.' I didn't want to enter in debates, I didn't want people accusing me, or seeing people unfriending people ... oh this person ... whenever I see a person with a photo of Mubarak as profile picture he is no longer my friend.

With the revolution the Facebook youth took to the streets and contributed to opening up a public space where different classes could interact, as they could not do on social media, a preserve of the middle class. However, when Mubarak resigned on the 11th of February, that exceptional space of encounter which the revolution had created dissolved. The sit-in was almost immediately lifted, and the 'Facebook people' who had initiated the revolution went for the most part reluctantly back to the dispersion of their own mediated friendships. They would reappear only intermittently during the various waves of protest that would later target the new power-holders: the military rulers of the Supreme Council of Armed Forces (SCAF), headed by Mubarak's former minister of defence, field-marshal Mohammed Hussein Tantawi.

THE TWITTER PASHAS

In Egypt the word 'pasha' has a number of complex connotations. It is used in everyday life much in the same way as the English expression 'sir'. But the word still holds its original meaning as the honorific title of the Ottoman aristocracy which ruled Egypt for centuries. As Galal Amin observes in his latest book, *Egypt in the Era of Hosni Mubarak* (2011), this class kept itself aloof from the doings of the local population. Pashas were of Turkish origins, and often flaunted this foreignness. For some participants in the revolution like Mohammed 'Saidi', the Egyptian Twitter activists who have become famous in the West after the uprising are just that: 'pashas', an aloof activist elite, detached from the feelings of common Egyptians. Even if one does not buy into the class hatred which seems to underlie opinions like Saidi's, it is evident that during the revolution the use of Twitter was for the most part restricted to a tiny activist community numbering a few hundred, and that it thus had a limited impact on the general mobilisation. If, as Mustafa Shamaa puts it, 'the revolution would have happened without Facebook', the same applies even more strongly to Twitter.

The micro-blogging website's penetration rate in Egypt is very low, standing at only 0.15 per cent in November 2011 (Dubai School of Government, 2011b). Naturally, the 'uptake rate' within the community of those participating in revolutionary protests is much higher than that. But of the 20 people I interviewed in Cairo, only around half were on Twitter (while almost all of them were on Facebook), despite the fact that my sample of interviewees exclusively comprised middle-class and upper-middle-class activists, the demographic with the highest degree of new media connectivity. Optimal Twitter use in fact requires owning a smart-phone which, given its expense, is materially inaccessible to the great majority of Egyptians, including many from the middle class. Moreover, it entails a higher level of education, and a better knowledge of the English language than does Facebook. As Hannah El-Sissi points out, 'you cannot use Twitter much if you are an Arabic speaker, things like hashtags, the main features of Twitter cannot be used if you only have an Arabic keyboard'. In fact, during the 18-day revolution itself, most of the tweets on popular hashtags like #jan25, #tahrir, #egypt were written in English (Wilson and Dunn, 2011: 1271).

Since the fall of Mubarak, and the increasing popularity gained by Twitter in the wake of the uprising, more people have started writing in Arabic or the local dialect Ammeya, but the top tweeps continue for the most part to write in English.

Given the limited audience that could be reached at home through Twitter, its main role was thus mainly as a means of eliciting 'external attention' (Aday et al., 2010), 'as a key resource for getting information to the outside world, perpetuating the feeling that the world was watching, which was an important factor for morale and coordination on the ground' (Wilson and Dunn, 2011: 1252). During the days of the revolution, famous activist 'tweeps' like Gigi Ibrahim (@Gsquare86), and Mahmoud Salem (@sandmonkey) allowed people abroad to follow minute by minute the events taking place in the Egyptian streets. Besides being a channel to the outside world, Twitter also served as a means of coordination within the activist elite, for which it came to constitute a sort of 'information HQ of the movement', as Ahmed Sabry puts it. As described by activist tweep Nora Shalaby:

> Twitter gave you an on the spot account ... Go from here don't go from there. Try to take this entrance not that one, because there you wouldn't be able to come in ... Don't go in that area because it is full of thugs ... we were trying to get as much information as possible for people to come in and know what was happening.

Such tactical use of Twitter was to be further refined in the protests taking place after the revolution, aimed at the SCAF. For example during the clashes in Mohammed Mahmoud street in November 2011, in which over 70 protesters were killed, activists used the #TahrirNeeds hashtag to share information about medicines and other materials required by field hospitals and other logistical issues. Arguably more important than these tactical affordances has been Twitter's role in creating a sense of emotional cohesion *within* the upper-middle-class activist community, as illustrated by the selection of messages published in the book *Tweets from Tahrir* (Nunns and Soueif, 2011). On the eve of the 25th of January protests, @TravellerW confessed 'Yes, I'm worried about tomorrow. Which is exactly why I am going – we cannot, will not let them scare us. #25Jan', while @monasosh condensed well the emotions of the eve in three words: 'scared, excited and hopeful #Jan25'.

While providing a platform for generating a sense of solidarity within the activist elite, their intensive Twitter use has, however, run the risk of isolating these leaders from the feelings and experience of poorer and less internet-connected Egyptians. It is worth noting that most of the Egyptian top tweeps are children of rich upper-middle-class families. They almost invariably live in luxurious neighbourhoods like Nasr City, Heliopolis, Maadi and Zamalek, and have been educated in English schools and then at the exclusive American University in Cairo. Their frequent visits to the US and the UK, to receive prizes or participate in TV shows, have drawn harsh comments from within the movement, and accusations that

Figure 2.3   Twitter hashtags painted on the walls of Tahrir square during the July 2011 sit-in against the military council. (Author: Paolo Gerbaudo)

they are detached from the experience of common people in Egypt. While some of these tweeps have become activist stars abroad, they are almost unknown inside Egypt, as testified by the fact that the bulk of my Egyptian interviewees had never heard of them. Indicative of this mismatch between global fame and relative local obscurity is the fact that those few Twitter activists who ran for the 2011 parliamentary elections were badly defeated. Among them was the witty blogger and tweep Mahmoud Salem (@sandmonkey), who enjoys a following of 70,000 people on Twitter, but managed to secure only 16,000 votes in the Heliopolis constituency.

In the months following the revolution, some activists have recognised this danger of disconnection from the broader populace and have developed new practices combining social media with street-level agitation. In fact, for some, the amount of time dedicated to maintaining their Twitter streams runs the risk of taking precious energy away from campaigning both on-the-ground and through more accessible forms of internet communication. This problem has been explicitly denounced by the activist tweep Hassan Hamad, one of the promoters of Tweet Shara'a (#tweetshare3), which translates in English as 'tweet the streets'. As part of this initiative young middle-class activists are invited to take part in street campaigning, to discuss politics with random passers-by, while documenting the event on YouTube and Twitter. Through this kind of interaction, activists hope to break out of the closed circles of like-minded people which inevitably tend to cluster on social media. Interviewed by the Egyptian state-owned daily newspaper *al-Ahram*, Hamad stated:

> Twitter is indeed isolated from the street; it is like there is an ocean between them. On Twitter you have these opinion leaders who have thousands of followers. These opinion leaders are usually activists who have their own political and ideological beliefs from the start, and they tweet what they believe is right whether it reflects the street or not. These followers retweet it and believe it, creating a gap between them and the street, which includes every political and social group and class in society.[11]

For Salma Hegab, a 21-year-old activist and co-founder of #tweetshare3, 'it is true that activists have been thinking too much about talking among themselves and that they did lose touch with Egyptian population at large. Many have enclosed themselves in a comfortable activist-only internet world.' The fact is that, as Nour Ayman Nour observes, 'internet circles become an echo room where everyone is hearing each other. They are hearing their own views being bounced back. And sometimes there is an increasing divide between the internet community and the people on the streets.' In the aftermath of the revolution, as protests continue against military rule, Egyptian activists are still trying to find a balance between the use of social media and local street campaigning. In so doing, they are creating a hybrid of the two, a mediated public space, as signalled by the appearance of Twitter hashtags as graffiti tags on the walls of Cairo during any renewed wave of mobilisation against the military council.

CONCLUSION

Social media played a crucial role in the Egyptian revolution, but not an exhaustive one. They were crucial for motivating the core constituency of the movement, the so-called *shabab-al-facebook* and for constructing a choreography of assembly to facilitate its coming together in public space. However, social media alone would not have 'done the trick' without young internet-connected activists also engaging in street-level agitation to cross the digital divide and engage with the lower classes. When social media are not used in interaction with face-to-face communication, they can exacerbate social tendencies towards fragmentation and seclusion as seen in the case of the 'Twitter pashas'. In conclusion, it is worth offering a general remark on the role played by social media in constructing the choreography of assembly during the Egyptian revolution, and on the digital activists who acted as the choreographers. The revolution has often been described by pundits and journalists as essentially leaderless and spontaneous; and indeed this supposed 'leaderlessness' is what made it so attractive to anti-authoritarian activists throughout Europe and the US. The account proposed in this chapter suggests a more complex picture. Although the revolution did not throw up a singular charismatic leader who grabbed all the attention (even if Wael Ghonim came close to being one), it was characterised by the leading role taken by one section of society, the *shabab-al-Facebook*, which came to act as the catalyst for the process of mass mobilisation.

Besides social media and street communication, a wide range of other forms of communication also played a role in mobilising participants. The television channels of course, in particular Al-Jazeera and its Egyptian spin-off Al-Jazeera Mubashir, which became a mass medium for the channelling of information about the events taking place (Miles, 2011; Cottle, 2011). More could also be said about the role of newspapers and street media like flyers and posters, which also had an important role in the ecology of communication of the movement. Given the very specific scope of this chapter, however, these elements could not be considered. What is particularly significant for the purposes of this book is the fact that the Egyptian uprising and its use of social media as 'choreographic' tools it foregrounded came to inspire copy-cat movements in the West. As we will see in the following chapters, activists in Spain and in the US were driven by a desire to imitate and build on the 'Tahrir model'. In some cases, however, failing to appreciate the specificity of the Egyptian case, they also failed to learn from the errors committed by Egyptian activists. In the following chapter I will turn to the indignados of Spain, and their attempt to import into the West the Tahrir model of protest, together with the social media practices it foregrounded.

3
'We are not on Facebook, we are on the streets!': The Harvesting of Indignation

Because we are more humane. Because we are more decent.
Because we are more respectable. Because we are more.
YouTube video of Democracia Real Ya promoting the 15th of May 2011 demonstration[1]

While the world was still under the spell of the Arab Spring, a new social movement, inspired by the events taking place in Tunisia and Egypt, made its tumultuous appearance in debt-stricken Europe. Spain, one of the European countries worst affected by the global economic crisis, became the first site in the West to adopt the 'Tahrir model' of popular protest, with its combination of social media and mass sit-ins. Beginning on the 15th of May 2011 (known in Spain as 15-M), the day on which the first demonstrations were called in 58 Spanish cities, it was a '#revolution' or, better, a '#spanishrevolution' in '#sol', as its supporters were to celebrate it in the language of Twitter hashtags. After the demonstrations, a handful of protesters occupied Puerta del Sol in central Madrid. Refusing to leave, they were soon joined by thousands of others summoned through the social media.

The protesters gathered in central Madrid, and soon in tens of cities across Spain, came to be known as the 'indignados', or the indignants, from the booklet *Indignez vous!* (2010) authored by the nonagenarian French politician Stephane Hessel, who by calling on young people to rise up against economic injustice had inspired some of the initiators of the movement. Rejecting any Left/Right identification, they announced that they did not feel represented by existing parties and trade unions and were opting instead for a form of participatory democracy, or 'democracy 2.0', using Facebook and Twitter. 'Nobody expects the #spanishrevolution' proclaimed one sign held by a protester, wearing a Guy Fawkes mask from the film *V for Vendetta*, introducing a slogan that was to be re-tweeted and reposted hundreds of times. But why was nobody expecting it? Where was the 'indignation' hiding before it came into public view in the cities of Spain? And what was the role of social media in bringing this indignation into view?

In this chapter I discuss the role of social media in the mobilisation of the Spanish indignados. I will show how social media contributed to fashioning a choreography of assembly, resembling a 'harvesting of indignation', the physical and symbolic concentration of a constituency, united by a common sense of victimhood and indignation around public squares like Puerta del Sol, acting as a symbol of the 'people'. Social media like Facebook and Twitter contributed to transforming individual sentiments of anger into a collective identity animated by a desire to take back the streets after years of demobilisation. The emotional tension that underscored this choreography was expressed in slogans like 'take to the streets' and 'we are not on Facebook, we are on the streets', reflecting a widespread desire to break out of a situation of isolation and passivity characterising Spanish society in the midst of the crisis.

The indignados or 15-M movement has often been described by its own participants using the imaginary of networks. For example, in her book *Nosotros los Indignados* (2011), Klaudia Álvarez, the communication coordinator of Democracia Real Ya, portrays it as a 'cerebro en red' (networked brain) made up of 'inteligencias conectadas' (connected intelligences) (Álvarez, 2011: 12). Castells himself, in a speech delivered at the protest camp in Plaza de Catalunya in Barcelona, described the movement as a form of resistance against the 'manipulation of brains',[2] and presented the emergence of the indignados as made possible by the greater scope for grassroots organisation available in the contemporary system of 'mass self-communication' (Castells, 2009).

As stated in Chapter 1, I am suspicious of this cognitivist understanding of social movements as networks of brains, and my aim here is to recuperate a sense of the role of the body and emotions in the process of contemporary mobilisation. In the specific case of the indignados movement, it is precisely the emotion of 'indignation' that deserves to become the focus of analysis. Interestingly, the movement is also described by its own participants as 'un estado de animo' (an emotional state), as seen in the collective experience of enthusiasm throughout the 'acampadas' (the protest camps). But how was this emotion harnessed and triggered by the movement's organisers?

OF ALCOHOLIC GATHERINGS AND ILLEGAL DOWNLOADS

To understand the rise of the indignados movement and the reasons for the high level of participation it attracted we need to take into account the exceptional gravity of the economic situation in Spain at the time. Alongside Portugal, Italy, Ireland and Greece, Spain was one of the 'PIIGS',[3] to use the infamous label applied by financial analysts to those European countries whose sovereign debt ratings plunged in the wake of the financial crisis of 2007–8. Of the national economic indicators, the most staggering one in the case of Spain is youth unemployment: at 41 per cent in 2010 and topping over 47 per cent in the third quarter of 2011 (Eurostat, 2011), the highest in Europe. Yet, as always happens with social movements, these grievances alone cannot explain the appearance of the indignados (Buechler, 2000). Why, otherwise, did the Spanish people not mobilise before the 15th of May 2011, given that such grievances were to a great extent there already?

Asking the activists who participated in the 15-M movement the reasons for the earlier lack of mobilisation, one often gets in response an array of adjectives like 'pasmaos' (stoned), 'anestetisados' (anaesthetised), 'atontados' (stupified), 'apalancados' (paralysed) – all terms conveying the sense of a society, and its youth in particular, incapable of voicing its discontent at the effects of the economic crisis. My interviewees almost invariably described Spain as a country in which people were trying to forget their troubles by indulging in the pleasures of Spanish nightlife and its *bar de tapas*.[4]

This widespread resignation must also be attributed largely to the incapacity of the existing institutions and organisations to become a focal point in the mobilisation of emerging popular demands. The Spanish Socialist Party (PSOE) of José Luiz Zapatero embraced the neoliberal response to the crisis, cutting public spending, and reducing labour rights. The trade unions, for their part, were accused of offering only a timid response to the government's austerity plans, given their traditional closeness to the Socialists. While in Greece in 2010, ten general strikes took place, in Spain there was just one, and even that had limited impact. Apart from the 'institutional Left' of parties and trade unions, the radical grassroots groups stemming from the anti-globalisation movement also seemed to be going through a phase of latency. Despite such lows, legally and illegally occupied social centres like the Tabacalera, the Patio Maravillas, and Casablanca in Madrid, maintained their role as outposts of alternative culture and sociability and would come to constitute an important resource in sustaining the occupation of Puerta del Sol.

Spain is well known the world over for its thriving street life. Yet in the period before the blossoming of the indignados movement, the country had been subjected to an intense sanitisation of public space, inspired by a 'fear of crowds', which affected both political and social gatherings in public space. Sofia de Roa, a 32-year-old journalist active in the 15-M movement and a member of the organisation Estado del Malestar (Badfare State), recounts how the government and the mass media had begun to stigmatise any outbreak of protest in public space:

> Before the protests of the 15-M, there was a strike by workers on the Metro (the underground railway system) here in Madrid. And newspapers and TV presented them like criminals, just because they were using their right to protest. And the same happened with air-traffic control workers. Independently of what you think of a certain struggle ... the government responded by issuing a decree on protests sending a message to society to be careful about protesting. The general sense was that if you protested you must be a bit crazy. And many progressive people were also disillusioned, because in the past there were a lot of protests which didn't achieve anything.

This stigmatisation of public gatherings also affected subcultural practices of youth sociability, as exemplified by the government's campaign against the 'botellon'. The botellon – literally 'great bottle' – is an outdoor gathering in which large groups of young people spend the night in public squares, drinking, chatting and listening to music (Baigorri and Fernández, 2004). The practice emerged in the 1980s among students and young people wanting to avoid the high costs of 'legitimate' establishments. Its increasing popularity in the 2000s led to the creation of national and regional laws against the botellon. In response, in 2006 young people coordinated on the web to organise a number of 'macro-botellones' which attracted thousands of participants. The organisers made it clear that they saw the banning of botellones not simply as a measure against 'vandalism', as the government had it, but as a veiled attack on people's freedom of assembly and use of public space.

In the face of this stigmatisation of public gatherings, in the months before the 15-M, a glimmer of hope for radicals came from a series of online campaigns protesting against restrictions on so-called 'internet freedom'. The Zapatero's government 'Ley Sinde' – a law aimed at curtailing file-sharing in a country which had been dubbed a piracy paradise by media-industry lobbyists[5] – angered many digital activists, who organised online to oppose the approval of the law. The campaign received a boost after US diplomatic cables released by Wikileaks revealed that the Spanish government was submitting to pressure from American majors. Seeing this as a betrayal of the people's mandate, Spanish activists initiated Twitter feeds with the hashtags #leysinde and #redresiste (the Net resists) and #nolesvotes (don't vote for them), to contest the approval of the law. Various blogs and popular download websites like Cinetube[6] and Series Yonkis[7] blackened their pages in protest. Profile pictures on Twitter and Facebook were changed to an image designed by the cartoonist Eneko, representing the internet as an endangered dove.

After being defeated in the Senate in December 2010, the law was finally approved in February 2011. In response, a group of activists including Ricardo Galli, professor at the Balearic Islands University, and Carlos Sanchez Almeida, known in Spain as the 'hackers' lawyer', set up the website nolesvotes.com. On the 16th of February they launched a manifesto asking people not to vote for those parties who had approved the Ley Sinde in the upcoming local elections scheduled for the 22nd of May. In a note posted on the blog of the lawyer Javier de la Cueva, one of the initiators of the campaign, the group proposed to 'develop ... citizens' initiatives based on the self-organisation of independent and reproducible territorial cells'. The note concluded on a techno-utopian note, claiming that 'the existence of the internet makes traditional representation unnecessary: a citizen can already represent himself without utilizing an alien voice'.[8] Hundreds of local groups coordinated through Google groups were created to spread the campaign locally, targeting specific candidates from the 'traitor parties', and the 'No les votes' campaign soon went beyond the single issue of 'internet freedom'. A Google map appeared on its website, documenting several cases of corruption, and the group circulated pictures accusing the two main Spanish parties of being united in resisting transparency and in maintaining their privileges.

The 'No les votes' campaign remained at the level of a diffuse online contestation and never managed to materialise into street demonstrations (Sampedro and Haro, 2011: 165). Nevertheless, around the time of its unfolding, a number of other campaigns were emerging emphasising the importance of re-appropriating public space, and which also came to influence the rise of the indignados: Juventud Sin Futuro (Youth without Future), Estado de Malestar (Badfare State), Plataforma de Afectados por la Hipoteca (Platform for Mortgage Victims) and Democracia Real Ya (Real Democracy Now).

Juventud Sin Futuro (JSF) was a radical student and youth movement coalition incorporating leftist activists of different ideologies. On its website it described itself as an organisation of 'young people, affected by unemployment and precarious jobs' and rallied behind the slogan 'sin curro, sin casa, sin miedo' (without a job, without a home, without fear).[9] Its novelty stemmed from its innovative use of social media like Twitter and Facebook as vehicles for mobilisation. At the same time the group also maintained a strong local footing. As Segundo Gonzales, a member of the group, explains: 'we always used social media, but we also always had a plan of physical action, because we are an organisation with some tradition and are rooted in different universities across the country'. JSF organised a demonstration on the 7th of April which, while attended by only a few thousand, would be seen in retrospect as an important 'dry run' for the 15th of May protests.

Not as ideologically explicit as JSF, but still recognisably 'progressive' in its discourse and imagery, was Estado de Malestar,[10] a group of activists campaigning against unemployment and cuts in public services. Since early 2011, Estado de Malestar had been staging protest performances every Friday in Plaza Callao and

Figure 3.1 The 'thumb down' logo of Estado de Malestar.

Puerta del Sol in central Madrid, and in 30 other Spanish cities. However, as Sofia de Roa admits, 'our Friday protests had only had a limited degree of success. People would pass by and briefly look with curiosity or disdain and just move on.' This group also focused on the use of social media in its communications – its very logo took the form of a Facebook 'thumb up' reversed into a 'thumb down' and accompanied by the words 'no me gusta' (I don't like it), and all its performances would be uploaded regularly on YouTube.

Less innovative in terms of its communications was the Plataforma de Afectados por la Hipoteca[11] (PAH), a group founded in February 2009 to defend people's right to housing and to protest against the eviction of 'mortgage victims'. PAH constituted an important link with the tradition of the 13-M housing rights movement, which in 2006 (from May 13th and through to June) had staged a series of sit-ins in public squares organised through SMS and emails (Sampedro and Haro, 2011: 159). While all these campaigns and organisations played an important role in the preparation of the 15-M protests, the group which gained most prominence was 'Democracia Real Ya'[12] (DRY), originally established online to campaign against austerity and corruption. Democracia Real Ya, the last actor to appear on the activist scene, would also be the one which came to act as focal point in the process of mobilising the indignados movement.

'WE ARE NORMAL, COMMON PEOPLE'

We are like you: people who get up every morning to study, work or find a job, people who have family and friends. People who work hard every day to provide a better future for those around us. Some of us consider ourselves progressive, others conservative. Some of us are believers, some not. Some of us have clearly defined ideologies, others are apolitical, but we are all concerned and angry about the political, economic, and social outlook which we see around us: corruption among politicians, businessmen, bankers, leaving us helpless, without a voice. This situation has become normal, a daily suffering, without hope. But if we join forces, we can change it. It's time to change things, time to build a better society *together*.[13]

This excerpt from the manifesto of Democracia Real Ya, published on the group's Facebook page, illustrates well the collective identity which came to define its online campaigning. Claiming to transcend the Left-Right spectrum, DRY's stated intention was to represent all those people who regardless of their political beliefs and lifestyles were affected by the ravages of the economic crisis and the politics of austerity imposed by Zapatero's government. Through the inclusivity, or some might say vagueness, of its identity, DRY would in the months before 15-M become an attractor for thousands of largely unpoliticised young people, creating a platform of emotional condensation to transform individual experiences of frustration and indignation into a collective political passion.

The initial nucleus of Democracia Real Ya was the result of an online encounter between two young people: 26-year-old Fabio Gandara and 23-year-old Pablo Gallego. Both Gandara and Gallego fell into Paul Mason's category of 'graduates without a future' (Mason 2012). Gandara had specialised in public law but after working for a time at a famous legal firm in Barcelona had been laid off. He had some minor activist experience having attended the European Social Forum in Paris in 2003 and then joined in the spontaneous protests against the ruling Partido Popular of José María Aznar after the Madrid bombing of March 2004. Pablo Gallego, a fresh graduate from the business school of Cadiz University, was without prior activist experience. He was motivated to engage in organising by his first-hand experience of the dire state of the Spanish job market. 'I realised that things were very bad, and there was no solution to anything', he explains.

The story of the emergence of Democracia Real Ya is the story of two individual manifestos, both published online months before the indignados movement would materialise in the streets. In October 2010, Fabio Gandara published his own manifesto in a Facebook group called 'Yo soy un/a joven español/a que quiere luchar por su futuro'[14] (I am a young Spaniard who wants to fight for his future), which later took the name of Juventud en Accion[15] (Youth in Action). 'This is not a movement of the Left or of the Right. We do not adhere to any theoretical groupuscule, be it Marxist, neo-Leninist, or anarchist. We are *simply* young people', proclaimed Gandara in the manifesto.[16] Although it managed to attract only a handful of signatories at the time, the manifesto already pre-figured in its tone and ingenuity the post-ideological refusal of Left and Right identifications which was to be a key feature of Democracia Real Ya. Unaware of Gandara's manifesto, in early 2011, Pablo Gallego published his own on his personal blog. 'A May '68 in Spain is possible' was the opening line of his 'Manifiesto Juventud' (Youth manifesto).[17] In simple almost amateurish language, the manifesto called on young Spaniards to break out of their state of passivity, to fight against corruption, a stalled two-party system, and trade unions by and large subservient to the ruling Socialist Party. Gandara came across Gallego's manifesto and began chatting with him online. Together they decided to set up a new Facebook group called 'Plataforma de coordinación de grupos pro-movilización ciudadana'[18] (platform for the coordination of groups for a civic mobilisation).

'Initially we were few people, me, Pablo and another person', recounts Gandara. 'Then bit by bit, people involved in different movements, from the internet movement to the student movement, started joining our forum.' In this phase the group organised exclusively online using the Facebook chat service as its means of coordination. As Gandara explains, the strategy agreed within the group was to 'use the power of the internet and the structure of the web to organise ourselves at the state level and develop a civic mobilisation for mass protest in the whole of Spain'. 'I initially had a leading role (voz cantante) in the group', explains Gandara, scrupulously adding that 'there was no administrator who had an exhaustive role. There was a debate every time a decision had to be taken.'

Once the group managed to attract more people, they began 'doing brainstorms, noting specific ideas, or slogans, and we would discuss what was the specific social and political change that we were asking for'. During chat sessions on Facebook the slogan 'Democracia Real Ya: no somos mercancia en manos de politicos y banqueros' (Real Democracy Now: we are not commodities in the hands of politicians and bankers) was coined and later came to be adopted as the group's name. Then, a 'bombarding work' began, as Gandara goes on to recount:

> We would enter internet forums of social and political discussion to see what they were saying in that group and to comment on what they were saying and inviting people to participate and adding comments to Facebook groups, and posting on profiles of any kind and sending emails to associations and NGOs and political groups and telling them a bit about this idea.

As testified by its emphasis on openness to new members, the identity of the group centred on its techno-libertarian emphasis on the possibilities of participatory democracy offered by the web, of the kind that had previously been invoked by the 'No les votes' campaign. But the group also strived to avoid being pigeon-holed as 'political', constantly emphasising its 'civic' character. For this reason, as Gallego explains, in all the group's communications words which might sound 'too political' or 'too ideological' would be studiously avoided, and substituted by a more colloquial language, such as those typical of Facebook status messages. For Gallego the 'secret of DRY's success was the use of euphemisms':

> A euphemism [for example] is to say that those at the bottom are against those at the top, instead of talking about class struggle. You are saying the same ... but you are not scaring people. The use of a new language has been fundamental to the movement's success ... At a moment when the citizenry is highly individualized and vulnerable in the face of the system it is a way to create an aggregate of people united not because of an ideological affinity, but by a protest affinity.

The same kind of anti-ideological spirit also animated the design of the group's website and publicity material. The main colour used as a background both in the website and in its publicity was a politically neutral yellow. This tint, similar to the one used in the public communications of the Spanish state, was the same as that adopted by Estado de Malestar and Juventud Sin Futuro, in an attempt to escape tight ideological identifications. A similar style characterised the group's logo, which carried only the organisation's name under 'DRY' in big letters. Written in a stencil font, the logo softly echoed the subversive language of graffiti and street art, thus giving the group's identity a youthful while studiously unobtrusive creative edge.

The online branding of the group, with its almost obsessive focus on inclusivity, registered its desire to move away from the antagonistic subcultural identity of the anti-globalisation movement and of the radical Left more generally. Aitor Tinoco, a key DRY organiser in Barcelona, speaks proudly of the fact that 'we were able to abandon flags and ideologies and talk about concrete problems to mobilise the citizenry'. While in some quarters this post-ideological approach earned DRY accusations of 'political childishness', it was also arguably precisely what allowed the group and its Facebook page to become 'a place to go beyond', as Sofia de Roa puts it.

Figure 3.2   The youthful logo of *Democracia Real Ya.*

While eschewing a clear ideological orientation, DRY owed the coherence of its identity to a direct appeal to the people against the system – a move which deeply resonates with Ernesto Laclau's description of populism as the construction of a popular unity against distant and corrupt institutions (Laclau, 2005). The clearest illustration of this orientation is offered by a YouTube video used to launch the demonstration on the 15th of May. At its centre stands a chessboard on which a standard set of black pieces is overwhelmed by a mass of white pawns. This was accompanied by a series of flashing captions which, after listing a series of grievances about corruption and unemployment, affirmed in Spanish: 'because we are more humane, because we are more decent, because we are respectable', ending with 'because we are more'.[19] This majoritarian orientation, clearly visible in this video as in all the communication of DRY, constantly highlighted the separation between 'politicians and bankers' and the 'common people', as illustrated by a scathing message posted on the Facebook page on the 3rd of April: 'thieving politicians and bankers remember that you are nothing and will never be anything without the people!'

Seeing in the campaign an opportunity to overcome division and inertia, different groups eventually decided to put their weight behind the 15-M call launched by DRY. The call was eventually supported by thousands of individual internet users and also by 200 civil society organisations, including well-established groups like the anti-globalisation group ATTAC and the environmental NGO Ecologistas en Accion (but not trade unions).

'REVOLUTION BEGINS ON THE 15TH OF MAY'

Besides being employed in the construction of a common identity, at the inception of the 15-M movement social media were also used as a means of generating an *emotional impetus* towards the protest, by firing up people's enthusiasm and constructing a contagious sense of anticipation for the upcoming event. 'The most important thing about these new tools was to give people an *ilusion*', Fabio Gandara explains, 'an *ilusion* that we could change things'. Interestingly, the word 'ilusion' in Spanish has a double meaning, the most immediate one being 'hope', the second one 'illusion'. This ambiguity captures well the way in which the DRY activists motivated prospective participants by putting forward a sort of self-fulfilling prophecy about the success of the demonstrations. Since the opening of the Facebook page in early March 2011, two months before the protests, organisers had worked hard to give the impression that the protests were going to be 'huge'. Despite the scarce resources they had at their disposal, and shielded behind the anonymity of the collective name of their Facebook group, they eventually managed to trigger a mood of collective euphoria among the page's users.

The page became a site for the accumulation of an emotional energy (Jasper, 2011), capable of motivating people to make the 'jump to the streets' (salto a la calle) and overcome their isolation and passivity. A cartoon published by the popular satirical magazine *El Jueves* in support of DRY a few days before the 15th of May illustrated the imaginary which underscored this operation. It depicts an overweight man, his eyes glued to a computer screen, in a sort of social media adaptation of the stereotype of the 'couch potato'. Instead of TV it is the internet which feeds his addiction. 'I am on Second Life' – says the character in the balloon – 'I go to many demonstrations'.[20] Against this perception of a widespread apathy, it is significant that the campaign adopted the simple but evocative slogan 'Toma la calle!' (take to the streets). Similarly to what had happened with the *shabab-al-Facebook* in Egypt, young internet-connected Spaniards were summoned to transform themselves from a secluded Facebook youth into a politically active street youth.

Just a few days after the opening of the Facebook page, the admins were already launching boastful messages like 'LA REVOLUCION EMPIEZA EL 15 DE MAYO'[21] (revolution begins on the 15th of May) and 'EL 15 DE MAYO ES NUESTRO DIA!' (15th of May is our day!). Almost every day they would report on the increasing numbers of supporters. Here are some of the examples of the motivational messages conveyed: 'Menos de 48 horas despues ... Ya somos 500!!!' (After less than 48 hours ... we are already 500!!!). 'En menos de 4 dias ya somos mas de 1,000!! Sigamos creciendo!' (Less than 4 days in and we are already 1,000. Let's keep growing!') 'Vamos a por los 10.000!!' (We are reaching 10,000 people). The increase in support – though nowhere near as momentous as it had been with the Kullena Khaled Said page discussed in Chapter 2 – was invariably celebrated by the page admins as a clear indication of a high turnout in the upcoming demonstrations. 'Esto va a ser algo grande' (This is gonna be big) wrote the admin on March 27th. Status messages abounded in exclamation marks and 'smilies', displaying an exuberance which proved very effective in grabbing users' attention and building up their motivation to act.

The admins skilfully exploited the interactive features of Facebook, striving to 'give people the impression that thanks to these instruments people could participate directly' in public affairs, in the same direct way in which they could post a message or a picture, as Fabio Gandara explains. They presented their group as being completely spontaneous and leaderless, and continuously restated that 'it was open to the participation of all and all those who want to get involved'. Status messages posted on the page constantly invited participants to help with the mobilising efforts by sharing the page and inviting their friends to 'like' it. 'Invita a todos tus amigos a la pagina. El 15 de mayo la calle tiene que ser nuestra' (invite all your friends to join the page. On the 15th of May the streets have to be ours) pleaded the second status message posted. 'Nos esta cuestando llegar a los 11.000 ... no puede ser hay que difundir!' (It is costing us to get to 11,000 ... it's not possible ... we need to reach out!) was one exclamation during the second week of the page's existence, when the growth in membership seemed to be slowing down.

Tens or hundreds of comments would follow each of these status updates, sometimes complimenting the admins, more rarely criticising them, almost always contributing to the collective sense of exaltation. As Wael Ghonim had done with the Khaled Said page, the DRY admins spent a lot of time acknowledging and replying to the comments, so as to sustain the impression that users were taking part in an interactive conversation rather than simply 'liking' the content fed to them. Moreover, they repeatedly asked users to contribute content to the page in the form of texts, pictures and videos. For example, on the 29th of April users were asked to record a video explaining their reasons for taking to the streets on the 15th.

Dozens responded to the invitation, recounting their own personal experiences of frustration with the economic and political system, thereby giving a series of faces and names to a phantom movement which was yet to make a physical appearance.

Besides the DRY page, in the months before the protest a number of other channels, including Facebook pages, blogs and websites, contributed to circulating the call to participate far and wide. Compared to Egypt, where it had a minor role as a means of mobilisation, in Spain Twitter played a significant part in attracting attention to the movement and creating conversations among activists, journalists, bloggers, academics and sympathisers. In the weeks preceding the 15th, the hashtag #15M became a trending topic several times on the Spanish Twitter, which itself sparked further waves of enthusiasm, triggering an avalanche of related tweets and Facebook messages. This and other hashtags like #indignados, #tomalacalle (take to the streets), #spanishrevolution became a venue not only for sharing pent-up anger against 'the system' but also for a collective cultivation of hope about people's ability to react. 'On the #15m we can be 10,000, 100,000 or 1,000,000, but we will always be one less without you' read a message posted on the DRY Twitter account a few days before the protests and re-tweeted 58 times. The tweet 'Real Democracy now: because we are fucking fed up' (estamos hasta los cojones) appeared on the 13th of May on *El Jueves* magazine's official Twitter account, using a brazen language quite typical in the warm-up for the 15th.

The launch campaign was to a great extent a web-based operation. But as had been the case in Egypt, as the day of the protest drew closer organisers progressively shifted their efforts towards street communication. The activists of DRY and other groups like Estado de Malestar and Juventud Sin Futuro were convinced that the movement had to become visible in the streets, in order to draw in those Spaniards cut off by the digital divide. Mobilising operations progressively came to encompass what Fabio Gandara calls 'a trabajo a pie de calle' (street work). As Sofia de Roa explains:

> Bit by bit people worked on outreach on the internet, and then in the last months the outreach for the event leapt onto the streets in the form of posters, debates, conferences and word of mouth and everything at that level, because it was necessary to do communication on the streets as well. There were posters in all the cities, and word of mouth worked very well.

Local groups printed out the posters made available on DRY's website or self-produced and put them up in main streets and public squares all across Spain. The intention of local organisers like Asun, an activist based in Salamanca, was to 'begin to make visible the movement on the streets, where people would pass by and see a poster we had put up, even those who were not on the internet, or did not have a Facebook account'.

The street communication campaign was particularly important because the demonstrations of the 15th were being organised not only in Madrid and Barcelona but in a total of 58 cities across the country. In order to ensure a decent turnout organisers were compelled to reach out locally to people beyond the core constituency of the movement. To help this street-level campaign, 'different local groups were created and there were face-to-face meetings in different cities, and this way we made the transition from the network to physical reality, and those two levels were made complementary' explains Fabio Gandara. These meetings saw the participation of experienced activists, but also hosted many people for whom this was their first experience in politics. Aitor Tinoco recalls how this 'was the first time that I was not seeing the same faces around the table'.

Throughout the work of preparation for the first day of protest, the main weakness appeared to be the scarcity of coverage in the mass media. National TV and press almost completely snubbed the event. In truth, activists were not counting heavily on the use of mass media as a mobilising channel. They were convinced that by using the internet and working locally 'they could jump over *Publico*, *El Pais*, and any other TV and newspaper' as de Roa puts it. However, given the wide support the protest was gathering, they thought it fit to try to use this channel as well, in order to broaden their outreach. In the weeks before the demonstration Pablo Gallego, Fabio Gandara and other spokespersons for the movement appeared on several radio programmes. But when a few days before protest they held an official press conference, they were astounded that only two news media showed up: the Left *Publico* and centre-Left *El Pais*. 'We asked ourselves what we had done wrong', says Gandara. The disinterest of the mass media provoked angry reactions among many activist tweeps. But paradoxically it also appeared to confirm the organisers' sense of worth: it seemed the upcoming protest was so significant that they needed to be censored, a view reflected in a number of tweets circulating at the time: 'Today's front pages are ignoring the protests. They demonstrate that the big media are part of the problem', wrote one tweep on the morning of the 15th. A few hours before the beginning of protest, user @grcanosa, an industrial engineer, condensed the collective indignation against the national news media: 'when in a country there are 60 simultaneous demonstrations and it does not go out on any media, something is happening isn't it?'

A MAGNETIC SUN

When I arrived to Calle de Alcalá and I saw all the people there I was very happy. And to see that there were so many people of different age, and to see that it was growing, and to see that we were a lot ... and now that I am telling you this I get goosebumps.. really I was so happy. When we arrived to Puerta del Sol, people started sticking big posters on the buildings. The people who were there were so unbelievably happy ... I remember that at the end of the demo I met some friends of mine. We sat on the square, and there were many people who also began sitting. And it was strange. Because normally after the end of a demonstration you go home.

Sofia de Roa's account of her experience during the 15th of May demonstration reflects the sense of exhilaration in witnessing a movement, nurtured online, eventually materialising in the streets of central Madrid. On the day, around 50,000 people marched in the streets in the Spanish capital alone, while thousands of others took to the streets in 57 other cities. The big turnout immediately sent emotional ripples across social networks. Pictures of the demonstrations were circulated to counter those who would say that 'we were 5 or 6' (from a tweet by user @kurioso), and angry accusations were launched at the big TV channels for not covering the protests. But it was what happened later in the night that would turn the 15-M protest from an isolated event into the beginning of a momentous protest wave. Instead of returning home at the end of the demonstration, some participants decided to camp out in Puerta del Sol. The square in central Madrid was turned into an 'acampada', a protest camp, which, also thanks to the intense social media messaging radiating from it, came to act as an almost irresistible *magnetic gathering* or *trending place* for the thousands of Spaniards who would flock there in the following days.

'Mas de 100 personas durmiendo en Sol en Madrid. Difundelo y unete!!' (More than 100 people sleeping in Sol in Madrid. Share and join!!!), was how @Anon_VV, a Spanish Twitter account connected with the international hacking group Anonymous, broke the news. After skirmishes with police at the end of the demonstration, a total of 50 people decided to spend the night in the square. Despite its reluctance to get involved in potentially illegal actions – wanting to retain its reputation as the moderate front in the indignados movement – Democracia Real Ya gave its stamp of approval to the occupation on its Facebook page. However, people like Gallego and Gandara decided to stay on the sidelines so as not to 'interfere in the spontaneous process' of the popular assemblies which developed in the camp. In fact, given their lack of experience in ground activism, these digital activists had little say on how the camp developed. The leading role in setting up the camp and its system of general assemblies and working groups was taken by people from the so-called 'okupa' or squatters scene in Madrid.

The taking of the square was celebrated as 'spontaneous', which indeed it was in the sense that nobody had planned it thoroughly in advance. But as Carmen Haro Barba, a press officer for the radical social centre la Tabacalera, one of the hotspots of the activist scene in Madrid, points out: 'while for some this was their first experience of politics, most of the people who slept there on that night were experienced activists, part of the active fabric of this city. Many of them were militants of the social centres, people for whom politics is a full-time endeavour.' Social centres like Tabacalera, Patio Maravillas and Casablanca, all located within walking distance from Puerta del Sol, contributed to the logistics and provided materials to set up the protest camp and keep it going. For all the importance of internet communication in reaching out to prospective participants and setting the scene for the protests, the actual construction and maintenance of the camp required a know-how which the digital activists who had launched the campaign did not possess. As had already happened in Egypt, once the movement 'camped out', the focus of communication and organisation progressively shifted from the internet to the streets.

The tipping point for turning the sit-in into a fully-fledged protest camp came on the 17th of May when in the early morning the police arrived to clear the square. 'I live in a country in which you can camp out to see Justin Bieber but not to defend your rights', commented @TheDirtyMachine sarcastically. If an episode of police repression had given the movement its first impetus, a second gave the occupation of Puerta del Sol an aura of legitimacy which over the following days attracted an inflow of thousands of supporters

Figure 3.3 Map of the protest camp in Puerta del Sol. (Courtesy: Lara Pelaez Madrid)

to the camp. Twitter hashtags like #nonosvamos (we don't go) and #yeswecamp (a pun on Obama's slogan 'Yes we can') became a channel for expressing support for the occupiers and for circulating information about how to help the occupation.

The number of tweets posted per day on the hashtag #15M shot up to 58,000 on the 17th, reaching more than 200,000 on the eve of the local elections of the 22nd. A video presentation prepared by a group of researchers at the University of Zaragoza represents the flow of tweets as a glow of blue light flowing out of Madrid, reaching a climax on the day preceding the elections.[22] This visualisation captures the way in which the enthusiasm experienced by those occupying the square was *radiated* out to those keenly following the events from afar. In the ensuing days many of these internet followers would turn into actual participants by joining the occupation either full time or part time. As Sofia de Roa recounts:

> On Monday, when there was the eviction in the night, there was a call [se convoco] on the social networks saying to everybody to go the streets at 8pm in Puerta del Sol. And at 8pm there were more people than there had been on the 15th of May. Which means that it was really impressive [especially given that it was a Monday night, rather than the weekend]. On that Tuesday the

support on social networks was growing exponentially with many people saying 'I go!', 'I go!', 'I go!' And people were really coming.

In the late afternoon of the 17th the first General Assembly after the re-occupation decided to erect an 'acampada'. In a matter of hours Puerta del Sol was turned into a Spanish adaptation of Tahrir square with a circle of tents in the centre – a powerful image which would later not only be popularised through social media but finally also reported by the newspapers and TV.

Since the first days of the encampment, social media, and Twitter in particular, constructed and sustained an emotional attraction to the occupation, facilitating the ongoing mobilisation of supporters and sympathisers. 'URGENTE! Hay que ir YA a #acampadasol, están cerrando los accesos' (Urgent there's a need to go to #acampadasol, they are closing access points) wrote @SpainRevolt on the 18th, when the occupiers had just set up the basic infrastructure of the camp and feared a new eviction. Later that day another user incited people to join: 'Estamos en #acampadasol y necesitamos mas gente. Tenemos q movernos y no dejar q los politicos hagan lo q quieran, por favor ...' (We are in acampadasol and we need more people. We need to move and not leave the politicians to do what they want, please...). Similar messages were sent in the following days informing people about the needs of the camp (which accepted only material donations and refused monetary ones), keeping them updated about the events taking place, as well as maintaining an ongoing conversation between those who were in the square and those who for whatever reason could not join the occupation, or could not join it just yet.

Exemplary of the way in which these and similar messages contributed not only in generating widespread sympathy but also in increasing the numbers involved is the story of Asun, a 40-year-old activist who joined the protests in Sol after having learned about them on Facebook. 'I knew through Facebook that people had decided to stay', recalls Asun, who had participated in the 15-M protests in Salamanca and went to Madrid as soon as she knew that activists had set up a protest camp there. 'It was a very quick decision, because I did not know that this would happen. I told myself "si hay una chispa hay que follarla"' (literally 'if there is a spark you need to fuck it': a figurative expression referring to an opportunity not to be missed). For many Spaniards the occupations in Sol and in tens of other squares appeared not only as an event not to be missed but also one that had to be experienced in person rather than simply followed through social media. Messaging on hashtags like #sol and #15M contributed to turning the squares into contagious or *magnetic gathering places*, creating a mediated spectacle from which emanated an irresistible sense of exhilaration capable of transforming 'spectators' into 'actors'.

When I visited the Puerta del Sol camp on the evening of the 20th of May, at the very peak of the occupation, what impressed me the most was the sheer bodily density in the square. Streams of people were trying to make their way into the square from the seven roads leading into it. Inside the square itself the crowd was almost suffocating, and indeed there were rumours that many people had fainted because of the crush. 'Please try to move to side streets and squares' pleaded a voice from the camp megaphone, 'we need to extend beyond Sol in order to avoid the crush'. I was also astounded by the sense of fellowship exuding from the General Assembly held every evening in the centre of the square. The interventions – delivered by people of different ages and class backgrounds and lasting no more than a couple of minutes to abide by the assembly rules – usually involved a testimony to the experience of personal hardship in the midst of the economic crisis, and almost invariably concluded with the ritual formula 'yo tambien soy un indignado' (I also am an indignant). It was as though the indignation which had previously been geographically dispersed and held together only symbolically on the web was now being physically 'harvested', stored in one place and given not only a collective name but also a physical centre, an anchoring point in public space.

THE NET WAS *NOT* THE SQUARE

Spanish academics José Manuel Sánchez Duarte and Victor Sampedro Blanco have interpreted the actions of the indignados movement as a sort of *transfer* to the streets of practices of cooperation first developed on the web. Their argument is summed up in the claim that before the 15th of May 'The Net was the square':

> The internet logic has been *transferred* to public life; from there those who do not understand the first, cannot understand what is happening. We don't either, but we do notice that the practices of the net (self-summoning, forum deliberation, consumption of counter-information, the weaving of affective and effective networks, to produce and to operate in peripheral and digital spheres) have become tangible. The traits of digital communication

– co-operation, instantaneity, self-nurturing, horizontality, de-
centralisation, flexibility, dynamism and inter-connection – have
become present in assemblies and camps.[23]

The protest camps in Puerta del Sol and several other squares
across the country cannot, however, be understood as a simple
transposition onto public space of practices first established on the
web. Rather, as documented in the course of this chapter, the use of
social media involved an emotional choreography, which effected a
deep transformation of the experience of solidarity and cooperation
constructed among an online public, and the symbolic and physical
harvesting of individual indignation. By contrast, the practices
developed in the square were characterised by an immersion and
corporeality which had little in common with the kind of 'virtual
proximity' constructed on the web in anticipation of the protests.
The process of mobilisation reached its climax in a re-appropriation
of public space and a reinvention of the tradition of street politics,
which to some extent developed in competition with the culture of
digital activism which had been crucial in the initial phase.

The oft-heard cry 'no estamos en Facebook, estamos en la
calle!' (We are not on Facebook, we are on the streets) came to
express the joy generated by the rediscovery of a sense of physical
communion that reversed the spatial and communicative dispersion
epitomised by social media interactions. Rather than posting status
messages, people stuck hundreds of post-it notes at the entrance
of Sol undeground station, where groups of people would stop
to read them. Instead of discussions held over internet forums,
participants immersed themselves in commissions, working groups
and assemblies (practices invented long before the appearance
of the Net). Rather than browsing through hundreds of profile
pictures they became acquainted with other people's faces. Instead
of Facebook 'pokings' they resorted to collective hugs like those
frequently seen during the first days of the camp. There was no
doubt among most of the people I interviewed that the face-to-face
interactions conducted in the square were by far superior to the
kind maintained on the web, seen by many as running the risk of
exacerbating people's isolation and loneliness. As José Ordóñez, a
protestor in his late thirties puts it: 'it is only when you go to an
assembly that your solitude disappears. The web runs the risk of
isolating you.' Thus while social media were undoubtedly important
in getting people 'there', once they were gathered physically in public

space, it was as though they were almost embarrassed about the way they had got there in the first place.

The protest camps became centres in the network, physical points anchoring a diffused movement. As Aitor of DRY notes, 'that's why the camps have been so important, in order to overcome the *fragmentation* of the net, to move from that social atomisation which is well reflected in the very structure of the net'. He describes the occupied squares as a site of 'incarnation', and as stages for a process of 'social recomposition' in which a new social body would be formed. This process of recomposition came to revolve around a symbolic and material *concentration*, of which the suffocating bodily density experienced in Puerta del Sol at the peak of the protest was the manifestation. The importance of physical centres as focal points for the action of contemporary popular movements goes against the grain of the claims to de-centralisation and irreducible multiplicity made by many activists inspired by the likes of Deleuze, Negri and Castells, with their allergy to centres of any kind. Nevertheless, it is an element which is crucial to understanding the indignados movement and their 'popular' or 'populist' character. Puerta del Sol, alongside other major occupations like the one in Plaza de Catalunya in Barcelona, became a 'nodal point' through which to transform the people from a phantom public into a tangible crowd.

Figure 3.4   An assembly in Puerta del Sol. The signpost reads 'they call it democracy and it is not'. (Courtesy: Lara Pelaez Madrid)

We must not forget that for Spain, Puerta del Sol constitutes the geographical and legal *centre* of the nation. It is the 'Kilómetro cero', the point from which all distances are measured and the point of departure for the *radial network* of roads. But it is also the 'national square', what the Place de la Bastille is for France, or Parliament square for Britain, and Tahrir square for Egypt – that is, the place in which, several times throughout history, people have petitioned or revolted against their national government. Bearing in mind this deep symbolic connotation, we can understand why the mere name 'Sol' seemed to say so much about the *unity* of the movement, its holding together despite its internal diversity, and its refusal of forms of delegation and representation. This toponym became a popular hashtag for activist Twitter feeds (#sol, #acampadasol), material for domain naming (acampadasol.org, sol.tv), a short-hand for the movement as a whole, and an imaginary point of reference for all those who were not physically present 'in Sol' but were nevertheless orientated towards it, following events closely through social and mass media alike.

Like a sun, its rays radiating through space, during the heyday of the occupation the 'plaza tomada' (the taken square) seemed somehow capable, thanks to the bodily density it attracted, of redeeming an economically down-trodden and politically humiliated nation. For Helena, an activist involved in acampada Sol, 'Puerta del Sol with its seven esoteric rays was the point of departure for the awakening of Spain and humanity.' This quasi-religious dimension should not be overlooked, given that the acampada in Sol, among its many (for some too many) commissions and working groups, also featured one devoted to 'love and spirituality'.

Naturally, the powerful ritual space constructed in Sol through the occupation could not last forever, and after almost a month, on the 19th of June, the indignados decided to lift the camp, given the strain on those maintaining it, and the growing complaints from local hotels and shop-keepers. But in an expression of the movement's emotional attachment to the square, they left behind 'InfoSol' – an info-point made of recycled material – so as to outlast the bodily gathering of the movement; though this popular 'monument' of sorts was soon to be trashed by the Spanish police.

After lifting the main occupations the movement focused on 'extending' itself, spreading the 'indignation' it had accumulated in symbolic spaces like Puerta del Sol and Plaza de Catalunya. Activists set up assemblies in different neighbourhoods throughout the big cities, while indignant marchers traversed Spain to encourage the creation of assemblies in remote Spanish towns. This was a remarkable attempt to give the movement a capillary presence throughout Spanish society by constructing local organisational structures. Nonetheless, arguably this emphasis on de-centralisation, which to a great extent reproduced practices and discourses dominant during the anti-globalisation period, also ran the risk of depriving the movement of its *concentration*, of the physical and symbolic density it had worked hard to harness. While in Madrid activists decided to continue holding a weekly assembly in Puerta del Sol, in Barcelona they decided to move completely to the neighbourhoods, without maintaining a central assembly. That decision proved 'a complete hara-kiri', as Aitor Tinoco puts it. 'We de-centralised our struggle to the neighbourhoods and thus lost a *central focus*.'

Bearing in mind the vital role of occupied squares as ritual *centres* and organisational *foci* of the movement, rather than simply as nodes in a network, we can appreciate the role played by social media during the phase of *sustainment* of the occupation, besides the phase of *initiation* discussed in the previous sections. Social media helped to sustain a sense of *emotional attraction* to the mass sit-ins. Facebook pages, tweets and posts were involved in the continuous weaving together of an emotional texture around the occupied public spaces, connecting these places with dispersed publics. Live-stream broadcasts by the website Sol.tv received almost 10 million visits during the first week of the protests,[24] just as the city council of Madrid switched off its webcam in Puerta del Sol in an attempt to black-out the protests. Hundreds of videos posted on YouTube conveyed the experience of collective enthusiasm in the square, while several dedicated websites, including tomalaplaza.net (take the streets) and tomalosbarrios.net (take the neighbourhoods), sprang up to give supporters and sympathisers timely reports on what was happening.

These and other websites also allowed the movement to connect with those who for whatever reason could or would not attend the protests. As Luis, an activist involved in the communication commission of the 'acampada' in Barcelona, explains: 'in the physical square are 2,000 people. But our Facebook page has received 2,000,000 visits in 15 days, with people from every part of the country, who are connecting, sharing and thanking.' The diffuse and distant forms of involvement which the 'acampadas' managed to attract through the use of social media allowed 'those who could not physically attend to feel part of the movement', as Teresa, a freelance web-designer involved in the movement, observes.

CONCLUSION

The 15-M movement in Spain was characterised by an intense and enthusiastic resort to social media as a means of mobilisation. In using social networking sites like Facebook and Twitter activists constructed resonant emotional conversations across the internet and managed to harness a widespread collective indignation transforming it into a political passion driving collective action in public space. Movement organisers wove together a 'choreography of assembly' which facilitated the gathering of a diverse and dispersed constituency around Puerta del Sol and the other main occupied squares of the movement, transformed into symbolic points of convergence for the movement. In the process, Facebook pages and Twitter feeds constructed loose collective identities characterised by an appeal to 'normality' (as in DRY's self-definition as 'normal and common people') aiming to intercept prospective users regardless of their political and cultural affiliations.

Naturally the process of mobilisation in the indignados movement was not all about Twitter and Facebook, however much these media allowed organisers to reach out to diverse sectors of the Spanish society and exploit the participatory imaginary of the web 2.0. Similarly to what happened in Egypt, activists soon resorted to street-level agitation to go beyond the movement's core constituency and break the barrier of the digital divide.

Furthermore, television stations like La Sexta and centrist and progressive newspapers like El Pais and El Publico contributed to shaping the image of the indignados, to mobilising people, and to building a consensus for the indignados far and wide. In an opinion poll published by El Pais on the 5th of June 2011, 66 per cent of Spaniards expressed their sympathy towards the indignados, and even 81 per cent agreed that they were right to be 'indignant'.[25] Such figures demonstrate that the indignados have to a large extent fulfilled their majoritarian ambitions, and drawn a diverse following of supporters and sympathisers. Furthermore, thanks to its numerous local occupations beyond the main squares, the movement has also managed to create local infrastructures accessible to people outside of the metropolitan areas. Compared to the anti-globalisation movement, whose mobilisation potential was for the most part restricted to an urban middle-class youth, this constitutes a major achievement.

Despite its initial success, however, the 15-M movement slowly began to wane during the last months of 2011. Local neighbourhood assemblies saw their numbers progressively drop, and within the movement itself the differences became more acute between the so-called moderates identified with Democracia Real Ya and the more 'radical' members represented by the so-called 'okupas' activists rooted in the squatters movement. At the time of writing, the movement was celebrating its first annual anniversary with protests beginning on the 12th of May, but was internally torn between the initiators of the movement led by Fabio Gandara, who had decided to turn Democracia Real Ya into a legal organisation, and others who wanted the movement to remain a 'network' without any formal structure.

The irksome question of leadership is thus finally coming to the fore and being openly discussed. This is a testament to the fact that the indignados, like other such movements, were not and are not 'leaderless'. As we have seen in the course of this chapter, a handful of young digital activists like Fabio Gandara and Pablo Gallego had a decisive role in steering the actions of the movement, by 'setting the scene' for or 'choreographing' public protests. While these activists' doings were hardly visible in the public spaces they contributed to creating, the way in which they used social media to construct collective identities and to fuel an emotional tension towards participation deeply shaped the way in which the movement emerged and developed.

4
'The hashtag which did (not) start a revolution': The Laborious Adding Up to the 99%

Im thinking about getting my lazy ass out of bed to go #occupywallstreet in the city.
My bed is just way too comfortable though :(
Tweet sent on the 22nd of September 2011

'It all started innocuously enough with a July 13 blog post urging people to #OccupyWallStreet, as though such a thing (Twitter hashtag and all) were possible. It turns out, with enough momentum and a keen sense of how to use social media, it actually is.'[1] The quote from a Reuters report encapsulates much of the myth created around the rise of Occupy Wall Street in mainstream news media. The story goes that one day someone put out a Twitter hashtag and then by some kind of social media magic a social movement was born. In fact, as we will see in this chapter, the emergence of Occupy Wall Street was a much 'messier' process than this kind of representation suggests. If *Adbusters* – the Canadian countercultural magazine which first published a call to protest on the 17th of September – had hoped that the #OccupyWallStreet hashtag, together with 'tactical briefings' published on its website, would ignite a 'revolution', this did not turn out to be the case. On the pre-announced day of protest, of the 20,000 'redeemers, rebels, and radicals' it had summoned only 300 turned up. The movement got up and running, and grabbed the attention of the US public and of the world, only after a messy and slow process of ground-level organising and a redefinition of its identity as a popular (rather than countercultural) movement representing the '99%': i.e., all those who were suffering the consequences of the economic crisis.

The emergence of Occupy Wall Street was characterised by a tortuous development in which social media were only partly used as a means for a choreography of assembly, setting the scene for public protest, and often became more a kind of channel for the reverberation of events taking place on the ground. Paradoxically, in the country where social media firms like Twitter and Facebook have their headquarters, campaigners initially failed to use them effectively as a means to 'choreograph' the movement before its materialisation in public space. Social media only acquired importance during the phase of sustainment of the movement, being used to create a *sense of attraction* to the occupations, and to invoke a sense of solidarity between 'physical occupiers' and 'internet occupiers', activists on the ground and people following events from a distance.

Occupy Wall Street (or 'Occupy' in the shorter form and 'OWS' in its acronym) followed in the wake of the Egyptian uprising and the Spanish indignados, from which *Adbusters* drew their inspiration for putting out the initial call. On the 17th of September protesters assembled in Zuccotti Park, a few tens of metres away from the New York Stock Exchange, and the occupation soon inspired tens of other camps across the US. Progressively the movement came to encompass a diverse constituency, including blue-collar workers, unemployed, retired, poor, homeless, all representatives of that 99% the movement purported to be fighting for. Before being evicted from Zuccotti Park and from most of its other camps between November and December 2011, the movement had managed to secure quite an impressive degree of public support. According to a poll published by the *New York Times* in mid October 2011, 46 per cent of American citizens agreed with the reasons given by the 'occupiers' for their action.[2]

Even if social media alone cannot explain the emergence and relative success of Occupy Wall Street, it is evident that they have played an important role in mobilising and coordinating participants. Unsurprisingly, this aspect of the movement sparked a huge news media hype. Technology journalists and social media gurus eagerly debated which social media gadget best represented the movement. Having gotten bored with Twitter, some of these pundits applauded the activists' adoption of Twitter's 'anarchist' alternative Vibe[3] and the location-based service FourSquare.[4] Social media start-ups immediately jumped on the techno-utopian bandwagon, hoping to find in Occupy a much needed PR boost for their newly introduced services.[5]

As in the preceding chapters, I am not much interested in the technical affordances of these tools, but in the cultural practices the activists developed in their use. I will highlight how, similarly to in Egypt and Spain, social media were crucially used for constructing a *choreography of assembly* facilitating the gathering of participants in public space, and generating an emotional tension towards participation. I begin by describing the crisis of public space which characterised American society at the inception of Occupy, and the incapacity of established organisations to act as the base for building a popular campaign against the politics of austerity. Looking at the interaction between *Adbusters* and the organisers on the ground, I argue that the launch campaign failed in creating that initial *emotional impetus* which characterised the protests in Egypt and Spain. The fixing of the date – 17th of September – was initially not accompanied by the construction of a resonant *popular identity* or by the accumulation of a *sense of anticipation* motivating a dispersed constituency to take to the streets. During the phase of initiation, all the organisers' attention was on Twitter, while Facebook, which had constituted the springboard for the other two movements, was initially snubbed. Only later, once the movement had pitched its tents in Zuccotti Park, did the 'We are the 99%' Tumblr page come to act as an emotional rallying point for the construction of an inclusive popular identity and the generation of an impetus towards participation.

In the second part of the chapter, I move to analysing the role played by social media in sustaining the protests once the occupation of Zuccotti Park began. Here Twitter was effectively used to weave together an emotional conversation and to sustain a sense of solidarity between the physical occupiers and their distant supporters or 'internet occupiers'. However, social media interactions did not manage to turn sympathisers into actual participants to any great extent. In the final section of the chapter I discuss the use of Twitter as a tactical device during protest events and emergency situations such as the eviction of occupiers from the park on the night of the 15th of November. I suggest that the use of Twitter on this occasion pointed to the presence of a group of core organisers, or 'choreographers', which contradicts the movement's claims to leaderlessness and absolute spontaneity.

RECLAIMING THE FIRST AMENDMENT

The First Amendment gives every New Yorker the right to speak out. But it doesn't give anyone the right to sleep in a park or otherwise take it over, to the exclusion of others. Protesters have had two months to occupy the park with tents and sleeping bags. Now they will have to occupy the space with the power of their arguments.[6]

When, on the morning of the 15th of November 2011, the Mayor of New York Mike Bloomberg went to a press conference to justify the eviction of the protest camp at Zuccotti Park in Downtown Manhattan, executed a few hours earlier by the New York Police Department, he saw fit to appeal to those higher values of public health and safety. Nevertheless, it was clear to anyone with any knowledge of recent American history that his action was not simply 'administrative' but deeply political and ideological. The eviction was but the latest instance in a history of attacks on the right of assembly, animated by that 'fear of crowds' Mike Davis has eloquently written about (see for example 1992a). Young activists just needed to think back to the police repression of the protests against the Republican National convention in 2008. Older ones might be reminded of by-now legendary events such as the violent eviction of the People's Park in Berkeley in May 1969 by then governor of California Ronald Reagan, who deployed the National Guard to stop a group of residents and students from occupying an abandoned patch of land near the Berkeley campus.

The eviction at People's Park was the inauguration of a long political cycle which has marked 'the end of public space' in American society (Mitchell, 1995). Different scholars and pundits have denounced how, in the subsequent decades, the dominance of neoliberal doctrine has involved an ongoing attack on spaces of political encounter and alternative sociability (Putnam, 2000; Brenner and Theodore, 2002). The consequences of neoliberal ideology for public space have been well described by Mike Davis, who highlights the 'destruction of any truly democratic urban space' brought about by neoliberalism. For Davis, 'the public spaces of the new megastructures and supermalls have supplanted traditional streets and supplanted their spontaneity. Inside malls, office centers, and cultural complexes, public activities are sorted out into strictly functional compartments under the gaze of private police forces' (Davis 1992a: 155). The call to 'occupy' chosen by activists was premised precisely on this sense of a crisis of public space, and on the conviction that in order to create a public space anew there was no other way than by physically 'occupying' it.

The absence of an established public space in which to voice public grievances has become particularly apparent since the inception of the global economic crisis. Similarly to the case of the Spanish indignados, the key reason for the surprising level of support earned by Occupy Wall Street was the dire economic conditions in the US, undergoing its worst crisis since 1929. As the Occupy activists were themselves to popularise, 30 years of neoliberalism had seen the rich getting richer and the poor poorer. According to the Congressional budget office, between 1979 and 2007 the richest 1 per cent of Americans saw its earnings rise by a whopping 275 per cent, while the rest saw only a 60 per cent rise along with a rising cost of living.[7] With the explosion of the economic crisis in 2008, the situation of economic inequality became yet bitterer for the majority of Americans, affected by unemployment, home repossessions, and falling earnings. Unemployment touched a record 10 per cent rate in 2009,[8] the highest since the Great Depression, dropping to 8.6 per cent in December 2011 but still well above pre-crisis levels.[9] The hopes raised by Barack Obama during his 2008 presidential campaign soon turned sour. Obama demonstrated he was not a new Roosevelt, with the determination to rein in a capitalism out of control, but a cautious centrist politician, ready to compromise on the economy with the Republicans, and careful not to antagonise corporate America from which the first African-American president of the US drew much campaign funding.

Confronted with this dire economic situation, the organisations of American civil society, including trade unions and established activist groups, have by and large proven incapable of coming up with a convincing and broad-based response. In the 30 years since Reagan took power and neoliberalism became the dominant political philosophy in Washington, American trade unions have been defeated in battle after battle, similar to what has happened in the UK since the era of Margaret Thatcher. They now represent just 11 per cent of the workforce in the private sector, and 25 per cent of the government workforce. It is true that events like the 2011 Wisconsin protests can be read as a sign of renewed vitality within the US labour movement. Yet trade unions in general have remained far too weak and corporatist to be capable of leading a powerful national campaign against the politics of austerity. Besides the unions, other social movements which might have otherwise constituted a focal point to gather around were not up to the challenge. The anti-war movement had fallen apart following internecine struggles and the progressive fading away of the 'war on terror' in the news agenda. The galaxy of direct action groups like DAN and Ya Basta, described by David Graeber in his book *Direct Action* (2009), was instead too small and subcultural to constitute a platform for the convergence of popular dissent.

Paradoxically, in recent years it has been the American Right rather than the Left that has taken the lead in reinventing a politics of the street, as well illustrated by the Tea Party movement. Since January 2009, hundreds of protests have been organised in different parts of the US to protest against the effects of the economic crisis and what participants considered an excessive level of government intervention in the economy. The protest movement peaked in a taxpayer march on the 12th September 2009 in Washington DC, in which the equation between 'Obama' and 'socialism' was all the rage. Some envious leftist activists have defined the Tea Party phenomenon as an 'astroturf' movement, that is, one orchestrated and bankrolled by powerful organisations. But it is undeniable that the Tea Party has skilfully managed to tap into a vein of discontent caused by the economic crisis, which to a great extent Occupy Wall Street would also do.

As in Spain and Egypt, in the US some glimmers of hope for radicals in recent years also came from online activism. Since the late 1990s, the 'free culture' (Kelty, 2008) developed by hackers, advocates of open source software, and internet rights campaigners, has come to constitute a major inspiration for the development of new forms of activism. The foremost representative of this emerging techno-utopian political culture is the hacker group Anonymous. 'Anonymous', a 'mass noun' used by several hackers around the world to sign their actions, originated in 2003 from an online encounter between hackers sharing funny pictures on the 'imageboard' website 4chan.[10] The group began its activity by engaging in light-hearted online mockeries, like defacing the homepage of the American epilepsy association with a flashy video. Only later did the group come to acquire a political profile through its attacks on the websites of government agencies and corporations (almost invariably accompanied by its 'suit without head' logo and the signature motto 'We are Anonymous. We are legion. We do not forgive. We do not forget. Expect us') as well as for its support for Wikileaks and Julian Assange.

Wearing Guy Fawkes masks inspired by the activist cult movie *V for Vendetta*, people identifying themselves with Anonymous have in recent years also made the leap onto the streets, in a demonstration that even hackers do not always content themselves with 'inhabiting' cyberspace. Since the Project Chanology protests of 2009, against the Church of Scientology and its censorship of a YouTube video featuring a clueless Tom Cruise, Anonymous has repeatedly invited its supporters to take to the streets to protest against corporations and organisations which it sees as countering its ideals of transparency and freedom of information. Occupy

Wall Street has been to date the most important public campaign Anonymous has put its weight behind. In anticipation of the protests the hacker group posted a YouTube video inviting its supporters to flood the streets of Downtown Manhattan on the 17th of September. Similarly to what happened in Egypt and Spain, the digital activist practices developed by groups like Anonymous, with its ideals of anonymity and leaderless organising, had a deep influence on the emergence of Occupy Wall Street, which I reconstruct in the following section looking at the interaction between organisers online and on the ground.

ADBUSTERS AND THE PEOPLE ON THE GROUND

> On September 17, we want to see 20,000 people flood into lower Manhattan, set up tents, kitchens, peaceful barricades and occupy Wall Street for a few months. Once there, we shall incessantly repeat one simple demand in a plurality of voices.[11]

It all began as a shot in the dark. The trumpet of war this time was first sounded not by a newly formed group of unemployed graduates who had met through social networking sites, as was the case with Democracia Real Ya, nor by an anonymous Facebook admin as in the Egyptian revolution. Instead, on this occasion the initiative was taken by an established alternative news media, the Canadian anti-consumerist magazine *Adbusters*. On July 13th the magazine's website addressed its network of supporters – '90,000 *redeemers*, *rebels*, and *radicals*' – asking 20,000 of them to morph into a revolutionary army by assembling in Wall Street, the financial centre of America and the world. The call suggested that

> If we hang in there, 20,000-strong, week after week against every police and National Guard effort to expel us from Wall Street, it would be impossible for Obama to ignore us. Our government would be forced to choose publicly between the will of the people and the lucre of the corporations.

Against the claims to spontaneity and leaderlessness which have since been associated with the movement, at its inception Occupy was a carefully orchestrated campaign, whose logo, copy and imagery had been professionally packed up by the creative graphic team of *Adbusters*. The idea behind *Adbusters*' call was to exploit what they saw as 'a shift in revolutionary tactics' introduced by the Egyptian uprising and the Spanish indignados: 'a fusion of Tahrir with the acampadas of Spain'. As we have seen in the previous two chapters, the Egyptian and Spanish movements were 'revolutions' with a set date, pre-announced on Facebook well in advance. *Adbusters*' call surpassed both in its ambition to 'design' a revolution, with almost no prior consultation with the political groups already established on the ground.

Behind the launch of the campaign lay the work of two key people inside *Adbusters*. The first was Kalle Lasn, the magazine's founder and main editor, a histrionic 69-year-old filmmaker and writer. The second was Micah White, a 29-year-old Berkeley-based activist and the senior editor on the magazine. Interestingly, Micah owed much of his fame as a writer to his harsh critique of 'clicktivism', a form of internet-only activism practised by organisations like MoveOn and Avaaz (White, 2010). He had also criticised Facebook which he blames for the 'commercialization of friendship'. Following the revolutions in Tunisia and Egypt, however, he had seen reasons for hope in the possibilities opened up by the use of social media, and had suggested that 'technology can birth the barricades of the 21st century' (White, 2011).

The call to occupy Wall Street was certainly not *Adbusters*' first attempt to take on the power of corporations. Since its foundation in 1989 the magazine had been an outlet of debate and visual experimentation for a crew of 'culture jammers', media activists dedicated to the mockery of mainstream culture through advertising spoofs, also known as 'subvertising', celebrated in the pages of Naomi Klein's *No Logo* (2000). Around the turn of the millennium it became one of the intellectual and creative powerhouses of the anti-globalisation movement. However the idea of 'jump-starting' a popular movement following the lead of the Arab uprisings and the Spanish indignados was in its ambition well beyond anything it had tried before. 'For 20 years we have been calling for a global uprising' – explains Kalle Lasn – 'and when that turmoil in Greece and in other parts of Europe happened and then in Egypt and Tunisia we saw an opportunity'. Unlike what had happened in Spain and Egypt, the date of the 17th of September was chosen on purely practical grounds: 'That was time enough to get the Twitter feed to go crazy and that was enough for the Facebook page to come together and we tried to do it as quickly as possible', Lasn explains.

In launching Occupy Wall Street, *Adbusters*' efforts were all focused on communication, rather than the actual organising of the event, as though hoping that advertising alone would suffice to create the momentum required for a popular movement to materialise. The very name of the campaign was turned into a hashtag – #OccupyWallStreet – so as to facilitate its 'viral' diffusion. *Adbusters* worked carefully on the campaign iconography, including the image of a ballerina dancing over the famous Wall Street bull sculpture. Moreover, Lasn and White decided that the movement should have only 'one demand', so as to imitate what they saw as the reason for the success of the Egyptian revolution. Where the Egyptians had tenaciously demanded the resignation of Hosni Mubarak, the American revolutionaries would have contented themselves with pleading for a presidential commission on the crimes of the financial system. In response to the criticisms raised by readers on its online forum, however, *Adbusters* decided to leave it to the people taking to the streets in New York what their one demand should be. Those gathered in Zuccotti Park eventually decided that they did not want to make any demands at all, fearing that to do so might legitimise those in power, who had nothing to offer them anyway, so they thought.

Adbusters' impromptu launch of the campaign did not go down well with the local activist community in New York. It was seen by many as a naïve operation given that it did not take into account the material resources that would be required to get the campaign up and running. Yet the local activists also recognised the 'political opportunity' (Tarrow, 1994: 17–18) the call opened up, and felt a sort of duty to set up the protests for those who were likely to make their way to Lower Manhattan on the day fixed by *Adbusters*. The sentiment then prevalent among ground organisers is well represented by David Graeber, an anarchist activist and anthropologist who had much influence in the nurturing phase of the movement throughout August and early September, and who has declared himself the 'inventor' of the 'we are the 99%' slogan: 'The *Adbusters* people said we have 90,000 subscribers; we're hoping to get 20,000' – recounted Graeber in an interview for *Vanity Fair*. 'We were like, Yeah, right. Those guys don't understand that these things just don't happen on the Internet. To make it *real* you have to do *real on-the-ground organising*.'[12]

It did not take long after the initial call was launched before the 'real on-the-ground organising' was initiated. Thus David Kroll, an activist and associate editor of the counter-information website *TomDispatch*,[13] recounts the early organising attempts in New York:

Figure 4.1   The 'launch' poster for #Occupywallstreet by *Adbusters*.

Months before the first occupiers descended on Zuccotti Park in lower Manhattan, before the news trucks arrived and the unions endorsed, before Michael Bloomberg and Michael Moore and Kanye West made appearances, a group of artists, activists, writers, students, and organisers gathered on the fourth floor of 16 Beaver Street, an artists' space near Wall Street, to talk about changing the world. There were New Yorkers in the room, but also Egyptians, Spaniards, Japanese, and Greeks. Some had played a part in the Arab Spring uprising; others had been involved in the protests catching fire across Europe. But no one at 16 Beaver knew they were about to light the fuse on a protest movement that would sweep the United States and fuel similar uprisings around the world. (in Van Gelder, 2011: 16)

For Kroll, 'without that worldly group that met at 16 Beaver and later created the New York City General Assembly, there might not have been an Occupy Wall Street as we know it today'. In turn it is fair to say that without *Adbusters*' call the small and highly subcultural activist scene in New York would have hardly found a way to bridge their sectarian divides and launch an ambitious and inclusive campaign like 'Occupy'. It is undeniable that *Adbusters*' call at least acted as a provocation shaking up the passivity and divisions within the American activist community.

Besides the anarchist scene gathering around countercultural spaces like 16 Beaver, ABC No Rio, and the C-Squat (the last two of which were actually closed for renovation at the time), other groups with a leftist orientation informed the development of the nascent movement. The idea of the protest camp had already been tried out by a small group of socialist activists called New Yorkers Against Budget Cuts. From June 14th to July 5th 2011 they had set up an encampment in front of City Hall to protest against a programme of budget cuts planned by Mayor Bloomberg. They called the sit-in (where they were not allowed by police to pitch tents) 'Bloombergville',[14] drawing their inspiration from the Hoovervilles, the shanty-towns which had mushroomed during the Great Depression of the 1930s and were named after President Herbert Hoover, held responsible for the economic disgrace. Besides this group, several others contributed in preparing the terrain for the nascent movement, including the newly formed activist group US Day of Rage, which took its name from the days of rage of the Arab Spring and called for an overturn of the system of party funding.

When on the 2nd of August these different groups met at the first General Assembly called at Bowling Green near to the bull sculpture sparks flied. Socialists organised the assembly as a rally with set speakers. David Graeber and other anarchists, seeing how things were panning out, invited people to defect from the meeting. 'I started tapping people on the shoulder who looked like they were as annoyed as I was and said, if we actually did a real general assembly, would you come?' Graeber recounted to *Vanity Fair*. 'We ended up forming a circle, and at that point everyone defected from the rally. There were maybe 60 or 70 people.'[15] The group which coalesced on that day started meeting regularly at Battery Park and then at Tompkins Square. Thus the first nucleus of the New York General Assembly, which would act as the main decision body of the movement, was formed, and started working on the organisation of the protests.

HOW *NOT* TO RUN A SOCIAL MEDIA LAUNCH CAMPAIGN

'We put out the hashtag ... and it was quite a blast', claims Kalle Lasn, the 'brain-father' of Occupy Wall Street, describing the launch of the movement in summer 2011. In truth though, there was not really much of a 'blast' on social networking sites in the two-and-a-half month period between *Adbusters*' first call and the occupation of Zuccotti Park. Compared to the activists in Egypt and Spain, the original nucleus of Occupy organisers by and large failed to construct a sense of anticipation around the 'landing' of the movement in public space. The level of attention on both Facebook and Twitter was almost flat until the movement made its physical appearance. As the social media company Social Flow noted in a report on the communication flowing through the #OccupyWallStreet hashtag: 'we are so used to seeing rapid information spreads on Twitter, yet what we see in this case is an extremely slow build-up'.[16] Moreover, according to the same report, many of the users who were initially using the hashtag were in fact Spanish tweeps connected to the indignados movement eager to see it making ripples across the Atlantic, rather than people based in the US. It was only in late September and early October, after two episodes of police repression and a threat of eviction, that Occupy started attracting attention on social media and eventually also on mainstream media.

There are a number of reasons for the relative failure of the Occupy launch campaign. Naturally the almost non-existent mass media coverage prior to the protests constituted a major obstacle to raising the awareness of the majority of the population. Arguably, however, the lack of public support was the consequence of a certain elitist attitude in the movement communications, reflected in its over-reliance on Twitter and its snobbery towards Facebook, a website with a much larger number of users. Starting with *Adbusters*, the Occupy organisers seemed to misunderstand the lesson of the use of social media in Egypt and Spain, where Facebook rather than Twitter had been the key website for launching the movement before its appearance in public space. In fact, from the very start Occupy was conceived as a 'Twitter movement', as evidenced by its very naming as a hashtag: #OccupyWallStreet. As a report published in October 2011 by social media company Attention highlighted, 'the data clearly shows that Twitter is the social network where all of the Occupy conversations are happening'. Twitter was getting 82.5 per cent of the mentions related to Occupy Wall Street, while Facebook was getting a very meagre 2.8 per cent, according to the report.[17] Many of the key Facebook pages were only established once the movement had already occupied Zuccotti Park. Among them the page of Occupy Together, which served as a platform for connecting all the occupations mushrooming around the US, and was opened only on the 24th of September.

The Facebook presence of the movement before the protests of the 17th was limited to the Occupy Wall Street page operated by organisers in New York, and an event page for the 17th opened by *Adbusters*. Both pages' performance in the preparation stage of the protest was very disappointing.[18] The page for OWS in New York[19] had been set up as far back as the 9th of August, at the time of the first General Assemblies. Yet by the 17th of September it had managed to attract only 891 'likes'. Compare this with the Kullena Khaled Said page in Egypt, which attracted 36,000 users on the first day of its existence! The OWS Facebook page began getting significant traffic only after activists had physically occupied Zuccotti Park on the 17th, with a rapid, though not explosive progression in the following days.

Looking at the kind of messages posted by the admin during the initial phase it is not difficult to understand why internet users did not 'like' the Occupy Wall Street Facebook page. Their status messages completely lacked that emotional component which, as we have seen, was the hallmark of both the Kullena Khaled Said page in Egypt, and the Democracia Real Ya page in Spain. The OWS admin wrote infrequently, and his status messages were telegraphic and

Table 4.1   Number of 'likes' on the Occupy Wall Street main Facebook page[20]

Date	Number of likes
Sept 12	374
Sept 13	382
Sept 14	401
Sept 15	449
Sept 16	526
Sept 17	891
Sept 18	2174
Sept 19	3391
⋮	⋮
Sept 24	13585

unappealing, often accompanied by annoying supplications of the kind 'share, share, share'. Below are some examples of early posts:

11 days until we visit Wall Street on September 17th. Like this video and then share it – September 6th [only 1 person liked the video and nobody shared it]

Share, share, share [with a link to an article about the 'super-rich' in the US] – September 7th
[only 5 people liked and nobody shared or replied]

Share, share, share. September 17th is real. – September 8th [only 4 people liked and nobody shared or replied][21]

As the reader can appreciate, the messages were not exactly designed to create an emotional connection with the public. They had a cold informative tone unlikely to elicit the enthusiasm of internet users. Many times these messages would just consist of links to articles or videos without any introduction framing them. All in all these Facebook communications amounted to an uninspired and uninspiring monologue, which failed to avail itself of the interactive features of social networking sites and thereby did not generate that collective conversation and contagious sense of enthusiasm which had played such a crucial role in both Egypt and Spain.

The same dullness characterised the Facebook event page opened by *Adbusters*. The page managed to secure around 20,000 positive RSVPs and 150,000 invitations before the first day of protest, but only a tiny fraction of these respondents would actually attend.[22] Also in this case the admin status messages were rather lifeless, and there was little conversation among users before the 17th. The disappointing performance in the use of Facebook as a campaign tool might well reflect some activists' personal lack of organisational craft and charisma. But more generally it betrays the fact that the Occupy organisers did not initially regard Facebook as an important channel in their communications. As a consequence they did not interact with a very large audience base, where many possible 'recruits' might have been found, and which, compared to Twitter, better approximated demographically to that 99% the movement purported to fight for.

But even on Twitter itself, where activists invested much more energy, the results were also initially disappointing. They did not manage to create that sense of enthusiasm prior to the protests that would have secured a high turnout on the first day of action. In fact, the #OccupyWallStreet Twitter hashtag never got close to becoming a trending topic, as the #15M hashtag had in Spain. Some tweeps raised the suspicion that the hashtag was not trending because of censorship by Twitter, which in those days was receiving investment from top banking firm JPMorgan. Twitter along with a number of independent analysts rebutted the accusation, pointing to the complexity of the algorithm defining which topics become trending ones.[23] Regardless of whether or not Twitter censored the Occupy hashtag, did this really matter so much for turning the attention of the public towards the movement?

What is evident is that it began to gain considerable attention on Twitter only when occupiers eventually pitched their tents in Zuccotti Park, and the police began their repression, as suggested in another passage of the report by social media firm Attention quoted earlier:

> In the first week, average mentions per day were an unimpressive 18.8 mentions per day. Not many people were talking about Occupy Wall Street. After the start of occupation on 9/17 and up until 9/23, average mentions per day increased by a whopping 2,004%. The following week had a 97% increase over the week prior, and the week after the Brooklyn Bridge arrests saw a 216% increase in average mentions per day.[24]

Thus what finally made the movement 'go viral' on social media was not what was happening 'independently' in the so-called 'twitter-sphere', but rather events taking place on the ground, which then reverberated in Twitter conversations. Specifically, as we have already seen in the case of the indignados and the Egyptian revolution, police violence against protesters was crucial in generating attention on the internet, gaining the movement new supporters and sympathisers.

Two events came to constitute the tipping point for Occupy's increasing visibility on social and mainstream media alike: the pepper-spray attack by NYPD officer Anthony Bologna, and the mass arrest on Brooklyn bridge on the 1st of October. On the 26th of September, Bologna was caught on camera pepper-spraying three female activists for no apparent reason during a small demonstration near Wall Street. The video quickly garnered thousand of hits on YouTube[25] and sparked many commentaries on TV shows like Jon Stewart's *Daily Show* and liberal broadcasters like MSNBC and CNN. The second episode was the arrest of over 700 protesters during a march on Brooklyn Bridge on the 1st of October. Ironically, the march itself had been organised by Occupy in protest at Anthony Bologna's actions the week before. In a demonstration of poor PR skills, the New York Police Department sparked a further wave of indignation by opting for a mass arrest of the kind the city had not seen for several years. These episodes highlight how the role of social media in the case of Occupy was more as a means to facilitate the *reverberation* of episodes taking place on the ground, rather than as a means of preparing the terrain symbolically for the protests. Paradoxically, in the home country of Twitter, Facebook, and several other social media firms, activists showed little ability for exploiting the emotional power of social media.

In order to understand the weakness of the initial social media campaign, however, we also need to take into account the confusion which early on lay at the core of the identity of Occupy Wall Street. This identity was torn between the radical countercultural imaginary proposed by the *Adbusters*' publicity, and the populist identity underlying the slogan 'We are the 99%' coined by David Graeber during the initial ground organising session in August. Only once the physical occupation had begun did the movement's identity eventually crystallise around a majoritarian orientation, aiming to represent the people as a whole rather than a bunch of 'redeemers, rebels, and radicals'. A crucial role in this process was played by the 'We are the 99%' Tumblr blog, whose contribution to the process of mobilisation is documented in the following section.

A TUMBLR WAILING WALL FOR THE 99%

'I am a two times felon with no job and I owe over $10,000 in medical bills. I am the 99%' – 15th of September.

'My parents put themselves into debt so that I could get a fancy degree. It cost over 100 grand $ and I have no job prospects. I am the 99%' – 25th of September
'I am 20 years old and I can't find a job because I have no experience. I have no experience because I can't find a job. I am the 99%' – 27th of September
'I am a single mum of four, college student, shelf stocker, I go hungry every day. I am the 99% per cent' – 28th September[26]

These sentences are a selection from the hundreds of 'photo messages' posted on 'We are the 99%' Tumblr blog.[27] The idea behind the project was simple: collecting the stories of all those who felt part of the 99%, all those who perceived themselves to be victims of the economic crisis irrespective of their political or cultural affiliations.

Most of the entries posted on the blog were generated by those 'graduates without a future' Paul Mason portrays as a sort of revolutionary subject of contemporary popular movements (2012). But among the hundreds of posts there were also stories of people coming from very different walks of life: working mothers incapable of providing for their children, older workers nearing the end of their career without the prospect of a pension, people needing surgery and unable to pay for it, Americans of different ethnic backgrounds, classes and ages confessing they were regularly going hungry or were 'one paycheck away from homelessness' as stated in one of the messages. For this diverse constituency of people – who shared in common not only their economic plight but also an anger towards the super-rich 1 per cent held responsible for the economic crisis – the website came to constitute a point of *emotional condensation*: a wailing wall on which the identity of a new-born movement might coalesce.

The Tumblr blog was created by a 28-year-old New York activist who made himself known only as 'Chris', and his friend Priscilla Grim, a 36-year-old activist and social media expert. They opened the website in early August, but began publishing posts only on the 15th of September, just two days before the occupation of Zuccotti Park. The website therefore had little influence during the initiation phase of the campaign, and in fact only began gaining momentum towards the end of September, around the same time as the movement finally began to make headlines in the mainstream media. In the text published on the homepage of the blog they proposed a simple but compelling description of the 99%:

We are the 99 percent. We are getting kicked out of our homes. We are forced to choose between groceries and rent. We are denied quality medical care. We are suffering from environmental pollution. We are working long hours for little pay and no rights, if we're working at all. We are getting nothing while the other 1 percent is getting everything. We are the 99 percent.[28]

Internet users who identified with this description were asked to photograph themselves holding a small sign with a message no longer than one sentence. In fact, almost all of the messages entered by users ended up being several lines long, as though reflecting an overflow of personal sentiment, their feelings incapable of being contained in a concise statement.

> Make a sign. Write your circumstance at the top, no longer than a single sentence ... Then, take a picture of yourself holding the sign and submit it to us. The 99 percent have been set against each other, fighting over the crumbs the 1 percent leaves behind. But we're all struggling. We're all fighting. It's time we recognize our common struggles, our common cause. Be part of the 99 percent and let the 1 percent know you're out there.

By taking a picture of oneself with a sign and sending it to the website users could symbolically subscribe to the identity of 99%, adding their own individual story to a collective assembling of anger and indignation. At the same time, they were asked to set aside their divisions in terms of political or cultural orientations, in a way which resonates with Laclau's discussion of the capacity of 'empty signifiers' (like the slogan 'We are the 99%') to create a 'chain of equivalence' connecting manifold issues throughout a movement's constituency.

The identity constructed through the Tumblr page was very different from the one reflected in *Adbusters*' initial call and the publicity it produced. The picture of the ballerina dancing over the bull evoked the format of the raving 'protest parties' of the anti-globalisation movement and its DIY culture (see for example McKay, 1998). Another picture used to accompany *Adbusters*' tactical briefings portrayed an activist hipster of some kind with a scarf and ski mask, running towards a target, implicitly Wall Street itself. This iconography was visually stunning, and the language used in the call and tactical briefings was infused with that taste for provocation and self-irony which has characterised *Adbusters*' departure from the rusty culture of the Old Left. But for all its beauty and inventiveness, this publicity did not capture the widely felt pain of many people in the US. *Adbusters* was basically re-hashing the imaginary of a 'politics of pleasure' (McKay, 1998) which was now past its expiry date and out of tune with the everyday experience of Americans at the time of the worst economic crisis since 1929.

The content of the 99% Tumblr blog completely departed from this avowedly minoritarian and voluntarist imaginary. The website contributed in spreading the 'meme' of the 99% and in giving this elusive and (almost) all-encompassing identification a concrete imagery: a series of faces and stories people could relate to, feel compassion for, and identify with. The 99% slogan fundamentally revolves around the creation of a popular identity, whose coherence lies in its opposition to those excluded from the 1 per cent of super-rich. The 'populist' cultural operation at play here is clearly similar to the claim of being 'normal, common people' made by Democracia Real Ya activists in Spain before the 15th of May protests. Some people have criticised the fact that the slogan reduces political identifications to a numerical factor.[29] Others have highlighted the risk of eliding differences among various categories of people inside the movement, and in particular ethnic and sexual minorities.[30] Moreover, it is clear that this collective name is connected with a sense of national identity, given that the 99% figure refers to the distribution of income in the American rather than the global economy. What it is disturbing for some is precisely the intention to represent the majority of Americans rather than simply an oppressed or idealist minority. This majoritarian ambition, however, constitutes precisely the difference between Occupy and the anti-globalisation movement, and arguably what has allowed the former to mobilise a diverse constituency, beyond young middle class people.

By collecting in one place the stories of Americans of different classes, the 99% Tumblr blog became a symbolic rallying point for a dispersed community of users called upon to recognise that its problems were not simply individual ones, but a consequence of the structural injustice of the economic system to which there was no 'biographical solution' (Beck, 1992), only a collective one. As Shawn Carrie, an Occupy activist points out:

> They always tell you that if you don't have a job it's because you are not good or trained enough. It teaches you that it's all about you but I think what people now realise is that it's a systemic

issue. It is one thing for one person not to have a job. But another thing when thousands and millions of people don't have a job. It is not just because people are not doing that. It is because it is the system that is broken.

This process of popular identification was paralleled in many of the discussions taking place in the protest camp in Zuccotti Park, where in the course of meetings small and large, and in the everyday life of the camp, people would continuously share their stories and their fears. For Bill Wasik, the main editor of *Wired!* magazine:

Those photos of struggling Americans essentially *virtualized* the occupation; the street protesters were merely the visible symbol of the giant, subterranean mob of Americans struggling to get by. What's really revolutionary about all these gatherings – what remains both dangerous and magnificent about them – is the way they represent a disconnected group getting connected, a mega-underground casting off its invisibility to embody itself, formidably, in physical space.[31]

In both its physical and web manifestations, the movement would come to amount to a 'documentation of disgrace' – in the words of Shane Gill, a member of Occupy PR team – a visible demonstration of how bad things were in America.

THE HEARTBEAT OF OCCUPY

A small park in Central Manhattan few people had ever heard of before the protest was to become the 'pulsing heart' of OWS, the focal point of a diffused space of participation. For the movement this small plaza made of granite tiles and decorative trees, deprived of sunlight because of the presence of tall buildings all around, came to constitute several things at the same time. On the one hand, it became a community space for those directly involved and a physical point of access for those who wanted to get involved or were simply interested in seeing the movement with their own eyes. On the other hand, it was also crucially a mediated place people engaged with from a distance following its activity through Twitter, Facebook and live streams on the web, besides the coverage offered by mainstream media. One message written on a piece of cardboard stuck to a tree in the middle of the park expressed this second role of the park by stating: 'this is the people's stage'.

Entering Zuccotti Park for the first time on the 5th of November, coming from Fulton Street subway station, I was initially a bit disappointed. 'Is that all?' I thought to myself. Having heard and seen so much about the park on TV and on the web before arriving there it was a bit of a shock to realise how small the camp was in comparison to those I had seen in Spain and Egypt. Yet the camp itself and the small community of a few hundred people occupying or spending much of their time there was only one piece in a much larger social interaction. The park became a symbolic place and a source of identification for a dispersed public of sympathisers following its doings through the media and on the internet. For David, an Italian IT researcher working in the US,

> Zuccotti was more like a symbol of thousands of people distributed around the globe. And the massive presence of Big Media operators was confirming the impression that something globally relevant was going on. I noticed a massive presence of smartphones, digital cameras – besides broadcast operators all around. You could almost hear the flow of tweets and Facebook posts spreading from there.

What made Zuccotti Park capable of becoming a sort of 'media spectacle' (Kellner, 2012), or more precisely a 'social media spectacle', was paradoxically precisely the richness of the face-to-face experience people could enjoy within it, and its exceptionality in the context of American society. For Stephanie, a young filmmaker who has been involved part-time in the movement, it was 'a sort of beautiful, exciting thing, which does not happen in public space in New York. Public space here is not really utilised in the way that it is utilised in the rest of the world'. She recounts one of the first evenings spent in Zuccotti Park:

> there were people who maybe they were there supporting a union, or there were people who were there with signs saying they were professors ... we just stayed there and talked, it was a beautiful fall night ... and we stayed there on a ledge of the park ... and sort of just listened to other people's conversations, and there were a lot of debates, and some people were just walking around saying – 'this is bullshit, I live in this neighbourhood get out of here'. And somebody would just approach him and say – 'tell me, let's just talk, we don't want to, we are not trying to bother

you, we are trying to help you'. It was like a spirit, something that had life in it, and it was really reaffirming.

Many of the interviewees I spoke with in New York after the eviction told me how much they missed the face-to-face conversations they had in the park: interactions for which there was no substitute on social media or web forums. As Shawn Carrie describes it: 'You [could] be talking with someone with whom you would have never talked to in your life, someone you would have never stumbled upon and talk to them. Because you have this space: this public space which has been activated for public discussions.' The camp was for the participants what, according to Richard Sennett, a city is supposed to be: 'a milieu in which strangers are likely to meet' (Sennett 1977: 48).

Around the immersive face-to-face environment experienced by the occupiers stood a diffuse emotional space: a space traversed by tweets, Facebook messages, and live streams. After the activists began establishing the camp on the 17th, Twitter streams on hashtags like #OccupyWallStreet, #OccupyWallSt, #OWS and #Occupy-wallstreetNYC became a channel for connecting those outside and those inside the camp. The minutes of General Assemblies were tweeted live by top movement tweeps like @DiceyTroop, while others would keep people posted on the different events taking place in the park. These Twitter feeds somehow read like the heartbeat of the movement, going up and down according to the evolution of the situation. The content of tweets and the overall mood they conveyed might signal euphoria or difficulty depending on events on the ground. As Michael Premo, an activist involved in Occupy in New York, recounts:

The only thing about those tools is that they provided a better platform to *radiate out* the love and emotion that was happening there ... I think it changed the texture of the tweets ... It had a different sort of relevance in terms of radiating that out to many people... and the sheer number of people also who were tweeting.

One example of the kind of emotional conversations going on between those in the camp and those outside is offered by a selection of tweets sent on the 24th, one of the toughest day during the first weeks. Heavy rain was making life more difficult for those sleeping in the park: 'Umbrellas needed! #OccupyWallStreet Large umbrellas!! Pls RT', implored one activist. '#OccupyWallStreet How many people

Figure 4.2 Activist snapping a picture of an event at Zuccotti Park on his iPhone. (Courtesy: Lara Pelaez Madrid)

there today? Growing? Same?', asked a concerned sympathiser. Reassurances promptly came. 'Not one person left. The 99% will prevail! #OccupyWallStreet #ourwallstreet #takewallstreet', wrote one of the occupiers. 'Head count still over 200 despite the weather. #OccupyWallStreet #ourwallstreet #takebackwallstreet #takewallstreet', added another. Towards the end of the day, when it finally stopped raining, someone saw fit to thank the hackers' group Anonymous for the relief: 'Whoa rain has stopped at #occupyWallStreet! Thanks anon for hacking the weather ;)'. Another tweep thanked 'hippie magic' rather than computer skills. Later in the evening the occupiers used Twitter to ask sympathisers to order pizzas for them at nearby Liberato's Pizza, whose name resonated positively with the former (and apt) name of Zuccotti Park: 'Liberty Plaza'. After being flooded with pizzas that night, someone cheekily tweeted '#occupywallstreet – we do eat more than pizza'.

The Twitter streams helped in maintaining a sense of solidarity between 'physical occupiers' and 'internet occupiers' (as Julian, a 24-year-old activist calls those supporters who did not spend much time at Zuccotti Park, or had never been there). Supporters would frequently send messages of encouragement like 'Today Is A Good Day For Revolution! For Everybody In #OccupyWallStreet! Keep It Up!' or #OccupyWallStreet about time … YES!' Other users would incite people to join the occupation or to partake in one of the many events and actions held within and around the camp. 'I hear #occupywallstreet has #cookies better hurry and go get some' read a message sent on the 27th. Finally, others tweeted to 'sign in', to use the metaphor utilised by the social media location-based service FourSquare, as exemplified by messages like 'Just arrived at #OccupyWallStreet representing brooklyn!' or 'I was going to go to this: [link] But might just go #occupywallstreet instead'. All in all these messages contributed to creating an *emotional attraction* around the occupation, facilitating the continuous in-flow of supporters, sympathisers, tourists and the curious, in a sort of ongoing pilgrimage which lasted until the camp was evicted.

Apart from its mediated symbolism, the park also constituted a physical point of access, a sort of recruitment booth, for those interested in joining the movement. Crucial at this level was the location of the park right in the middle of Lower Manhattan, a place traversed not only by bankers, but also by construction workers such as those employed in the building site of the adjacent Freedom Tower, janitors and waiting staff working in nearby offices and bars, as well as American and international tourists on a visit to the Big Apple. For OWS activist Shane Gill:

> Initially people were coming to the park, based on this first day of action that had been called, and then in the days after there was this escalating enthusiasm that probably attracted the more typical activist circle, but then consolidated also among those who outside of it wanted to physically participate in things. And then they carried it through for a couple of the first days and weeks ... partly the location being so central in Lower Manhattan ... it's really a high traffic, and foot traffic, and I think that *gathered* a lot of crowd.

Likewise the impression of another Occupy activist, Shawn Carrie: 'for people outside, for people who are not in the movement, if they want to find out they know where to go. If for example they have found out about it by reading on a newspaper, but are not involved yet, they know where to go to know more about it and get involved.' As these comments suggest, the presence of Zuccotti Park and then of hundreds of camps, large and small, across the US was crucial in allowing outsiders to see the movement with their own eyes, and for organisers to have a point of outreach to the population at large.

Figure 4.3   Activist holding a sign inviting people to join actively the occupation.
(Courtesy: Lara Pelaez Madrid)

The face-to-face interaction between occupiers and outsiders was, however, made more difficult by the tight policing in the area. The barricades erected by the NYPD, and the white observation tower, nicknamed the 'Star Wars tower' (Writers for the 99%, 2011: 128), demarcated the site as some sort of criminal area to enter at your own peril. During my visit to Zuccotti Park in early November 2011, I noticed how visitors for the most part remained outside of the barricaded perimeter of the camp, for the most contenting themselves with snapping photos of people holding cardboard signs (often used pizza boxes), or of the picturesque mass of tents, as though visiting some weird activist zoo. Very few of these visitors engaged with the camp beyond this superficial interaction. For their part, many occupiers put much effort in getting these people involved. One day I noticed a group of young male activists repeatedly shouting to the passing crowd: 'Don't be that guy! Don't be that guy!' The sense of their message was apparent: do not just stand outside and watch what we do, get involved, join us. Yet the invitation did not seem to find many receptive ears. As Caiti Lattimer, a 23-year-old participant, remarked to me: 'it takes a great amount of bravery for someone who isn't involved to even go down there because it is intimidating. Everything is intimidating when there is a large group of people involved.'

In the case of Occupy Wall Street, the widespread sympathy for the movement, mustered among other ways through social networking sites, failed to a great extent to translate into mass physical participation. Compared to both Egypt and Spain, the turnout for the different US protests, and for the day-by-day participation in the camp, was around one tenth or less. For example, while the indignados and the Egyptian revolutionary movement saw protests with over a million participants, the Occupy protests never went above the tens of thousands. Many sympathisers contented themselves with following events from the safe haven of their computer screens. Julian, a 25-year-old activist and a teacher in a New York primary school, for example, tells of a colleague of his who had never gone to Zuccotti Park or any of the occupations but became an obsessive follower of the movement online.

> She has watched the live feed for hours and hours and hours, and knows everything that is going on now ... and it's funny. I go in and she says ... oh my God, do you know what happened in Oakland? No! Then I go on my email and I say oh shit! And then she sent me an email saying that Zuccotti might be shut down any day now ... And I ask myself how do you know about this shit?

As Caiti Lattimer notes: 'the internet has allowed people that kind of voyeurism ... The internet has allowed people to watch the movement from afar and even to keep track of it daily without having to be there in person ... Therefore I assume that there are a lot people who are closet supporters of Occupy Wall Street.' The difficulty in transforming sympathisers into actual supporters, already noted by Klandermans (1984), is a reminder of the fact that the new forms of connection facilitated by the use of social media and the increasing availability of information they offer does not automatically translate into additional participation, unless organisers are capable of creating a powerful emotional connection with these constituencies.

INSIDE THE TWITTER HQ

We have seen how Twitter and other social media were very important for sustaining an emotional space around the OWS movement, connecting occupiers and sympathisers. Yet there is clearly another aspect of Twitter use which needs to be discussed: its tactical role as a platform for real-time coordination during action and in emergency situations. While in Egypt this had only a minor relevance, given the limited penetration of Twitter among the protestors, the case was different with Occupy. Almost all the people I interviewed in New York owned a smartphone and were Twitter users.

Occupy organisers created a number of Twitter accounts to be used for circulating tactical information. During different actions around Wall Street and in other parts of the city, these accounts provided a minute-by-minute coverage of events. Sometimes they went further, giving people specific directions or suggestions on what to do, or on how to divert police crowd-control attempts, in a kind of activist equivalent of military Command, Control and Communication. Thus, for example, experienced activists would be fielded on the ground to work on 'reconnaissance', walking some metres ahead of a march to tweet or text back details about the manoeuvring of police forces. Shawn Carrie, manager of the aptly named account @OWS_tactical, recounts the way he employed Twitter during the action held on the 17th of December 2011 against the NDAA (National Defense Authorization Act), a law releasing funding for defence. The target of the action was Grand Central Station, upon which people were invited to converge in scattered groups:

> Police didn't know where it is coming from ... because everybody is just moving, and everybody is just doing it at the same time, and they cannot point to the *centre* of it ... and so, from my tactical account I put out something like 'tactics'. And then I gave people tips about what to do, like just act inconspicuous ... or wait in line and pretend to be a tourist ... just hide out, and act nonchalant and don't look suspicious.

This use of Twitter as a tactical device appears at first sight to confirm the network or swarm-like view of movement coordination, as described among others by Arquilla and Ronfeldt in their seminal essay on 'net-wars' (2001). The basic idea being that mobile media devices allow for the de-centralised coordination of participants, as suggested by Carrie's own claim in the comment above that the police could not 'point to any *centre*'. However, in this kind of coordinating operation there often tends to be a neuralgic centre of communication, much like what happens with an army. From the interviews I conducted with a number of highly involved Occupy activists it emerged that the key Twitter tactical accounts were managed by a core group of movement organisers, composed of around 20 people. These people also tended to be highly involved in ground operations, in the General Assembly, and in the different commissions. During the occupation in Zuccotti Park this core group used an office space made available by the New York Teachers Union. A lot of controversy erupted among occupiers about the existence of this space, which the mainstream media were quick to call the 'Occupy HQ' or 'Occupy Media HQ',[32] given that its presence went against the grain of claims to leaderlessness.

The clearest illustration of the use of this 'Twitter war room' for the centralised coordination of 'combat operations' is offered by the events of the night of the 15th November, when the NYPD violently evicted protestors from the square. Andrew 'Foo' Conner, one of the core organisers, managed to leave before the police encircled the camp. After meeting up with others at the office space, Conner helped direct the dispersing crowd to a common re-gathering area. It is worth giving his account of that night at length:

> We were basically put in charge of taking the dispersed campers and getting them back to I guess *coherence* ... Because you have to remember we have lost a thousand or so people sleeping there at night and the police were doing their damn best to run people off this way, and run people off the other way and across the bridge and they dispersed us ... and there is no way they could disperse us because we live at Zuccotti Park! We can't go home ... and there was that very weird mentality. So, people were calling us because they knew that we were safe in one sense or another and we used Twitter to do everything we could. What ends up happening is that we send out three bike couriers and they were able to find people in each of the groups that were protesting and to get their phone numbers. And we were able to go to Twitter, and then with the three bike couriers and then getting their numbers, and then with emails, we were able to get everyone back to Broadway and Pine. So at this point we have a map on the wall trying to figure out where everyone is, because there were about five different groups split off. And then through Twitter we just said go to Broadway and Pine. We were able to take a bad situation for us and turn it into a moderately OK situation.

Conner's testimony is interesting for at least two reasons. First, this scene clearly shows that the practice of coordination does not correspond to the idea of a completely leaderless movement – on the night, the process of re-gathering the occupiers was led by a handful of core activists. Secondly, this centralised mediated coordination was made particularly urgent by the fact that the movement had lost its fixed base in space, that it had been deprived of that minimum of coordination offered by the camp, acting as a sort of beacon for the movement. It is as though having been deprived of a 'nodal point' in space, the movement had to resort to a mediated one in order to be able to act in concert.

The core organisers I interviewed were for the most part honest in admitting the contradictions of this situation. In fact, they had themselves tried to develop protocols to make the management of key Twitter accounts more 'horizontal'. Nevertheless, the practical constraints of this type of work appeared to make upholding such a lofty ideal virtually impossible. This tension is reflected in Shawn Carrie's description of the management of the main Twitter account @OccupyWallStNYC, which at the time of the interview in December 2011 counted 300,000 followers:

> There's maybe 20 people who have access, and maybe 8 of those people who can approve ... What it is, is a system of privileges and permissions. Everybody has access to the account but it has a little bit of a structure where anybody can write tweets, but then they get put into a list which needs to be approved and the whole group looks at it ... and it is happening all the time 24/7 ... it is a running list ... we use a program to streamline it. Somebody submits something he/she wants to be tweeted and all the group has the possibility to look at it ... and they can edit it. Basically we have an open process to edit our tweets.

Carrie added that the group tried to make access to this account more open but that it proved practically impossible to make it completely open:

> we are always bringing in more people ... We definitely didn't want it to be too few people ... because one person cannot do all the work, for all the Twitter accounts ... But obviously we cannot make it completely democratic because otherwise it would be a *mess*. But it is a very fair and horizontal way to actually exercise a consensus process. And we wanted it very specifically to be that way.

The discrepancy between the movement's claim to leaderlessness and its own organisational practices did not seem to be just limited to the use of Twitter, but had a more general bearing throughout the movement. Formally, the life of Occupy in New York as elsewhere was regulated through a General Assembly held three times a week (Writers for the 99%, 2011: 25–32). However, in the day by day life of the occupation, there was a small group of highly experienced and highly involved activists who people turned to 'get things sorted out'. As Stephanie recounts:

> Leaders have emerged who are people who have the ability to be present and participate in that typical way, at every meeting all day long, or who have access to valuable internet space, or who have access to Occupywallstreet.org. They may not have what they are doing consented upon by any larger group. But because they have that valuable internet space that people turn to and look at, they become leaders in their own way.

While in its publicity OWS made frequent claims to being a 'leaderless movement', its organisational practices saw a handful of leaders emerge in its day by day evolution. Those who had access to the key communication channels of the movement became automatically not just 'opinion leaders' but also organisational leaders. In the following comparative chapter I will discuss how this continuing presence of leaders is in fact a more general feature of contemporary popular movements.

CONCLUSION

The vicissitudes of Occupy Wall Street demonstrate that the 'social media magic' does not work unless it is accompanied by a resonant narration, capable of motivating people to take to the streets. While from the beginning organisers, starting with Kalle Lasn and his team at *Adbusters*, placed much hope in the mobilising power of social networking sites and Twitter in particular, they failed to use these media as means for a 'choreography of assembly' setting the scene for public protests. Only once the movement became visible in public space did it begin receiving attention on social and mainstream media alike. Blogs like the 'We are the 99%' Tumblr page contributed to forging a popular identity very different to the minoritarian and voluntarist one advanced by *Adbusters*.

Twitter was instead adopted for constructing a sense of solidarity between physical occupiers and internet occupiers as well as for coordinating the actions of participants during actions and in emergency situations.

Occupy has been associated with anarchist claims to absolute leaderlessness. However, as was seen when looking at the 'Twitter HQ', the practices of communication and organisation of the movement contradict the claims to leaderlessness and absolute spontaneity often made by activists, especially in relation to their use of social media. While social media allowed for participatory conversations within and around the movement, as happened in other movements these conversations were led and moderated by a handful of core organisers managing influential movement Facebook and Twitter accounts. Such activists came to acquire a role as invisible choreographers who by using social media to publicise the movement's plans and events have had much influence in shaping its manifestations. If the activist spaces created by Occupy and other groups are indeed characterised internally by a strongly participatory character, their initiation and maintenance nevertheless requires the work of a few committed activists.

There are a number of aspects which have not been possible to cover in this chapter for reasons of space. Specifically, as has been the case in previous chapters, here it has not been possible to cover the role of mainstream media as a channel for mobilisation, even though this was, as Shane Gill puts it, 'the way in which most Americans got to know about Occupy'. Moreover, the discussion in this chapter has been limited in geographic scope given that I have focused all my attention on Occupy Wall Street in New York. Like the Spanish indignados, the Occupy movement demonstrated a remarkable capacity to extend itself across the national territory, creating a diffuse network of local protest camps, allowing also those living outside of New York City and other metropolitan centres to participate physically in the protests.

But a more general question arises concerning the future of Occupy. At the time of writing, in Spring 2012, all the main occupations had been evicted. Activists were preparing for new actions scheduled in May. But all in all the movement, now deprived of its novelty factor, seemed to be experiencing a phase of latency. This once again highlights the difficulty of sustaining a contemporary popular movement, especially when accompanied by a categorical refusal to explore new forms of formal organisation to give more continuity to a campaign. The future of Occupy and of similar movements will largely depend on the degree to which they manage to reinvent their activities beyond the tactic of the long-term encampment and to rethink the use of social media in the context of facilitating new forms of gathering in public space.

5
'Follow me, but don't ask me to lead you!' Liquid Organising and Choreographic Leadership

'I will just tell you one thing which is very important. We don't have leaders. OK?' So wrote a user on one of the Democracia Real Ya Facebook pages, in reply to a request from me for an interview with him. He declined, but his response was possibly richer than any interview I might have otherwise conducted. The comment encapsulates in few words the fundamental idea dominating contemporary activist discourse. From the pro-democracy movement which toppled Mubarak to the indignados of Puerta del Sol and the Occupiers of Zuccotti Park, activists constantly stress that they have no leadership, and appeal to the spontaneity of participation as a fundamental source of their legitimacy. Occupy Wall Street, for example, boldly states in its publicity that it is a 'leaderless resistance movement'.[1] But is this really the case? Is it true that social media allow contemporary social movements to become leaderless and horizontal spaces?

This chapter endeavours to develop a comparative analysis of the use of social media across the different social movements and national contexts discussed in this book, focusing on the crucial and controversial question of leadership in social media practices. The target of my critique is the discourse of leaderlessness and the ideology of horizontalism which dominates contemporary activism. 'Horizontalists' believe that thanks to the availability of modern technologies of communication social movements do not need the kind of linear command structure characteristic of bureaucratic organisations. Instead, they can rely on a form of 'swarm intelligence' (Hardt and Negri, 2005) within which, in the words of Shawn Carrie, 'no one is a leader because everybody is a leader'.

The analysis developed in the previous chapters has already largely contradicted this vision of contemporary movements as leaderless, by identifying individuals and groups who had a pivotal role in the various processes of mobilisation. From Facebook admins like Wael Ghonim in Egypt and Fabio Gandara and Pablo Gallego in Spain, to prominent activist tweeps with thousands of followers, like the Egyptian Mahmoud Salem (a.k.a. Sandmonkey), social media activists have deeply shaped the actions of social movements throughout the phases of both initiation and sustainment. However much these and other social media activists refuse the label of leaders, the communicative and organisational work they conduct through Facebook and Twitter amounts to a form of leadership, as a relatively centralised influence on the unfolding of collective action (Barker et al., 2001).

To grasp the workings of this form of 'soft' leadership, I begin by asserting that within contemporary movements the use of social media does not augur the end of organisation as such but the emergence of 'liquid' forms of organising. Within this model, stemming from a critique traditional or 'solid' organisations, communication and organisation become almost indistinguishable, and the 'communicators' of a movement become also automatically its organisers and leaders. In spite of the egalitarian ideology of contemporary popular movements, the forms of communication characterising social media are characterised by a 'power law distribution' in which a handful of people control most of the communication flow. This imbalance reveals the de facto presence of a form of leadership, which makes use of the participatory and interactive environment of social media for the channelling and triggering of participants' emotionality.

The nature of this 'choreographic' leadership will be further illuminated by looking at activists' use of Facebook and Twitter. Facebook, as we have seen, has been employed as something akin to a recruitment and training ground, to facilitate the emotional condensation and common identification of a largely un-politicised middle-class youth. Twitter, in contrast, has been mainly used as a vehicle for 'live' internal coordination within the activist elite, besides its many largely 'external' uses, including as a means for citizen journalists to document police brutality. Because of its lesser reach compared to Facebook, this medium – the most popular of social media within the core activist community – runs the risk of isolating movement leaders from the less internet-savvy sections of their constituency. Activists' use of social media thus reveals the inherent tendency of mediated communication to isolate even while connecting (Ling, 2004), with possibly nefarious consequences for the development of collective action.

In the final section of this chapter I reflect on the relation between social media, public space and locality. I argue that social media can be seen as involved in 'focal practices' (Borgmann, 1984) which direct people's attention towards specific places and events, symbolically gathering many dispersed individuals around the same actions. Symbolic places like those occupied by the mass sit-ins of the popular movements of 2011 come to constitute the nodal points in the texture of participation of contemporary social movements. They appear in the guise of impersonal leaders, fixed spatial referents making up for the absence of a visible leadership and the evanescence of its liquid organisational practices.

LIQUID ORGANISING

The only new thing about these tools is that you are not a member in an organisation anymore, you are a member in a cause or a movement. And you don't need to have a physical membership. You don't need to go to the meeting. You are not organising things underground anymore. You do everything over the internet. So you get the instructions … and if the instructions are convincing you, you yourself start to play a little bit of a part. You start to tell your friends, your family. You know what the goal is, which is to spread the information, and you start to give it to people. You start to create from the tools you have. You start to spread the information by word-of-mouth as much as you can. You send text messages to all your contacts. You send your people emails. You communicate with colleagues at work.

These comments by Ahmed Samih, a human rights activist involved in the revolutionary movement in Cairo, sum up well the way in which activists in Egypt, Spain and the US see the use of social media as bringing about new forms of organising. What Samih describes here is a situation in which *stable membership in an organisation is substituted for a continuous communicative engagement with the 'movement' at large*. In this situation of 'disintermediation', individual activists (note Samih's repeated reference to 'you' in the singular) rather than groups are seen as the basic units of the movement, responsible for relaying messages to their personal networks of friends and acquaintances.

The imaginary evoked by Samih resonates with Clay Shirky's description of social media as allowing for 'organising without organisations' (Shirky, 2008). It is remarkable how the mere mention of the word 'organisation' is capable of raising suspicion among activists, as I witnessed in some of the interviews. The idea that 'organisations have become an obstacle to organising ourselves' (Invisible Committee, 2009: 7) has a strong resonance with many of the activists I interviewed in Spain, Egypt and the US. Activists constantly present their politics as a reversal of the doings of large-scale institutions like banks, corporations and state agencies, with their top-down forms of communication. Moreover, they are also largely critical of the institutions of mass popular organisations, such as political parties, trade unions and other established forms of association.[2] Finally, they for the most part refuse the option of building new formal organisations to pursue long-term campaigns on the issues raised by social movements. This became particularly evident in the wave of disapproval sparked by the decision of some core members of Democracia Real Ya, including Fabio Gandara, to register the group as a legal organisation in the early months of 2012. One could say that while prizing freedom of expression (on the internet), and freedom of assembly (in public squares), contemporary movements are much less interested in exploiting freedom of association.

One way to identify the specificity of the organising forms facilitated by the use of social media is through the use made by Egyptian activists of the term 'organic' to mark their difference from established organisations, and in particular from the Muslim Brotherhood. 'They are very mechanic, we are very organic' says Egyptian activist Noor Ayman Noor, referring to Tom Burns and G.M. Stalker's analysis in the *Management of Innovation* (1961). It works like the 'traffic in Cairo', explains Mahmoud al-Banna, 'it is outrageous when you look at it, but there is an order to it, there is a pattern'. Similar views can be heard across the Atlantic, among the activists of Occupy Wall Street. Thus Will, a 25-year-old activist from San Diego involved in OWS New York, expresses his distrusts towards 'hierarchical organisations':

We have traditionally been used to hierarchical organisations like governments which are very top-down or business-like. These organisations put their ideas out through the media who can then use them to have a discussion. You can have a debate about 'this is wrong' and 'this is right', but only within these two fixed boundaries. And everyone is basically just repeating their opinions, no matter if they watch CNN, Fox News, or other mainstream media. There is not much independent thought. The hierarchical system supposes that we as individuals are not able to organise ourselves, that we need help.

As these comments illustrate, the rejection of solid organisations is accompanied by a striving for disintermediation and an investment in forms of bottom-up organising or 'open organising' (Jordan, 2002: 69) among 'individuals' rather than groups. These 'liquid' forms of organising stress the importance of direct involvement and authentic engagement – values which are part of the heritage of anarchism (see for example Vaneigem, 1983).

The notion of 'liquidity' (Bauman, 2000) as applied to these forms of organising has a strong resonance with the evanescent character of social media themselves. Social media messaging is often described as 'streaming' (an Al-Jazeera English TV programme on social media and activism was aptly titled *The Stream*). When following tweets posted on popular hashtags, or Facebook status messages, the impression is of an ever-changing communicative flow which can sometimes make people dizzy with information overload. As I will argue in the conclusion, this liquid character of the information flow in contemporary social movements raises important questions about their long-term sustainability.

In the framework of the liquid organising practised by contemporary movements, social media intervene in expanding and brokering connections between friendship networks. The flexible relationships they allow for are characterised by an informality or 'personalism' which Paul Lichterman describes as 'a way of speaking and acting which highlights a unique, personal self'. For Lichterman, 'personalism supposes that one's own individuality has inherent value, apart from one's material or social achievements' (Lichterman, 1996: 6). Social media are means through which a highly personal engagement with social movements can be constructed, while at the same time rejecting a well-defined and stable collective identity, an element which Lichterman sees in opposition to personalism.

Within contemporary social movements, with their stress on informality and the adoption of 'friendship' as the frame for interpersonal interaction, *communication and organisation become by and large impossible to separate from one another – so deeply embedded, so tightly woven together that they become indistinguishable.* In a way, communication is always also a form of organisation, as argued by, among others, François Cooren in *The Organising Property of Communication* (2000). Again one can think back to Lenin's affirmation of the newspaper as a 'collective organiser'

(1902/1969: 156). Interestingly, when Lenin was accused of thinking that he could make a party out of a newspaper, he replied that this was not his intention. The newspaper was only a tool in the hands of the Party, the visible manifestation of an entity which could not be reduced to this medium. For some contemporary activists, by contrast, it seems as though a movement's organisational structures can really be completely subsumed by Facebook pages, tweets, and other evanescent forms of communication.

What we are witnessing here is thus not only an equivalence between organisation and communication but arguably also a reversal of their mutual relationship. 'We organise ourselves in a certain way and we communicate accordingly', said Dario Azzelini, one of the leading figures of the German socialist group Fels, during my previous research on the culture of the anti-globalisation movement (Gerbaudo, 2010: 86). Contemporary activists could well reverse the statement: we communicate in a certain way and we organise ourselves accordingly. *It is communication that organises, rather than organisation that communicates.* As a corollary, 'communicators' also automatically become 'organisers', given the influence they can have through their communications on the unfolding of collective action. When an influential Facebook admin posts a status message he or she is not simply expressing an opinion but also inviting a certain kind of emotional response from page users. Similarly, when an activist 'tweep' sends a message about an incident involving the police, he or she is not only 'informing' but also eliciting a physical reaction from those receiving the message. These digital activists are not 'giving orders' to anybody. Yet their messaging influences the way in which people act together, by setting the scene in which their collective action is manifested, or, to use the terms employed in this book, by constructing a *choreography of assembly*.

RELUCTANT LEADERS

If among contemporary activists the word 'organisation' raises suspicion, the word 'leader' is capable of provoking an immediate rejection. Activists from the Arab World to Europe and the US frequently assert that the movements they participate in are 'leaderless' or 'horizontal', treating this as a crucial element in their identity and sense of worth. Moreover, crucially, many believe that the use of social media is what helps social movements achieve the goal of leaderlessness. An example coming from my background interviews conducted in other countries illustrates this belief well. Tim, an organiser in the British anti-austerity group UK Uncut, states that 'Facebook and Twitter allow us to be truly horizontal.'

But despite assertions like these, the adoption of social media within contemporary social movements does not allow them to become leaderless or horizontal automatically. They do not magically introduce a level playing field. Very much to the contrary, *it is precisely through the use of social media that new forms of leadership are constructed*. It is true that social media allow for participatory communication, but this feature does not mean that everybody has the same degree of influence on collective action and that hierarchy is eliminated. Rather, top Facebook admins and activist tweeps come to acquire a disproportionate degree of influence on movement communication, and thus also on the choreographing of its actions. The leadership constructed at this level is no doubt diffuse rather than concentrated in one person, and characterised by a charismatic (Weber, 1978: 1948) and 'organic' character in which 'authority is settled by consensus' (Burns and Stalker, 1961). Nevertheless, it remains a form of leadership as a relatively centralised (albeit distributed) influence on the unfolding of collective action.

Arguably the type of confusion which underlies the ideology of 'horizontalism' can be traced back to an erroneous equation between informal or 'liquid' organising and leaderlessness. The assumption is that if you do not have an elected chair, with legal status, that automatically means there are no leaders or leading groups. This idea had already been disputed by Burns and Stalker (1961) in their classic study of 'organic' organisations (as opposed to 'mechanic' ones), in which they asserted that forms of stratification continued to exist. This same phenomenon was also noted by feminist theorist Jo Freeman in her classic essay the 'Tyranny of Structurelessness' (1972), already cited in Chapter 1. Many of the remarks made by Freeman, commenting on the feminist movement in the US in the 1970s, could perfectly apply to contemporary social movements. Despite claims to leaderlessness, leaders or core organisers continue to exist, and possibly they will always exist in one form or another given that the dynamic character of the process of mobilisation always implies the presence of imbalances and asymmetries.

To assert that these movements have leaders is not to deny that they are highly participatory, and that they create genuine spaces for self-expression. This feature is well represented by the General Assemblies (GAs) which became a hallmark of both the Spanish indignados and Occupy Wall Street. General Assemblies, as an alternative to rallies with a prescribed list of speakers, have offered ordinary people a stage on which to voice their concerns, have their stories heard, and contribute to collective decision-making. Institutions like GAs are used to a great extent precisely to enforce horizontalism and leaderlessness. Yet it would be naïve to think that the mere presence of GAs magically transforms social movements into horizontal spaces of participation. This is so for at least two reasons.

Firstly, General Assemblies themselves, alongside similar organisational platforms, are affected by the dilemma of the 'hierarchy of engagement' described by Haunss and Leach in relation to the autonomous direct action scene in Germany (2009). This means that while these decision-making bodies are in theory open to everybody, *de facto* they tend to be mostly attended by people highly involved in the movement. Those who have work or family commitments, and for these or other reasons cannot attend regularly, can feel sidelined. Conversely, a disproportionate influence comes to be acquired by those who have what we could call the 'privilege of presence', that is, the time and energy to participate fully in the movement's actions.

Secondly, in the day-to-day life of social movements, the practical organisation of collective action relies heavily on the intervention of highly involved and experienced participants, or core organisers, who are responsible for 'getting things done' as Stephanie, an Occupy activist, puts it. There is in other words a gulf between the decision-making and the execution of the different activities of the movement. This phenomenon becomes particularly evident at the level of communications, as we saw in the case of OWS's management of their tactical Twitter accounts – the activists originally adopted 'horizontal' procedures, but soon had to restrict access to the accounts because they would have become 'a mess' if left completely open.

The presence of a leadership in contemporary popular movements is the most evident in the phase of their initiation, in the months and weeks before they become publicly visible, which in some but not all cases is also the phase at which the impact of social media is the highest. At the very beginning of the process of formation of contemporary popular movements we recurrently encounter a tiny group of people, initially often just one or two people who have been responsible for triggering the process of mobilisation: Wael Ghonim, the admin of the Kullena Khaled Said Facebook page, Pablo Gallego and Fabio Gandara, the first initiators of Democracia Real Ya, and

Kalle Lasn and Micah White editors of *Adbusters*. Naturally these initiators did not create the movement all by themselves. If it had been for them alone, there would have been no movement at all. However these people in collaboration with other activists and in interaction with sympathetic internet users launched an idea which progressively came to act as the initial nucleus of a symbolic gathering which would later precipitate into a material gathering, into a protest in public space.

The level of influence of these activists varied a lot according to the specific circumstances of the social movements they contributed in initiating. For example, Lasn and White had very little say once ground organising began in New York, also given that they were acting from the distance of Vancouver and Berkeley. In the case of the Egyptian uprising and the indignados instead, these leaders had an evident role in guiding the launch campaign from beginning to end. Working as admins of their Facebook pages, Ghonim as well as Gandara and Gallego, shaped the identity of a nascent movement, and had much power in defining its action in its initial stages of development. Yet, as soon as the movement landed onto public space, they lost a great deal of this influence. Given that their leadership was channelled exclusively through a Facebook page, once people did not need Facebook anymore to be gathered together, having found a site to *gather around* in a physical place like Tahrir square or Puerta del Sol, these Facebook leaders lost grip on their following. Similarly, influential 'activist tweeps', especially in countries with high Twitter penetration rates like Spain and the US, definitely had an influence in sustaining the action of participants on the ground, not just in the form of tactical coordination, but more crucially through the construction of an emotional tension towards protest participation.

The new forms of leadership emerging in the field of digital activism are paralleled by the continuing importance of street-level leadership. Once a movement is out on the streets, there is more room for ordinary participants to shape its action, as the influential individuals and groups are physically submerged 'in a much bigger crowd'. At this level also, however, we regularly find the presence of leading groups involved in giving collective action a sense of unity and of direction. In the case of Egypt, for example, a leading role was played by a number of organised political groups, such as the Muslim Brotherhood and the 6th of April movement. Moreover, the football ultras of el-Ahly and Zamalek, with their highly pyramidal structures, were crucial in coordinating and waging street fights with the police. In the case of Spain, direct action activists from the 'okupas' scene contributed significantly to informing the organisation of the *acampadas*, drawing on their previous experience in the anti-globalisation movement and direct action protests. Finally, activists involved in the tiny but vocal anarchist community in New York definitely had a leading role in managing the set up of General Assemblies.

As we saw in Chapter 5, without the people who had met at the 16 Beaver arts space in New York in August 2011, 'there would not have been an Occupy movement as we know it today' (Kroll in Van Gelder, 2011: 16). But what were those people if not leaders of some kind? Or does the fact that most of them were anarchists automatically preclude that possibility? Personally I am convinced that historical anarchists like Errico Malatesta, Mikhail Bakunin and Nestor Makhno were also precisely that: leaders. They were people who 'led' by initiating social movements, inspiring actions and acting as focal points or symbolic centres for anarchists scattered across geographic space to look towards. The role played by contemporary activists, and digital activists in particular, is very similar.

It is ironic that social media commonly held to facilitate the leaderlessness contemporary movements strive for become precisely the means through which new forms of leadership emerge. This phenomenon reflects the fact that, contrary to what theorists such as Castells think, the internet is anything but a non-hierarchical communication environment. As different analysts including Yochai Benkler (2006) and Clay Shirky (2010) have observed, communication on the web is characterised by a 'power law distribution' whereby a tiny minority of internet users produces the content the great majority consumes (Wikipedia – to which only 2 per cent of users ever contribute material – being a case in point [Shirky, 2010: 125]). The same hierarchical tendency underscores Twitter communication. This is exemplified by the distribution of messages sent on the #jan25 hashtag used by Egyptian activists during the uprising against Mubarak. Alexandra Dunn and Christopher Wilson found that out of over 106,563 unique users who employed the hashtag, the great majority of messages were sent by 200 'power accounts' (Wilson and Dunn, 2011: 1265). Similarly, a study of tweets related to the Spanish indignados conducted by the university of Zaragoza in Spain found that the working of Twitter streams connected to the 15-M contradicted the ideology of equality propounded by the movement. Researchers retrieved a 'tendency toward hierarchical structure' in which a small group of 'opinion leaders' gathered most of the attention (Borge-Holtoefer et al., 2011: 8).

Twitter interactions epitomise the new forms of hierarchy created in the use of social media. This is also because in this medium, unlike on Facebook, relationships are asymmetrical. By following someone you are not automatically followed, hence the huge disparity between average users and popular ones in terms of number of followers. The very naming of the relationship as an act of 'following' alerts us to the fact that this medium involves or encourages some form of leadership. Or are we to believe that there can be 'followers' without leaders? The type of interaction available on Twitter reveals a structural imbalance in online communication, an imbalance which in organisational terms means the presence of a leadership, however diffuse, distributed or networked it might be.

To sum up, social media have become a means through which leadership is exercised while at the same time concealed, so as to maintain an impression of absolute spontaneity and fulfil the criteria of horizontalism. This phenomenon is perfectly illustrated by the controversy surrounding the existence of the 'HQ' of Occupy Wall Street, an office space near Zuccotti Park, where a dozen activists worked on communications as described in Chapter 5. Some militant anarchists got very angry about the existence of this space, which they saw as a command centre trying to control the movement. It is clear that this space was very troublesome for them because it materially embodied the fact that for all the talk about leaderlessness which populated the publicity of Occupy Wall Street the movement fundamentally relied for its day-to-day survival and public relevance on the work of a committed bunch of media-savvy activists. At least in the case of Occupy Wall Street in New York, people were not trying to make this presence of a group of core organisers a completely hidden secret. What was scandalous in other words was not the presence of organisers, but the fact that organisers were 'housed' in a specific space, instead of being invisible in the crowd or hidden behind a computer screen somewhere in town.

Interestingly, many Facebook and Twitter accounts used by contemporary social movements go under anonymous names, or collective names, thus contributing to the impression of leaderlessness, while they often tend to be operated by a core group of organisers. Social media create the impression that nobody is leading because it is assumed that these media are inherently 'participatory', and that by using them people are 'simply' communicating, interacting, sharing, 'participating'. *However, enshrined in 'simple' communication, there are forms of 'soft' leadership, which make use precisely of the interactive and participatory character of the web 2.0 environment.* Indicative of this phenomenon is the assertion of Egyptian activist Ahmed Sabry, a 48-year-old architect, that 'Facebook was our training ground and Twitter was our HQ.' Interesting here is the opposition between physical structures for organising (a training ground, and a headquarters as a building), and 'immaterial' and evanescent channels of communication like Twitter and Facebook, which itself reads like a celebration of *liquid organising*. To put it in a more extended form Facebook was used by movement leaders, or to use a more neutral term 'organisers' or 'activists' to mobilise people from the outside of the space of participation, while Twitter was important for purposes of internal organisation.

FACEBOOK WAS OUR TRAINING GROUND...

When Mark Zuckerberg developed the first version of Facebook at Harvard, what he aimed to cater for was young students' craving for flirting and friendship (Kirkpatrick, 2010). In fact, these are to a great extent still the kind of desires which animate most Facebook users. For many contemporary social movements, however, this most popular of all social networking sites has come to constitute a platform for political organising and mass mobilisation – the equivalent of what the counter-information website Indymedia was for the anti-globalisation movement, as a point of contact between activists, supporters and sympathisers and an arena for public discussions. The contrast between Indymedia and Facebook immediately highlights one key difference between these movements. While activists using Indymedia were addressing an already politicised public, contemporary activists using Facebook attempt to 'recruit' and train (prepare for political action on the streets) a following among a largely un-politicised youth, epitomised by the Egyptian *shabab-al-Facebook* discussed in Chapter 2.

As we have seen, in advance of the movement appearance in public space Facebook pages and groups like Kullena Khaled Said and Democracia Real Ya have acted as an emotional rallying point around which to condense a common identity capable of assembling symbolically a diverse constituency of dispersed and individualised participants. Moreover, they have been a springboard for constructing an impetus facilitating the 'jump to the streets' as uttered by Spanish activists. The use of Facebook varies greatly across the social movements studied in this book. While the website played a crucial role in the Egyptian uprising, and an important one in the case of the Spanish indignados, it had almost no role in the preparation phase of Occupy Wall Street, given its snubbing by American activists. The reason why activists turn to Facebook to 'recruit' participants is fairly easy to understand from a purely strategic perspective. Facebook is the most popular of all social networking sites, approaching one billion global users in 2011. Few media give access to a larger audience, and certainly not in the interactive way this medium allows for. Across the countries considered in this study Facebook penetration rates vary greatly. In the US, 42 per cent of adults were on Facebook in 2011, while in Spain the penetration rate was 33.5 per cent.[3] Compared to these countries, Egypt has a very small percentage of Facebook users: only 4% of the adult population, though steadily growing (Dubai School of Government, 2011c). Regardless of these differences, at the time of the study, Facebook was in all three countries the social networking site with the largest number of users (in the case of Egypt, for example, a microscopic 0.15% were Twitter users). Thus, in using Facebook as a ground for their mobilising efforts, activists were focusing on the one site where they could potentially reach the largest number of users.

The popularity gained by the website as a platform for recruitment is, however, not reducible merely to the size of its user base. Arguably, what makes this medium so effective for drawing people in, including those with no previous experience of political participation, is the fact that it allows activists to tap into people's 'real' local social networks. In general, Facebook is used to mediate one's relationship to and engagement with a local community of friends and acquaintances: 'to articulate connections that have some basis offline' (Ellison et al., 2011: 134) and to maintain and extend users' 'social capital' (Bourdieu, 1984). In fact, many of those my interviewees interacted with on Facebook were indeed their real friends or close acquaintances, rather than 'Facebook friends' (in the sense of Facebook-only friends). In this sense, Malcom Gladwell is partly wrong in asserting that social media allow only for the construction of 'weak ties' (or at least he is wrong with regard to the type of interaction people engage in on Facebook).

At the same time, even such 'weak ties' can come to constitute a vehicle of mobilisation. As sociologist Mark Granovetter (1974) famously contended, it is in fact through weak ties that information is transmitted across groups, rather than simply within them. For Caiti Lattimer, an Occupy activist:

Facebook allows you to share things with people that you only have an acquaintanceship with ... The interesting thing with Facebook is that it truly allows you to reveal your private opinions and self to people that often times you have met just once and don't really know at all. So for example out of the 2,000 people I am friends with on Facebook I have close relationships with maybe 20 of them, maybe 30 if I am lucky.

It was remarkable that many of the people I interviewed in both Egypt and Tunisia, and to a lesser extent in Spain and the US, went to their first demonstration all by themselves. Fathma Righi, a 24-year-old Tunisian activist, recounts how on the 14th of January – the day of the decisive protests in the capital – 'I went by myself, because none of my close friends was sure to come.' For Fathma, as for other interviewees, the mere declared intention to participate uttered by many on the revolutionary Facebook pages she had joined seemed enough to persuade her to turn out. In Fathma's case, it was also because she felt that 'all Tunisians were my brothers. I did not need to be with friends. I was not scared.' Facebook had become for her a thermometer of the mood of the nation rather than simply a means to interact with her friends.

The use of Facebook as a mobilisation tool reflects not only the technological affordances of the medium, but also the peculiar forms of appropriation activists have devised, turning it from a symbol of corporate entertainment into a tool of resistance. Needless to say that this process has not been frictionless. Activists have had to face repeated censorship from this corporate service, such as the closing of pages and accounts. Furthermore, they have had to invent new forms of communicative engagement tailored to the forms of interaction allowed on the website. This has been visible in the forms of imagery and language adopted by activists in using this medium and tapping into its audience.

First and foremost, Facebook is a medium which privileges visual material, pictures, videos and the like. As Segundo Gonzales, a member of Juventud Sin Futuro in Spain, notes: 'on Facebook you do not read a text of 6 paragraphs, you do not share it. Nobody does. But if you write a sentence or a picture, people do share it. It is a culture of images, a culture of instantaneity.' For Occupy activist Andrew Conner, the challenge in using the website as a channel for mobilisation is the fact that 'Facebook is dumb audience':

> If you put a stupid photo, or a silly post, it will always get more likes than a political post that says 'this is really important come out to the park tonight'. And the problem is that it is unconscious. More people will like the image of a cat than they will like an OWS message saying that we are getting evicted.

But despite the levity and sometimes vulgarity of its content, it is arguably precisely this non-political and 'mass' character of Facebook, together with the breadth of its user base, that makes it such a powerful venue for social organising. Here activists can make connections with others outside of the narrow activist community, people who will not automatically share its idealism and commitment.

As Ethan Zuckerman has claimed in his own 'cute cat theory of social media', while the web 2.0 was designed 'to share pictures of funny cats', this does not mean that it is not suitable for activism. 'There's a real challenge within the world of lolcats – making activism viral probably means making it funny as well as political and heart-wrenching' (Zuckerman, 2008). In other words, activists need to be able to turn the type of communications prevalent on these platforms to their own ends. Since contemporary movements are supposed to be 'popular', given their claim to represent the people, campaigning on Facebook at least forces them to deal with an audience which uses social networking sites primarily for the purposes of entertainment rather than for political reasons. By the same token, the use of dedicated activist social networking sites – like the Spanish N-1[4] adopted by the indignados movement – only increases the danger of isolating activists from society at large, secluding them in an activist-only bubble.

Secondly, in their use of Facebook, activists have resorted to the informal and intimate language which characterises communications among its users. As we have seen in previous chapters, activists like Wael Ghonim and Fabio Gandara created emotionally charged interactions with their audiences to sustain a process of collective identification among people sharing a common sense of victimhood in the face of an unfair power system. The identities constructed on their Facebook pages were characterised by that deep elusivity which Ernesto Laclau considers a feature of populist movements (Laclau, 2005: 118). In the case of the Kullena Khaled Said page, it was the figure of Khaled Said himself that constituted the initial nodal point in the process of identification. Later, the page resorted to the imaginary of the nation and Egyptian-ness to construct a more wide-ranging identification, while the police force, deeply hated by different sectors of Egyptian society, came to act as a negative focal point, strengthening participants' sense of solidarity. Likewise in the case of Democracia Real Ya, the self-identification as 'normal, common people' was extremely loose. What gave it some coherence, apart from its appeal to the imaginary of cyberdemocracy and its promise of unrestrained participation, were vibrant verbal attacks levelled at bankers and politicians. The coherence of these identities was thus dependent not on some form of internal solidity, but rather on the opposition 'us vs. them': the people against the system.

In the case of Occupy Wall Street the process of popular identity-building found its venue not on Facebook, but mainly on the Tumblr blog 'We are the 99%', which, posting the stories and pictures of struggling Americans, managed to capture the imagination of many supporters and sympathisers. Within Occupy Facebook was initially snubbed as a mobilising platform. And when it was used there was little sign of that compelling emotional narration which was so important in both Egypt and Spain. Yet, also in the case of Occupy Wall Street, from the first week of occupation organisers came to realise the importance of improving their Facebook presence and exploiting its potential for emotional condensation. Here too the identity of the 99% was characterised by a deep indeterminacy, despite its apparent mathematical precision. What gave it some cohesiveness was once again its opposition to an enemy: in this case the financiers of Wall Street.

Besides serving as an emotional rallying point for constructing a popular identity, Facebook has also been appropriated as a 'springboard' for protest participation. Movement leaders in Spain, Egypt (this again does not apply to the US) used Facebook to fuel an *impetus* towards upcoming protest events capable of persuading people to take to the streets. The phenomenon has been observed analysing the doings of Wael Ghonim in Egypt, and Fabio Gandara and Pablo Gallego in Spain. These Facebook 'activist admins' constantly invoked an enthusiastic sense of anticipation, a sense of urgency about the need to take to the streets, and a sense of optimism about the turnout. The overall gist of these messages is summed up by one of the admin posts on Democracia Real Ya page back in March, two months before the protests, which proclaimed 'this is going to be big!' and bombastically anticipated 'revolution starts on the 15th of May'. As Andrew Conner puts it: 'you need to fake enthusiasm, until you have real enthusiasm'. Similarly, we have seen the effort Wael Ghonim put in to counter the defeatism of some page members, constantly reasserting his *trust* in users' honesty about their intention to participate in the 25th of January protest.

Indeed the question of trust is crucial in understanding the problems activists need to deal with in their use of social media. Social psychologist Bert Klandermans has observed that one of the key things that convinces individuals to participate in protests is 'the impression that also other people will participate' (Klandermans, 1984: 586). But one of the main problems with online organising is that the lack of face-to-face contact can become an obstacle to the construction of trust (Tarrow, 1998), making it difficult for users to be reassured about other people's intentions. In a way, one can see the popularity of the RSVP count function on Facebook event pages as being an attempt to cope with precisely this constitutive distrust of online interactions, by conveying the impression that 'we will be many'. Naturally, as we have seen across the different case studies, such counts hardly reflect how many people will actually take part in demonstrations. In the protests in Egypt, Spain and the US actual attendance tended to be between 10 and 50 per cent of those who promised to participate on Facebook. Nevertheless, the RSVP count with all its capacity for over-estimation creates the impression, or at least the necessary illusion, that there is an enthusiasm behind the event, and that one will not end up with only a few others facing overwhelming police forces.

...TWITTER WAS OUR HQ

'Nowadays most activists seem to use Twitter', says Egyptian activist Nour Ayman Nour. This sums up well the evidence that has emerged from our different case studies, at least if by 'activists' we mean those heavily involved social movement participants or core organisers (Oberschall, 1973: 383). If Facebook constitutes the equivalent of what Indymedia was for the anti-globalisation movement, one could say that Twitter is now analogous to what mailing lists were for the earlier activists: a platform for internal organisation and coordination. Here again, the differences between the two media are immediately evident, not only because of the mobile and real-time character of Twitter, but also because the micro-blogging site has a generalist rather than activist-specific character, and does not require a special subscription as do activist mailing services like riseup[5] or aktivix.[6]

As we have seen, with its rapidity and conciseness, Twitter has proved attractive to activists as a means to convey minute by minute updates about events taking place on the ground, as a sort of movement equivalent to the military C3 (Control, Command, and Communications): a movement HQ, to use Egyptian activist Ahmed Sabry's own definition, or channel for internal tactical communications about the movements of security forces, about attacks and other incidents, and about the needs of protest camps, such as medical supplies and technical equipment. Sally Zohney recounts how 'Twitter for me was the minute-to-minute update of the 25th of January, 26th and 27th. And I said OK … we are gathering in Nasr City in that area and we should avoid that area because there is police etcetera.' Similarly, in Spain, the protesters at Puerta del Sol used Twitter to give updates about police attacks and to inform supporters about the material needs of the camp. Within Occupy Wall Street Twitter has been adopted as an all-purpose tool, to coordinate people in the course of demonstrations, organise supplies, and publicise actions. For contemporary movements Twitter has thus come to constitute a *centre* or focal point in their real-time communications: a single platform where all information can be collected, and by being *gathered* in one place made available to a dispersed public of participants and sympathisers.

As with Facebook, the importance of Twitter naturally varied across the three different national contexts. While it had only a limited impact in Egypt, mainly reflecting the low Twitter penetration rate there, it was very important in Spain, and extremely important in the US, countries with a much higher penetration rate. (Twitter's penetration rate was 7 per cent in the US in 2011; though I was not able to find reliable figures for Spain, it can be estimated as a bit lower than in the US). Beyond the penetration rate one would also need to consider the 'uptake rate': the percentage of protesters who used the service. In the absence of relevant and reliable data it is understandable that this uptake rate should be much higher than the overall penetration rate, given the prevalence of a young and middle-class demographic among protestors.

While the use of Twitter as a tactical device has been well documented (see for example Aday et al., 2010), no attention has been paid to its contribution to the *emotional* construction of a sense of togetherness within social movements. This phenomenon can be seen in many Twitter conversations going on between those who are 'on the ground' and those who are following events from a distance.

Some activists have also attempted to use Twitter as a tool for activating and recruiting prospective participants, a task more usually covered by Facebook. However, this has mostly proven a failure, as we saw in the case of Occupy's overly Twitter-focused launch campaign. This is to a great extent a consequence of the website's communicative architecture, through which, as Ahmed Samih puts it, 'you do direct group communication about very *specific* issues', because 'it is organised around issues with hashtags'. When there are incidents or notable events taking place on the ground Twitter streams like those used by the activists can see hundreds of messages exchanged every minute. However, these discussions generally attract the attention of a fraction of all participants.

The specificity of Twitter conversations can also prove an obstacle when it comes to reaching out to people outside of the activist community. The people following hashtags like #OWS, #Tahrir, or #indignados are not exactly average internet users, nor average Twitter users either. Unless these hashtags become trending topics, which they rarely do, users have to look for them proactively, which presupposes they have an interest in the topic already. While Twitter communication gathers people closely around issues of common concern, and allows for focused discussions, this specificity also runs the risk of enclosing activists in their own 'virtual walled community' (Ling, 2004: 190). This is something that Egyptian activists in particular have become aware of, motivating the development of new practices of activist communication, such as #tweetashara3 (literally: tweet the streets) which combines new media practices with the classic repertoire of street level agitation.

The activist predilection for Twitter cannot just be reduced to technical issues, or to the site's supposed superiority vis-à-vis Facebook, but needs to be understood as a reflection of activists' striving for distinction (Bourdieu, 1984) from the vulgar mass of Facebook users. Through their engagement with Twitter, participants can gain a certain status, a 'symbolic capital' in Bourdieu's terms, which to a great extent comes down to the fact that Twitter is more exclusive than Facebook, given among other factors its emphasis on textual information. Two testimonies from activists will illustrate the point. Elizabeth, a participant in Occupy Wall Street, explains:

I don't do Facebook, I don't believe in it. I think it is a great business tool but personally I don't like the idea that people make money out of watching what you do. I have issues with it. Twitter maybe they do the same thing. But what you get there is the news by the second. That's the most valuable thing about it. So if you want news the best thing is to use Twitter, rather than to go to any of the websites, or even the newspapers.

Similarly Khaled, a 24-year-old Egyptian activist:

> I am not a big fan of Facebook. So I don't follow it closely. I had an account and then I de-activated it because at that point Facebook was very personal and people would take pictures of themselves in bikinis and this and that and put it up. It was an important tool to connect with old friends. But at the same time I felt it was a waste of time. Everyone was just showing off. I didn't feel there was much substance to it. So it just kind of pissed me off. I don't want to do this. It is wasting my time. There are more important things I need to do.

It is easy to empathise with this sense of frustration faced with the idleness that characterises so many Facebook interactions. This 'dislike' for Facebook, however, also highlights the risk inherent in what Bourdieu calls 'elective affinities', that is, the tendency that 'brings together people that go together' (Bourdieu, 1984: 241), in this case activists with other activists.

This risk of isolation which, as seen in Chapter 1 is a negative side-effect of increasing possibilities of connection offered by social media, is well captured in the testimony by Egyptian activist Sally Zohney who thus explains the difference between the forms of interaction available on Twitter and Facebook:

> On Twitter you follow and are followed by people who have very similar views ... On Twitter you surround yourself with a community of like-minded people. With Facebook it is different because it is your friends. So it is usually people you met before the revolution, people who are friends or friends of friends you met at school, or people you met at work. So it is people who don't necessarily have the same mindset or the same ideologies. So they get into lot of flames and arguments, and stuff ... My sister for example unfriended a lot of people during the revolution, friends she had since high school.

As Sally goes on to explain, 'because everyone you are following in your timeline, everyone is the same. So you think everybody in Egypt thinks the same way we all want the removal of the SCAF, all want this... but then you realise this is only the people who think like me ... the rest of the country doesn't think the same'. This risk of becoming trapped in an 'activist bubble' is particularly evident in activists' Twitter interactions, but clearly, though to a lesser extent, the same also applies to Facebook. This is not to claim that Facebook is inherently better, or more efficient than Twitter because of its specific communicative architecture, or the services it offers. It is not really a matter of technology, efficiency or quality of service, but a question of the social and cultural practices conveyed through this new medium. As we saw earlier, social media and Twitter in particular reflect the tendency of mobile communications to 'bring us together' while 'tearing us apart' (Ling and Campbell, 2011). This threat is a reminder of the continuing importance of street-level communication, which by and large continues to be the best way in which social movements can reach out to mainstream society, without the mediation of mainstream media.

TRENDING PLACES

To further understand the dynamics of contemporary social movements we need to dissect the complex interaction between social media, public space and locality which is hinted at by the metaphor of choreography. The case studies considered in this book highlight how the rise of social media does not entail a lessening of the importance of street politics or of face-to-face communication in physical spaces. Street-level communication – in the form of face-to-face agitation, fly-posting, leafleting and similar practices – continues to play a crucial role as a means of mobilisation. As seen in the context of the Egyptian revolution, fundamental for the success of the revolution was the face-to-face interaction between the *shabab-al-Facebook* and the *shaabi*, the lower classes on Cairo's streets. Similarly, the Spanish indignados, after having initiated the launch campaign towards the 15-M soon invested in the creation of local groups responsible for reaching out to those people bereft of an internet connection or of a Facebook account. In the case of Occupy this work of street level mobilisation had a lesser role compared to Egypt and Spain, for how much activists also resorted to posters, flyers and face-to-face networking to mobilise people. All in all, while social media were important to coalesce a core constituency of young middle class people, street level communication is what has allowed these movements to expand and become truly 'popular', by breaking the barrier of the digital divide, and allowing members of the so-called 'internet generation' to engage with 'those who do not have a Facebook account' to use the expression of Occupy activist Andrew Conner.

Apart from exploiting existing forms of public space, activists also actively engaged in creating new contexts of proximity. Contrary to the view of network theorists like Castells, who have argued that the new media automatically entail a lessening of the importance of place, contemporary activists' use of social media is involved to a great extent in reconstructing and facilitating forms of physical proximity. Social media contribute in the construction of a sense of political locality or a political 'net locality' (Gordon and de Souza Silva, 2011), giving the movement a grounding in public space. Occupied squares like Puerta del Sol, Tahrir square, Zuccotti Park – but also Syntagma square in Athens or the Kashba square and Bourghiba avenue in Tunis – have acquired an extraordinary symbolic importance in contemporary movements, as spaces for the gathering of a constituency that does not feel represented by existing organisations and institutions. The intense messaging about these sites through Facebook pages, Twitter streams and activist blogs has turned them into what we could call (playing with the Twitter notion of a 'trending topic') *trending places*: venues for *magnetic gatherings*, face-to-face assemblies whose alluring power depends to a great extent on the intense flow of messaging radiating out of them and in turn attracting people towards them.

Social media are often blamed for distracting us from what we are meant to be doing, or inundating us with messages and thus adding to the misery of information overload. In their activist use, however, they often serve as a means of 'concentrating' people's attention and emotions, functioning as what technology theorist Albert Borgmann has called 'focal practices', practices which 're-center' us, giving us a sense of our location in the world (Borgmann, 1984). Hence the popularity of Twitter hashtags carrying the name of a specific place associated with the movement, like #Tahrir, #Sol, #Zuccotti, which then becomes the target of an emotional investment, exemplified by messages like 'I believe in #Tahrir'.[7] We can here refer back to Paolo Virno, cited in Chapter 1, who playing with the Greek term 'topos' which covers both place (as in topology) and language (as in topic), asserted that the multitude does not have a common place but it does have a common a common language (Virno, 2004). In a way it is as though with contemporary movements one needs to reverse such statement. In contemporary popular movements it is as though the *topos* of topic comes to be identical with the *topos* of place. Matters of discussion as 'matters of concern' (Latour, 2005) can hardly be extricated from the specific places in which activists fight upon them.

As a consequence of this heavy symbolic investment in occupied squares, the space of participation of contemporary popular movements acquires a concentric and centripetal structure which resonates with the description of 'texture' developed by Henri Lefebvre in his *Production of Space*. According to Lefebvre, textures are 'made up of a large space covered by networks or webs' (Lefebvre, 1974/1991: 222). Though shaped by communicative processes which by nature are wide-ranging, they tend to centre on places or '*monuments* [which] constitute the strong points, nexus or anchors of such webs ... the properties of a spatial texture are fixed upon a single point: sanctuary, throne, seat, presidential chair or the like' (Lefebvre, 1974/1991: 222, 225). Likewise, the occupied squares of contemporary protests come to resemble a kind of 'monument' at the centre of the texture of participation. They are fixed points that *transfix*, points that capture and attract internet publics from a distance. Alongside the 'empty signifiers' which dominate the activists' online communications and the identities they construct, these places offer 'full signifiers': signifiers filled with histories, political traditions, and the bodily density or 'collective effervescence' of popular reunions (Durkheim, 1912/1965: 162). In face of the flexibility and elusivity of contemporary movements' organisational structures, but also in face of the indeterminacy of the identities these movements construct through social media interactions, the role of such places as focal points is what allows the movements to come together and hold together.

The reader might well ask at this point: have not specific places always been important for revolutionary movements? What makes contemporary protest sites so exceptional? It is true that all revolutions have had their symbolic places which have acquired an almost sacred quality for the movements invested in them – the Bastille in 1789, the Winter Palace in October 1917, the Sorbonne in May 1968. Yet with the 'take the square' movements of 2011 there appears to be something even more compelling. Occupied squares have become not simply stages for protest performances but also sources of identification for the social movements that have appropriated them, nodal points capable of holding together movements otherwise deprived of a solid organisational structure. In this way, places like Zuccotti Park, Puerta del Sol and Tahrir Square have themselves come to act as 'impersonal leaders', making up for the lack of a visible leadership and the reluctance of *de facto* leaders to be seen as such. Not being able to cling to a flag, a political party, or a personality cult, and having to temper the liquidity of its social media communications, the contemporary social movement clings to a place, as the stage of its history, the cradle (and grave) of its development.

CONCLUSION

The *liquid organising* practised by contemporary activists in their use of social media does not mean automatically the elimination of leadership. To the contrary, social media adoption among activists is accompanied by the rise of forms of soft and emotional leadership, which are by and large indirect as well as invisible but nonetheless effective in giving collective action a certain degree of coherence and a sense of direction. It is this kind of soft and dialogical leadership that the term 'choreography' endeavours to capture. Thus, the doings of contemporary movements are ridden with a deep contradiction between the discourse of leaderlessness and horizontality and organisational practices in which leadership continues to exist, though in a dialogical or interactive form. And possibly it will always continue to exist thanks to the asymmetrical character of the process of mobilisation and the need for focal points in the process of people's assembling in public space.

A further issue to be taken into account is the fact that the forms of soft leadership and liquid organising made possible through the use of social media, while effective in setting the scene for action and choreographing specific protest events in the short term, can prove ineffective in the long term in giving a direction to the collective action of social movements. This risk has been highlighted by the crises experienced by all three movements discussed in this book once their main occupations, from Tahrir square to Zuccotti Park, were lifted and they were deprived of that space to which, to a great extent, they owed their identity and sense of unity. The consequences and limits of this model of liquid organising and the 'invisible' choreographic leadership that underlies it will be discussed in the Conclusion, looking at its theoretical and political implications, and paying particular attention to the question of sustainability of contemporary social movements.

Conclusion

I believe in #Tahrir
@Aujo808, 14th November 2011

'The streets are dead capital' proclaimed the artistic collective Critical Art Ensemble in 1995, explaining that 'for an oppositional force to conquer key points in physical space in no way threatens an institution' (Critical Art Ensemble, 1996: 11). Instead of physical strikes one will have to organise virtual strikes, instead of physical sit-ins, virtual sit-ins, instead of physical demonstrations, virtual demonstrations. This call was indicative of the spirit prevalent among many activist groups in the mid 1990s. Francis Fukuyama had just announced that we had reached the 'end of history' (Fukuyama, 1992), and Thatcher's war cry 'There is No Alternative' still rang true for the majority of the population in Western countries. The global financial meltdown of 2008 was still far away and the bubble of the 'new economy' had not yet burst. The only glimmers of hope for radicals were coming from the mountains of South-Eastern Mexico, where the Zapatistas had begun their uprising, to which the Critical Art Ensemble provided virtual support by hacking the Mexican government's websites.

In face of the social and political latency and the emptying out of public space from protest politics which characterised those years, the rise of the internet came to be hailed as opening up a new space where a 'free culture' (Kelty, 2008) could develop. While John Perry Barlow of the Grateful Dead was seeing the web as a new 'Electronic Frontier', many activists came to welcome it as a new political playground. The rise of 'hacktivism' led many to see the internet as offering an escape from the emptied out public space (McCaughey and Ayers, 2003). Closeted in their rooms, their eyes glued to flickering screens, browsing through thousands of websites and databases, hacking governmental and corporate servers, activists would form virtual communities and waged their battles against the corporate state through the recesses of cyberspace, much like the characters in a William Gibson novel.

The social media practices of the 2011 popular movements urge us to depart from this escapist vision of the internet as a virtual space wherein to refuge ourselves from the crisis of public space. What we are witnessing now is a use of social media in the service of re-appropriating physical public space (Lefebvre, 1974/1991), rather than its substitution with a virtual one. A use we have tried to capture with the notion of a 'choreography of assembly'. At this level, the choice of the term 'choreography' stands to suggest that this process of reconstruction of public space is not completely spontaneous and improvised. In fact, *despite their repeated claims to leaderlessness, contemporary social movements do have their own 'choreographers' and these choreographers are not identical with the 'dancers' or participants.* As it happens in the field of dance, in contemporary movements these choreographers or 'soft leaders' are for the most not visible on the stage or at least do not take centre-stage as it were. But by harnessing participants' emotionality and directing it their actions nevertheless do have a deep influence on the display of collective action. In these final remarks I want to reflect on the theoretical and political implications of this use of social media within contemporary popular movements. To this end, I focus on three fundamental questions which have emerged from the foregoing study: the emotional character of social media use in social movements; the tension between spontaneity and organisation; and the threat of evanescence.

THE EMOTIONAL COALESCENCE OF THE 'PEOPLE'

Reading through the thousands of Facebook status messages, comments, tweets and blog posts which first anticipated and then celebrated the 'landing' or 'parachuting' of the popular movements of 2011 into public space, one frequently comes across metaphorical spatial expressions like 'jumping out' or 'jumping downward' or 'breaking out of the bubble' of internet activism. These messages reflect the construction of an *emotional striving* to depart from a sense of isolation, dispersion and passivity that activists see as the hallmark of social experience not only in authoritarian regimes like Mubarak's Egypt, but also in societies fallen prey to neoliberalism's attack on all forms of public space. *In front of this situation of crisis of public space, social media have become emotional conduits for reconstructing a sense of togetherness among a spatially dispersed constituency, so as to facilitate its physical coming together in public space. This finding clearly goes against much scholarship on new media which has tended to locate them in a 'virtual reality' or in a 'cyberspace' (McCaughy and Ayers, 2003), or in a 'network of brains' (Castells, 2009) detached from geographic reality. But it is corroborated by recent research identifying a revival of locality in new media practices (Gordon and de Souza Silva, 2011).*

There is no doubt that for almost all the activists I interviewed, the internet alone is not the solution to the crisis of public space. In fact, while the movements discussed in this book have seen their first nuclei emerging in the form of online discussions, they are marked by a sense of embarrassment at being simply internet-based publics in the first place: 'We are not people of comment and like.' Exploiting this embarrassment, even the Mubarak regime tried to debunk the credibility of the pro-democracy movement, precisely by ridiculing them as 'Facebook people', armchair revolutionaries who would have never make precisely that jump from the 'screens to the streets'. 'We are not on Facebook, we are on the streets' chanted the Spanish indignados in response, expressing their conviction that physical rather than virtual space is the primary *locus* for grassroots politics. 'This is not a cyber-utopia' says Shane Gill in a similar vein, criticising those 'techno-utopians' who want to reduce the movement to its internet communications.

It is true that Democracia Real Ya and other groups have some of their meetings online, and the Occupy groups use video and voice conferencing services like Mumble to engage in forms of interaction which transcend the physical limits of location. But what is most exciting and 'contagious' about these movements, what has captured the public imagination, are not abstract discussion sessions on internet forums, but the protest camps, assemblies, demonstrations, sit-ins and popular marches on the ground: multiple variations of a politics of the streets performed 'shoulder to shoulder' rather than 'peer to peer'. Internet communication and social media in particular are important only as the means towards facilitating such gatherings. These technologies cannot substitute public space for a 'virtual public sphere' (Papacharissi, 2002), but only re-weave a new sense of public space, refashioning the way in which people come together on the streets. When they are not connected to the construction of public gatherings social media can also run the risk of isolating activists from the broad constituency of the movement, as seen when talking about activist obsession with Twitter in the foregoing chapter.

To understand the working of this mediated reconstruction of public space operated by activists in their social media use, it is crucial to appreciate the conspicuously emotional rather than 'informational' character of this operation. Digital activists like Wael Ghonim in Egypt, and Fabio Gandara in Spain have skilfully exploited the personal character of social media, their capacity to become channels of intimate while at the same time public conversations. They have used social media to construct an *emotional tension*, connecting the highly dispersed and individualised interactions people maintain through Facebook, Twitter and other social media to the bodily immersion of collective gatherings. These forms of communication have contributed in creating a contagious sense of anticipation or *impetus* in advance of the protests, and an *emotional attraction* around mass sit-ins to sustain participation after the movement's landing in public space.

The emotional quality of the communications of contemporary movements needs to be understood in conjunction with the 'popular' character of these movements. In his discussion of 'populism' Laclau had already noted that the symbolic construction of the 'people' as a political subject has a profound 'affective' dimension (Laclau, 2005: 227). As we have seen from our case studies, social media can be used to construct a sense of solidarity within a diverse constituency, sharing a common sense of indignation, anger, frustration and perception of shared victimhood in face of a corrupt system. Social media become the pole of 'aggregation', or better 'concentration', of these individual sentiments, turning them into political passions within a narrative of *popular reunion*.

The implications of this emotional quality of the forms of mobilisation practiced by contemporary popular movements, revolve around the need to depart from techno-deterministic and cognitivist understandings of social media as informational channels advanced by theorists like Clay Shirky (2008, 2010) and Manuel Castells (2009). This line of analysis has popularised a vision of social media as some sort of C3 (Command, Control and Communications) devices of contemporary social movements, bestowing them with a technological edge over a sluggish state apparatus. This vision understands social movements as quasi-military insurgent groupings, swarms or smart mobs (see for example, Arquilla and Ronfeldt, 2001; Rheingold, 2003; Hardt and Negri, 2004) reducing their communications to pure questions of efficiency.

It is true, as it has been documented at different points in this book, that contemporary movements use social media also for tactical, that is, 'practical' purposes: to exchange information about the situation on the ground, and make up for the lack of a linear command structure. Nevertheless, tactical communication also has a deep emotional dimension, as seen for example in the

Occupy activists' use of Twitter for coordination after the eviction at Zuccotti Park. All in all though, as has been demonstrated in the course of the book, the most important role of social media lies in the construction of an emotional sense of togetherness among dispersed participants, rather than in the coordination of 'combat' operations on the ground.

This emotional quality of activist use of social media is a reminder of the fact that the understanding of social movement communications cannot be reduced to purely technical factors, and, more importantly, that there can be no 'technological fix' to the problem of collective action. No Android or iPhone App, no mapping software, no instant messaging or social networking service, no arrest alerting system, no online voting platform will ever solve technically the question of collective action, of how to mobilise and organise participants. This might well be a designer's dream, but by the same token it should also always be an activist's nightmare. The success of popular movements still lies to a great extent in the organisational skill of its activists and in their capacity to create a compelling sense of togetherness capable of initiating the coalescence of a disparate constituency. Arguably, contemporary movements could get by well enough without the tactical affordances offered by social media. But what they cannot do without (or what they do better with) is the capacity of such media to become the instruments of an *emotional narration* capable of motivating individuals to take to the streets.

SPONTANEITY BY DESIGN

The move 'from the web to the streets' has not only been undertaken for instrumental reasons, in order to cross the digital divide and engage with those (many) people 'who are not on Facebook'. It is also a reflection of contemporary popular movements' anti-author-itarian valuing of immediacy and face-to-face relationships. These movements fight against institutions which they criticise for being bureaucratic, alienating, pyramidal, over-structured and opaque. Rejecting the distance between people and power these institutions are seen to establish, contemporary movements are characterised by a striving for directness of anarchist inspiration: direct action, direct democracy, direct human contact. Directness as a desire for disin-termediation, visible in the movements' distrust towards traditional organisations' mechanisms of delegation and representation and in their embracing of liquid forms of organising.

The paradox, though, is that this disintermediation and personalised interaction, designed to allow for the construction of immediacy and 'authentic' human relationships, is itself premised on complex processes of technical and symbolic mediation, of which social media are just the most evident manifestations. It is in fact remarkable how, despite the claims to spontaneity made by these movements, they are characterised by attempts to manage or design the 'revolution' which are historically unprecedented – as exemplified by the use of Facebook for fixing protest dates. When did it happen in the past that people would announce 'the revolution begins' on this or that date, as was done by Wael Ghonim in Egypt and Fabio Gandara and Pablo Gallego in Spain? *It is as though in the context of a 'mediatised' society, immediacy (by definition the absence of mediation) cannot be sustained without being thoroughly mediated.* It is at this level of mediation that soft, indirect, and invisible or 'choreographic' forms of leadership develop.

Activists are perpetually having to dispel conspiracy theories claiming that there is someone or something 'behind' their protests – be it Israel, the CIA, Hamas, or Serbia (sic!) in the case of Egypt; the Democratic Party, George Soros' money, or 'the Canadians' (sic!) in the case of Occupy; or the Socialist Party PSOE, or even the Jesuits (sic!!) in the case of the Spanish indignados. The suspicion that social movements have to counter again and again is the idea that their endeavours are just a 'cooked-up' venture, that they are merely the ingenuous puppets of someone pulling their strings from behind. Naturally, these conspiracy theories are almost invariably ludicrous, and inadvertently make for good movement counter-propaganda in showing the obtuseness of their political opponents. And yet they are right in raising the suspicion that these movements are not completely 'spontaneous', and that there is in a sense 'someone pulling the strings'. But the 'puppeteers' here are the participants themselves, and in particular those highly committed members who dedicate much time to the movement, and thus become its communicators and organisers, or 'leaders'.

Contemporary social movements put a lot of emphasis on individual participants' active contribution; there is, however, no such thing as unrestrained participation and 'pure' spontaneity (Gramsci, 1971: 196). It is true that general assemblies, protest camps, working commissions, and the like are spaces which allow for self-expression and improvisation. But here we run into a paradox: *in order for this spontaneity to unfold, there is the need for a hidden work of scene-setting conducted by a nucleus of core organisers, around which further rings can progressively crystallise and without whose presence they seemingly would not crystallise.* The spontaneity of contemporary movements is thus a highly organised one, precisely because it is a highly mediated one, in a context in which communication and organisation become almost indistinguishable from one another.

The ethical problem raised by this kind of 'choreographic' leadership is not the presence of leaders as such but rather the categorical denial of the existence of leaders of any kind. What worries me about this denial is its capacity for encouraging a lack of responsibility among movement leaders. Look for example at Wael Ghonim, who has always trenchantly rejected the label of leader. 'This is Revolution 2.0: No one was a hero because everyone was a hero', he wrote on the 13th of February 2011 in a tweet re-tweeted more than a hundred times. No doubt there is some truth in this statement. The Egyptian revolution succeeded because of the heroic and creative participation of hundreds of thousands of people, hundreds of whom lost their lives during the glorious '18 days' and thereafter. But who could deny that Ghonim, alongside many influential activists like 6th of April's Ahmed Maher, had a major role in shaping the emergence of the movement? He indeed was a leader of some kind, a Facebook admin and a 'Facebook leader', who, alongside many leaders on the ground, was instrumental in opening up that highly participatory space which constituted the stage of the Egyptian revolution.

On a negative note, however, Ghonim was also instrumental in shutting that space down. When Mubarak resigned on the 11th of February, Ghonim famously tweeted: 'Mission accomplished. Thanks to all the brave young Egyptians. #Jan25'. Ironically, this mimicked the message which a few years earlier had been delivered from an aircraft carrier by George Bush, who would himself later repent of having thought the war in Iraq was over. Likewise Egyptians were soon to realise that they had not won, or not as fully as they had hoped. They learned from experience that the military council (SCAF) which succeeded Mubarak was not that different from its departed master. They would later regret having left the square without ensuring that the military top brass would not continue in the dictator's steps. As Egyptian activist Nora Shalaby reports, many people in the movement resented Ghonim for his famous tweet, precisely because of the perception that his Facebook page had such an influence on people's action that by sending the message he had convinced many that it was time to go home.

Ghonim's tweet was not just an opinion, however much it pretended to be merely that. His message had a concrete, though indirect and invisible, emotional effect. It contributed to the creation of a collective celebratory mood, which led many people to think that really the revolution had accomplished its aims and that they could go back to their own private lives. This is the problem with the 'anti-leaders',[1] or *reluctant leaders*, of contemporary social movements – by refusing to admit to being leaders at all, they can then be let off the hook when they do something wrong. The problem, in other words, is unaccountability: the very problem Jo Freeman identified when looking at the feminist movement of the 1960s and '70s. It seems like again and again we are faced with the same problems, and communication technology has not lived up to its promise of fixing organisational problems by means of its wondrous affordances.

My remarks about the de facto leadership in the movements considered in this book should not be taken as moralistic. In fact, I have nothing but praise for the people who put so much effort in creating and sustaining the various movements, and for all their mostly invisible work of choreographing the collective actions. Moreover, I do not think that leaders, or 'organisers', or highly involved and influential participants – if you prefer the term – are not living up to or are betraying their movements' ideals. On the contrary, I think that it is the ideals, and in particular the ideology of 'horizontalism', that is 'betraying' activists by being incapable of capturing empirically the gist of the actual practices taking place on the ground. In other words, this is *not* an 'immanent' critique of the Adornian kind (Adorno, 1976: 112–13), that of not living up to one's ideals. It is, as it were, a transcendental one: a critique of not 'thinking up' to one's practices.

In sum, I would argue that activists do not need to change their communicative and organisational practices so as to make them more 'horizontal'; they need not labour under the optimistic compulsion to achieve a utopian equality of involvement which will never be realised however hard we try. Rather, *we need to invent new concepts and practices better suited to capturing the fact that, for all its participatory ideals, the process of mobilisation always involves inequalities and asymmetries in which there are people who mobilise and people who are mobilised, people who lead and people who follow, and the two categories only ever partly overlap.* This is not an invitation to return to the old reassuring dogmas of Leninism with its class essentialism, its theory of the vanguard party and the like, but a call for the invention of new ways to make sense of the processes by which social movements are triggered and guided, processes which do not fit the imaginary of horizontal networks. The metaphor of choreography might just be one theoretical device that would aid in developing this alternative understanding.

BETWEEN EVANESCENCE AND CONTINUITY

At the heart of the culture of contemporary social movements there lies a third fundamental tension: that between evanescence and fixity. On the one hand, contemporary popular movements are characterised by 'liquid' forms of organising; in which the use of social media by social networking sites is geared towards superseding the authoritarian tendencies of 'solid' organisations like parties and trade unions, in the effort of avoiding the 'iron law of oligarchy' (Michels, 1999). On the other hand, these movements require the invocation of a sense of locality or 'net locality', which involves bestowing them with some degree of fixity, a 'nodal point' in their texture of participation.

As we saw in Chapter 5, the activists' choice of social media as their preferred means of communication is paralleled by their embrace of a culture of instantaneity, perfectly matched by social media like Twitter and Facebook with their focus on the 'here-and-now' – or, more negatively put, with their constitutive evanescence. These media can thus be seen as the contemporary equivalent of traditional movement 'ephemeras' like flyers and posters. In fact, they are even more ephemeral: 'ephemeral ephemeras' as it were. It is remarkable how in their activist use social media come to be tightly linked to specific actions or events, as exemplified by the functionality of Facebook events which has become so popular among activists. Once these events are over, the messages linked to them disappear into the electronic dustbin and become of interest only to the researcher or the abnormally curious, not to mention very difficult to retrieve. Indicative here is the fact that one can go back only five days in search of past tweets. 'Last things first' would be an apt slogan for Twitter, a medium which constantly focuses users on the *very* latest news and events.

Besides the evanescence actively nurtured through the use of social media, contemporary movements are also characterised by a striving for continuity and permanence, as testified to chiefly by their long-term occupations of public spaces. The practices conducted in the occupied squares come to resemble not only rituals of popular reunions, but also rituals of rootedness, reminiscent of the planting of the liberty tree in public squares during the French Revolution. The movements' construction of these *centres*, whose logic goes against the grain of visions of contemporary society as a 'network without centres', urges us to depart from the apology for dispersion which underlies both Castells' and Hardt and Negri's theorising, and to pay attention to the continuing importance of 'centring' practices in social groupings (Laclau, 2005).

This commitment to establishing fixed points in public space marks a clear break with the practices of the anti-globalisation movement. The earlier protests followed the logic of 'summit-hopping' – having been summoned through mailing lists and Indymedia websites, a diverse coalition of activists would converge from different corners of the West towards the same location to contest the global order. After a week or so of communal life, and fighting with police, the participants would return home to their local activist scenes, with their squats and occupied social centres. In a reversal of this orientation, contemporary popular movements are marked by an urge to make themselves semi-permanently visible in public space, as a way of sustaining a direct everyday interaction with those outside the movement, with passers-by, with the 'people'. Rejecting the nomadic spirit of the anti-globalisation movement, protest changes from being an 'event' into a durable 'all-out' occupation, endeavouring to give the movement a physical anchoring so as not to be washed away by the vagaries of an era of social liquidity.

The process of localisation, in which social media communications are heavily involved, is understandably not without its risks. Occupied squares, protest camps, mass sit-ins and the public geographies they construct can also become an object of 'fixation', as in the sense of 'mental fixation'. The almost obsessive focus on such 'trending places' can hinder a social movement's ability to reinvent itself and generalise its practices. Moreover, once deprived of that central point of attraction and beacon of coordination which the all-out mass sit-in provides, whether because of police repression or internal collapse, contemporary movements run the risk of a rapid dissipation. The challenge here is well condensed by a tweet sent by Egyptian activist Nora Rafea in July 2011, during one of the several sit-ins in Tahrir square after the 18-day revolution, in which she asserted 'Tahrir is a state of mind.' What she meant was: 'Tahrir is beyond the square. Go out of the square. If you think that the revolution is all about the square this is wrong.' The word 'Tahrir' and the connected Twitter hashtag '#Tahrir' have condensed a revolutionary spirit, which cannot be reduced to the site known as 'Tahrir square' in Downtown Cairo, but which at the same time is difficult to extricate from the place and the experiences associated with it.

To conclude: the strategic question facing contemporary social movements and their use of social media today is that of how to maintain a degree of continuity once, for whatever reason, they can no longer rely on the role played by occupied squares as nodal points in their texture of participation. Finding solutions to this dilemma will involve a deep organisational rethink (there were signs of this already taking place as the book went to print), and at the same time a rethink of the ways in which various forms of protest communications and social media in particular are utilised as means of mobilisation. Whatever the solutions, the commitment of these movements to the symbolic reconstruction of a new sense of public space will continue to be of fundamental importance in the coming years, both in the West and in the Arab World.

Appendix

This book draws on 80 interviews conducted with activists, social movement participants and sympathisers. Interviewees were recruited by spending time at protest sites and identifying possible initial interview candidates, and then proceeding through 'snowball' sampling, with an eye on ensuring diversity and balance in terms of gender, age and level of involvement in the movement. Interviews followed a semi-structured format, and lasted between half an hour and two hours. The interviews began by reconstructing the interviewees' personal background and experience of participation in social movements, before moving on to their use of social media for protest purposes, and their self-reflections on the opportunities and threats of these forms of communication.

Interviewees were later sent interview transcripts via email, to make sure everything they said had been correctly transcribed and to allow me or them to add any further information. The interviews were initially coded with an open-coding method, through which a series of key themes and sub-themes were progressively identified. None of the interviewees requested anonymity. However, some asked to have only their first name used as illustrated by the ensuing list of interviewees.

On top of these interviews, the book draws on ethnographic field notes collected during research visits to the different sites covered in this volume and on an analysis of archived social media material, including Facebook pages and Twitter feeds. At an initial stage this material was coded on its own, separately from the interviews. Later, some overarching master codes were identified to construct a general interpretive narrative.

US – OCCUPY WALL STREET

	Name	Surname	Age	City	Group	Profession
1	Malav	Kanuga	32	New York	Occupy	Researcher
2	Linnea	Palmer Paton	23	New York	Occupy	Student
3	Caiti	Lattimer	22	New York	Occupy	Student
4	Mark	–	25	San Diego	Occupy	Travel Writer
5	Noah	–	28	New York	Occupy	Student
6	Richard	–	42	New York	Occupy	Community organiser
7	Elizabeth	–	46	New York	Occupy	Teacher
8	Thanu	–	27	New York	Occupy	Student
9	Julian	–	25	New York	Occupy	Teacher
10	David	Boardman	33	New York	–	IT designer
11	James	–	22	New York	Occupy	Unemployed
12	Andrew	Conner	26	New York	Occupy	Event organiser
13	Shawn	Carrie	23	New York	Occupy	Unemployed
14	Laurel	–	27	New York	Occupy	Student
15	Emily	Kokernak	36	New York	–	Fundraiser
16	Shane	Gill	32	New York	Occupy	Unemployed
17	Stephanie	–	27	New York	Occupy	Filmmaker
18	Kalle	Lasn	70	Vancouver	Occupy	*Adbusters*' main editor
19	Cari	–	32	New York	Occupy	–
20	Michael	Premo	30	New York	Occupy	Community organiser

EGYPT – REVOLUTIONARY MOVEMENT

	Name	Surname	Age	City	Group	Profession
1	Hannah	El-sissi	22	Cairo		Student
2	Marwa	Hussein	32	Cairo	–	Journalist
3	Ahmed	Samih	38	Cairo	–	NGO worker
4	Noor	Ayman Noor	22	Cairo	–	Musician
5	Kamal	–	28	Cairo	–	Employee
6	Mohammed	'Saidi'	22	Cairo	–	Journalist
7	Nora	Rafea	25	Cairo	–	NGO worker
8	Nora	Shalaby	32	Cairo	Revolutionary Socialist	Archaeologist
9	Sally	Zohney	27	Cairo	–	NGO worker
10	Mahmoud	Al-Banna	24	Cairo	Socialist	Architecture student
11	Mustafa	Al-Shamaa	21	Cairo	Socialist	Student
12	Ahmed	Sabry	41	Cairo	–	Architect
13	Osama	Hoon	42	Cairo	6th of April	Security guard
14	Abdallah	–	26	Cairo	El-Ahly 'ultras'	Accountant
15	Salma	Hegab	21	Cairo	Tweetashare3	Student
16	Mohammed	El-Agati	43	Cairo	Arab Forum for Alternatives	NGO worker
17	Ahmed	Sharquaui	22	Zagazig	6th of April	Student
18	Khaled	–	24	Cairo	–	Teacher
19	Carlos	Latuff	43	Brazil	–	Activist cartoonist
20	Ali	Hamad	22	Cairo	–	Tourism worker

SPAIN – 15-M MOVEMENT

	Name	Surname	Age	City	Group	Profession
1	Laura	Blanco	28	Madrid	–	Researcher
2	Taiz	–	28	Madrid	–	Unemployed
3	Luis	Ordóñez	37	Madrid	–	Self-employed
4	Sofia	de Roa	32	Madrid	EDM	Journalist
5	Segundo	Gonzales	25	Madrid	JSF	Student
6	Asun	Villar	48	Madrid	DRY	Unemployed
7	Aitor	Tinoco	28	Barcelona	DRY	Unemployed
8	Gregorio	Herrero	72	Malaga	–	Retired
9	Feliz	Herrero	70	Malaga	–	Retired
10	Fabio	Gandara	27	Madrid	DRY	Lawyer/Unemployed
11	Pablo	Gallego	23	Madrid	DRY	Unemployed
12	Pablo	Rey Mantoz	32	Madrid/ Boston	–	Researcher
13	Ana	Turull	27	Barcelona	–	Architect
14	Vicente	Martin	33	Barcelona	–	Unemployed
15	Jorge	Izquierdo	36	Barcelona	–	IT worker
16	Helena	Candelas	40	Madrid	–	Unemployed
17	Teresa	Marcos	26	Madrid	–	Freelance web designer
18	Carmen	Haro Barba	24	Madrid	Tabacalera	Researcher
19	Marina	–	28	Madrid	–	Designer
20	Francisco	–	30	Madrid	–	Teacher

BACKGROUND INTERVIEWS (UK, TUNISIA, GREECE)

	Name	Surname	Age	City	Group	Profession
1	Tim	–	28	London	UK Uncut	Student
2	Bernard	Goyer	24	London	Student Movement	Student
3	Kirsten	Forkert	32	London	Student Movement	Lecturer
4	James	Haywood	23	London	Student Movement	Student
5	John	Jordan	43	London	Climate Camp	Activist
6	Brian	–	23	London	Student Movement	Student
7	Ahmed	–	24	Tunis	Revolutionary movement	Student
8	Mohammed	–	42	Tunis	Revolutionary movement	Accountant
9	Haithem	–	28	Tunis	Revolutionary movement	Lecturer
10	Hamza	–	23	Tunis	Revolutionary movement	Student
11	Ismail	–	27	Tunis	Revolutionary movement	Worker

continued

	Name	Surname	Age	City	Group	Profession
12	Fathma	Arrighi	26	Tunis	Revolutionary movement	Employee
13	Ibrahim	–	32	Tunis	Revolutionary movement	Employee
14	Dimitris	–	24	Athens	Aganaktismenoi	Student
15	Krinis	–	42	Athens	Aganaktismenoi	Researcher
16	Erasmos	–	37	Athens	Aganaktismenoi	Student
17	Georgios	–	46	Athens	Aganaktismenoi	Unemployed
18	Nikos	–	27	Athens	Aganaktismenoi	Unemployed
19	Eleni	–	32	Athens	Aganaktismenoi	Teacher
20	Sissy	–	48	Athens	Aganaktismenoi	Politician

Notes

INTRODUCTION

1. 'Tweep' is an expression used to describe a Twitter user.
2. *Time* magazine's 'Person of the Year' cover for 2011 was dedicated to the 'protester'.
3. See for example A. Houslaner, 'Is Egypt About to Have a Facebook Revolution?', *Time*, 24 January 2011; http://www.time.com/time/world/article/0,8599,2044142,00.html
4. http://www.bambuser.com
5. J. Halliday, 'Hillary Clinton Adviser Compares Internet to Che Guevara', *Guardian*, 22 June 2011; http://www.guardian.co.uk/media/2011/jun/22/hillary-clinton-adviser-alec-ross
6. E. Morozov, 'The Brave New World of Slacktivism', *Foreign Policy* (blog), 19 May 2009); http://neteffect.foreignpolicy.com/posts/2009/05/19/the_brave_new_world_of_slacktivism
7. Subcomandante Marcos, 'Marcos is Gay', 5 November 1997; http://www.greenleft.org.au/node/16118
8. See for example A. Nunn, 'Greece: More Than a Demonstration, Less Than a Revolt', *Red Pepper*, April 2012; http://www.redpepper.org.uk/greece-more-than-a-demonstration-less-than-a-revolt
9. See for example Takethesquare.net, 'Call to Unity', 2011; http://gst.maito.name/occupy/squares
10. Expressions like 'spontaneous' and 'leaderless' to describe the popular movements of 2011 abound in many media articles and reports across the different countries considered in this study. See for example H. Gautney, 'What is Occupy Wall Street? Story of a Leaderless Movement', *Washington Post*, 10 October 2011; http://www.washingtonpost.com/national/on-leadership/what-is-occupy-wall-street-the-history-of-leaderless-movements/2011/10/10/gIQAwkFjaL_story.html

CHAPTER 1

1. L. Penny, 'Out with the Old Politics', *Guardian*, 24 December 2010; http://www.guardian.co.uk/commentisfree/2010/dec/24/student-protests-young-politics-voices
2. A. Callinicos, 'Student Demonstrators Can't do it on Their Own', *Guardian*, 26 December 2010; http://www.guardian.co.uk/commentisfree/2010/dec/26/student-protests-laurie-penny
3. M. Castells, 'Fearful Around the World, United on the Web', Lecture delivered at Berkeley University, 27 May 2011; http://takethesquare.net/2011/10/08/conclusions-of-the-speech-of-the-sociologist-manuel-castells-on-15m
4. http://www.meetup.com
5. http://www.doodle.com

CHAPTER 2

1. International Telecommunications Union (2011), *Yearbook of Statistics Telecommunication/ICT Indicators 2001–2010*.
2. See for example F.W. Salah, 'Bloggers' Street Movement and the Right to the City: (Re)claiming Cairo's Real and Virtual "Spaces of Freedom"', *Environment and Urbanization*, 21:1 (January 2009), 89–107.
3. S.M. Shapiro, 'Revolution, Facebook Style', *New York Times*, 22 January 2009; http://www.nytimes.com/2009/01/25/magazine/25bloggers-t.html?pagewanted=all
4. D. Wolman, 'Cairo Activists Use Facebook to Rattle the Regime', *Wired!*, 12 March 2012; http://www.wired.com/techbiz/startups/magazine/16-11/ff_facebookegypt?currentPage=all
5. Tor is the acronym of the Onion Router, which allows users to protect their internet privacy by way of a complex process of encryption to hide the origin, content and destination of messages. For more information visit the project website at https://www.torproject.org
6. The 'ultras' – fans of the Cairo football teams el-Ahly and Zamalek – played a crucial role in the revolution against Mubarak. See for example J. Montague, 'Egypt's Revolutionary Soccer Ultras: How Football Fans Toppled Mubarak' *CNN*, 29 June 2011; http://edition.cnn.com/2011/SPORT/football/06/29/football.ultras.zamalek.ahly/index.html
7. A. Mafhouz, 'Asmaa Mahfouz and the YouTube Video that Helped Spark the Egyptian Uprising', *Democracy Now!*, 19 January 2012; http://www.democracynow.org/2011/2/8/asmaa_mahfouz_the_youtube_video_that
8. http://www.indybay.org/newsitems/2011/01/29/18670645.php
9. Tilly coined the term 'contentious gatherings' to describe the actions of modern social movements (Tilly 1978: 115). A contentious gathering is fundamentally a protest gathering.
10. J. Gilinsky, 'Egyptian "Sandmonkey" Blogger Unmasks Himself in Cairo', *PBS*, 14 February 2011; http://www.pbs.org/mediashift/2011/02/egyptian-sandmonkey-blogger-unmasks-himself-in-cairo045.html
11. Z. El-Gundy, 'Twitter's Role in Revolutionary Egypt: Isolation or Connection?', *El-Ahram*, 10 January 2012; http://english.ahram.org.eg/NewsContent/1/114/32610/Egypt/-January-Revolution-continues/Twitters-role-in-revolutionary-Egypt--isolation-or.aspx

CHAPTER 3

1. My translation from the Spanish of an excerpt from a video of Democracia Real Ya posted on YouTube: Anonymous, 'Porque somos más, toma la calle', 4 April 2012; http://www.youtube.com/watch?v=1SAfFFpGF3E
2. Quotation taken from the YouTube video of the speech delivered by Manuel Castells in Plaza de Catalunya in Barcelona, 27 May 2011; http://www.youtube.com/watch?v=2nWa32CTfxs&feature=related
3. PIIGS is an acronym encompassing Portugal, Ireland, Italy, Greece and Spain, all European countries with a high public debt and/or budget deficit.
4. Bar de tapas are traditional Spanish establishments in which customers are traditionally served free appetizers called 'tapas' to accompany their drinks.

5. See for example this report: 'Ending the Open Season on Artists', *Economist*, 17 February 2011; http://www.economist.com/node/18184458
6. http://www.cinetube.es
7. http://www.seriesyonkis.com
8. J. de la Cueva, 'No les votes', Personal blog, 14 February 2011; http://derecho-internet.org/node/554
9. http://www.juventudsinfuturo.net
10. http://malestarmadrid.wordpress.com
11. http://afectadosporlahipoteca.wordpress.com
12. http://www.democraciarealya.es
13. Democracia Real Ya, *Manifiesto de Democracia Real Ya*, 16 March 2012; http://www.democraciarealya.es/manifiesto-comun
14. http://www.facebook.com/yosoyunjovenespanolquequierelucharporsufuturo
15. http://www.juventudenaccion.info/?p=459
16. Excerpt from the Manifesto of the Facebook group 'Yo soy un/a joven español/a que quiere luchar por su futuro' (I am a Spaniard who wants to fight for his/her future); http://www.facebook.com/yosoyunjovenespanolque quaccerelucharporsufuturo#!/note.php?note_id=163314650381790
17. Excerpt from Pablo Gallego's manifesto 'Un Mayo '68 en Espana es posible' (A May '68 in Spain is possible), 8 February 2011; http://manifiestojuventud. blogspot.com
18. It was not possible to retrieve the Facebook page at the time of writing. Here is a post on the social networking site meneame, publicising the call: http:// www.meneame.net/story/indignate-inminente-convocatoria-plataforma-coordinacion-grupos
19. My translation from the Spanish of an excerpt from a video of Democracia Real Ya posted on YouTube: Anonymous, 'Porque somos más, toma la calle', 4 April 2012; http://www.youtube.com/watch?v=1SAfFFpGF3E
20. Image posted on the Facebook page of Democracia Real Ya.
21. This and the following messages have been selected from a pdf archive of the Facebook page of Democracia Real Ya; http://www.facebook.com/ democraciarealya. The posts are rendered in my own translation from the Spanish.
22. From the website of Zaragoza University's department of Biocomputacion y Fisica de Sistemas Complejos; http://15m.bifi.es
23. J.M. Sánchez Duarte and V. Sampedro Blanco, 'La Red era la plaza', Ciberdemocracia, 27 May 2011; http://www.ciberdemocracia.es/articulos/ RedPlaza.pdf
24. Figure taken from the website of Sol.tv; http://www.soltv.tv/soltv2/index.html
25. F. Garea, 'Apoyo a la indignación del 15-M', *El Pais*, 5 June 2011; http:// politica.elpais.com/politica/2011/06/05/actualidad/1307231940_787459.html

CHAPTER 4

1. B. Berkowitz, 'Occupy: From a Single Hashtag a Protest That Circled the World', Reuters, 18 October 2011; http://www.huffingtonpost.com/2011/10/18/ occupy-wall-street-hashtag_n_1017299.html
2. J. Zeleny and M. Thee-Brean, 'New Poll Finds a Deep Distrust of Government', *New York Times*, 25 October 2011; http://www.nytimes.com/2011/10/26/us/

politics/poll-finds-anxiety-on-the-economy-fuels-volatility-in-the-2012-race.
html

3. See for example this report on the technology news website Betabeat: A. Jeffreys, *Betabeat*, 29 September 2011; http://www.betabeat.com/2011/09/29/vibe-the-anonymous-anarchist-version-of-twitter-being-used-at-occupy-wall-street

4. 'Occupy Wall Street Across the United States, on Foursquare', *Washington Post* website, n.d.; http://www.washingtonpost.com/wp-srv/special/nation/occupy-america-map

5. An example of social media start-ups trying to engage with occupiers is the case of the mass-texting service Celly, as illustrated by this report on the Betabeat website: A. Jeffries, 'Celly: A Mass-Text Social Network for the Occupy Wall Street Movement', *Betabeat*, 18 November 2011; http://www.betabeat.com/2011/11/18/celly-a-mass-text-social-network-for-the-occupy-wall-street-movement

6. B. Jeffrey, 'What's Next for Occupy Wall Street Protests After Judge Bars Camping in Park?' (video), *PBS* website, 15 November 2011; http://www.pbs.org/newshour/bb/business/july-dec11/occupyws_11-15.html

7. R. Pear, 'Top Earners Doubled Share of Nation's Income, Study Finds', *New York Times*, 25 October 2011; http://www.nytimes.com/2011/10/26/us/politics/top-earners-doubled-share-of-nations-income-cbo-says.html

8. F. Norris, 'U.S. Jobless Rate Likely to Pass Europe's', *New York Times*, 22 May 2009; http://www.nytimes.com/2009/05/23/business/economy/23charts.html

9. C. Rampell, 'Jobless Rate Dips to Lowest Level in More Than Two Years', *New York Times*, 2 December 2011; http://www.nytimes.com/2011/12/03/business/economy/us-adds-120000-jobs-unemployment-drops-to-8-6.html

10. http://www.4chan.org

11. #Occupywallstreet: A Shift in Revolutionary Tactics', *Adbusters*, 13 July 2011; http://www.adbusters.org/blogs/adbusters-blog/occupywallstreet.html

12. M. Chafkin, 'Revolution Number 99', *Vanity Fair*, February 2012; http://www.vanityfair.com/politics/2012/02/occupy-wall-street-201202

13. http://www.tomdispatch.com

14. D.W. Chen, 'Bloombergville' *New York Times*, 15 June 2011; http://cityroom.blogs.nytimes.com/2011/06/15/in-bloombergville-budget-protesters-sleep-in

15. M. Chafkin, 'Revolution Number 99', *Vanity Fair*, February 2012; http://www.vanityfair.com/politics/2012/02/occupy-wall-street-201202

16. G. Lotan, '#OccupyWallStreet: Origin and Spread Visualized', *Social Flow* (blog), 18 October 2011; http://blog.socialflow.com/post/7120244404/occupywallstreet-origin-and-spread-visualized

17. E. Chambliss, 'Occupy Twitter: Data Reveal Passion', *Attention USA* (blog), 11 October 2011; http://blog.attentionusa.com/2011/10/occupy-twitter-data-reveals-passion

18. The analysis of Occupy Facebook pages was conducted by archiving the pages as pdf files before conducting qualitative analysis on the text and images posted on them.

19. http://www.facebook.com/OccupyWallSt

20. The data used in the chart was provided by Michael Premo, who currently acts as co-admin of the page, though he was not responsible for managing the page at its inception.

21. The quoted messages were all selected from the main Occupy Wall Street Facebook page http://www.facebook.com/OccupyWallSt.

22. The number of RSVPs mentioned here was that recorded on the Facebook page on 12 January 2012, when the analysis was conducted. In fact it is likely that the number of RSVPs before 17 September 2011, the first day of action against Wall Street, was lower than that, given that the event was left open for further positive RSVPs until 31 December 2011.

23. G. Lotan, 'Data Reveals That Twitter Trending Topics is Harder Than it Looks', *Social Flow* (blog), 12 October 2011; http://blog.socialflow.com/post/7120244374/data-reveals-that-occupying-twitter-trending-topics-is-harder-than-it-looks

24. E. Chambliss, 'Occupy Twitter: Data Reveal Passion', *Attention USA* (blog), 11 October 2011; http://blog.attentionusa.com/2011/10/occupy-twitter-data-reveals-passion

25. The Other 99, 'NYPD Peaceful Female Protestors Penned in the Street and Maced!' (#OccupyWallStreet video), 24 September 2011; http://www.youtube.com/watch?v=moD2JnGTToA&feature=youtu.be

26. All the messages listed here were selected from the collection available on the Tumblr blog; http://wearethe99percent.tumblr.com

27. http://wearethe99percent.tumblr.com

28. Website description available on the homepage of the Tumblr blog; http://wearethe99percent.tumblr.com

29. See for example this article by Marxist autonomist writer Federico Campagna: 'I Am Not the 99%', through-europe (blog), 28 October 2011; http://th-rough.eu/writers/campagna-eng/i-am-not-99

30. G. Tate, 'Top 10 Reasons Why So Few Black Folk Appear Down To Occupy Wall Street', *The Village Voice*. 19 October 2011; http://www.villagevoice.com/2011-10-19/news/greg-tate-top-ten-reasons-why-so-few-blackfolk-appear-down-to-occupy-wall-street

31. B. Wasik, '#Riot: Self-Organized, Hyper-Networked Revolts – Coming to a City Near You', *Wired!*, 16 December 2011; http://www.wired.com/magazine/2011/12/ff_riots/all/1

32. S. Captan, 'Inside Occupy Wall Street Media HQ', *Wired!*, 16 November 2011; http://www.wired.com/threatlevel/2011/11/inside-ows-media-hq

CHAPTER 5

1. Excerpt from a flyer collected on 6 November 2011 at Zuccotti Park in New York.

2. In fact the relationships between popular social movements and traditional organisations have been more complex than the anti-organisational spirit prevalent in activist discourse admits. For example, Occupy Wall Street has collaborated with trade unions, while in the Egyptian uprising organisations like the 6th of April movement and the Muslim Brotherhood played an important role in sustaining the protests.

3. The figures for internet penetration are taken from the International Telecommunications Union (2011), Facebook (2011), and Arab Social Media Report (2011).

4. More information on the 'N menos uno project' can be found on the project's website: https://n-1.cc

5. https://riseup.net

6. https://aktivix.org
7. Tweet by user @Aujo808, 14 November 2011.

CONCLUSION

1. The expression 'anti-leader' was used by D. Bennett in 'David Graeber, the Anti-Leader of Occupy Wall Street', *Bloomberg Business Week*, 26 October 2011; http://www.businessweek.com/magazine/david-graeber-the-antileader-of-occupy-wall-street-10262011.html

Bibliography

Abaza, M. (2011). Cairo's Downtown Imagined: Dubaisation or Nostalgia? *Urban Studies*, 48: 6, 1075–87.

Abdulla, R. (2007). *The Internet in the Arab World: Egypt and Beyond*. New York: Peter Lang.

Aday, S., Farrell, H., Lynch, M., Sides, J., Kelly, J., and Zuckerman, E. (2010). *Blogs and Bullets: New Media in Contentious Politics*. Washington, DC: Institute of Peace.

Adorno, T.W. (1976). *Introduction to the Sociology of Music*. New York: Seabury Press.

Alexander, J.C. (2011). *Performative Revolution in Egypt: An Essay in Cultural Power*. London: Bloomsbury Academic.

Alexander, J.C., Giesen, B., and Mast, J.L. (2006). *Social Performance: Symbolic Action, Cultural Pragmatics, and Ritual*. Cambridge Cultural Social Studies. Cambridge: Cambridge University Press.

Altheide, D.L. (1995). *An Ecology of Communication: Cultural Formats of Control*. New York: Aldine de Gruyter.

Álvarez, K. (2011). *Nosotros, los indignados: Las voces comprometidas del #15-M*. Barcelona: Destino.

Amin, G.A. (2011). *Egypt in the Era of Hosni Mubarak: 1981–2011*. Cairo: American University in Cairo Press.

Anderson, B. (1991). *Imagined Communities: Reflections on the Origin and Spread of Nationalism*. London: Verso.

Arendt, H. (1958). *The Human Condition*. Chicago: University of Chicago Press.

Arquilla, J. and Ronfeldt, D.F. (2001). *Networks and Netwars: The Future of Terror, Crime, and Militancy*. Santa Monica, CA: Rand.

Augé, M. (2006). *Non-Places: Introduction to an Anthropology of Supermodernity*. London: Verso.

Baigorri, A., Fernández, R., and Grupo de Investigación de Estudios Sociales y Territoriales. (2004). *Botellón: Un conflicto posmoderno*. Barcelona: Icaria.

Barker, C., Johnson, A., and Lavalette, M. (2001). *Leadership and Social Movements*. Manchester: Manchester University Press.

Barnett, C. (2003). Neither Poison Nor Cure: Space, Scale and Public Life in Media History. In Couldry, N. and McCarthy, A. (eds), *Mediaspace: Place, Scale and Culture in a Media Age*. London: Routledge.

Barnhurst, K. (2011). The New 'Media Affect' and the Crisis of Representation for Political Communication. *International Journal of Press and Politics*, 16:4, 573–93.

Baudrillard, J. and Poster, M. (1988). *Selected Writings*. Stanford, CA: Stanford University Press.

Bauman, Z. (2000). *Liquid Modernity*. Cambridge: Polity Press.

—— (2001). *The Individualized Society*. Cambridge: Polity Press.

—— (2003). *Liquid Love: On the Frailty of Human Bonds*. Cambridge: Polity Press.

Bayat, A. (2007). *Making Islam Democratic: Social Movements and the Post-Islamist Turn*. Stanford, CA: Stanford University Press.

—— (2010). *Life as Politics: How Ordinary People Change the Middle East.* Stanford, CA: Stanford University Press.

Beck, U. (1992). *Risk Society: Towards a New Modernity.* London: Sage Publications.

Beck, U. and Beck-Gernsheim, E. (2002). *Individualization: Institutionalized Individualism and its Social and Political Consequences.* London: Sage.

Benford, R.D. and Hunt, S.A. (1992). Dramaturgy and Social Movements: The Social Construction and Communication of Power. *Sociological Inquiry*, 62:1, 36–55.

Benkler, Y. (2006). *The Wealth of Networks: How Social Production Transforms Markets and Freedom.* New Haven, CT: Yale University Press.

Bennett, W.L. (2003). New Media Power: The Internet and Global Activism. In Couldry, N. and Currans, J. (eds), *Contesting Media Power.* Lanham, MD: Rowman and Littlefield, pp. 17–37.

Ben-Ze`ev, A. (2004). *Love Online: Emotions on the Internet.* Cambridge: Cambridge University Press.

Borge-Holthoefer, J., Rivero, A., García, I., Cauhé, E., Ferrer, A. et al. (2011) Structural and Dynamical Patterns on Online Social Networks: The Spanish May 15th Movement as a Case Study. *PLoS ONE*, 6:8.

Borgmann, A. (1984). *Technology and the Character of Contemporary Life: A Philosophical Inquiry.* Chicago: University of Chicago Press.

Bourdieu, P. (1984). *Distinction: A Social Critique of the Judgement of Taste.* Cambridge, MA: Harvard University Press.

Boyd, D.M. and Ellison, N.B. (2007). Social Network Sites: Definition, History, and Scholarship. *Journal of Computer-Mediated Communication*, 13:1, 210–30.

Bradley, J.R. (2008). *Inside Egypt: The Land of the Pharaohs on the Brink of a Revolution.* New York: Palgrave Macmillan.

Brenner, N. and Theodore, N. (2002). *Spaces of Neoliberalism: Urban Restructuring in North America and Western Europe.* Malden, MA: Blackwell.

Browers, M. (2007). The Egyptian Movement for Change: Intellectual Antecedents and Generational Conflicts. *Springer Netherlands*, 1:1, 73.

Buechler, S.M. (2000). *Social Movements in Advanced Capitalism: The Political Economy and Cultural Construction of Social Activism.* New York: Oxford University Press.

Burns, T. and Stalker, G.M. (1961). *The Management of Innovation.* London: Tavistock Publications.

Cammermats, B., Mattoni, A., and McCurdy, P. (eds) (2012). *Mediation and Social Movements.* Intellect: Bristol.

Carey, J.W. (1989). *Communication as Culture: Essays on Media and Society.* Boston: Unwin Hyman.

Castells, M. (1983). *The City and the Grassroots: A Cross-Cultural Theory of Urban Social Movements.* Berkeley: University of California Press.

—— (1996). *The Rise of the Network Society.* Malden, MA: Blackwell.

—— (2000). Materials For an Exploratory Theory of the Network Society. *British Journal of Sociology*, 51:1, 5–24.

—— (2004). *The Network Society: A Cross-Cultural Perspective.* Cheltenham: Edward Elgar Pub.

—— (2009). *Communication Power.* Oxford: Oxford University Press.

—— (2012). *Networks of Outrage and Hope: Social Movements in the Internet Age.* Cambridge: Wiley-Blackwell.

Cauter, L. de. (2004). *The Capsular Civilization: On the City in the Age of Fear.* Rotterdam: NAi.

Chayko, M. (2008). *Portable Communities: The Social Dynamics of Online and Mobile Connectedness*. Albany: SUNY Press.

Clausewitz, C. (2004). *Von Clausewitz, On War*. London: Routledge.

Cooren, F. (2000). *The Organizing Property of Communication*. Amsterdam: J. Benjamins.

Cottle, S. (2011). Media and the Arab uprisings of 2011: Research Notes. *Journalism*. 12:5, 647–59.

Couldry, N. (2000). *The Place of Media Power: Pilgrims and Witnesses of the Media Age*. Comedia. London: Routledge.

—— (2003). Passing Ethnographies: Rethinking the Sites of Agency and Reflexivity in a Mediated World. In Murphy, P. and Kraidy, M. (eds), *Global Media Studies: Ethnographic Perspectives*. New York: Routledge.

—— (2004). Theorising Media as Practice. *Social Semiotics*, 14:2, 115–32.

Couldry, N. and McCarthy, A. (2004). *MediaSpace: Place, Scale, and Culture in a Media Age*. Comedia. London: Routledge.

Critical Art Ensemble. (1996). *Electronic Civil Disobedience*. Brooklyn: Autonomedia.

Csordas, T.J. (1994). *Embodiment and Experience: The Existential Ground of Culture and Self*. Cambridge: Cambridge University Press.

Dahlberg, L. (2009). Libertarian Cyber-utopianism and Globalization. In El-Ojeili, C. and Hayden, P. (eds), *Utopia and Globalization*. London: Palgrave, pp. 176–89.

Davis, M. (1992a). Fortress Los Angeles: The Militarization of Urban Space. In Sorkin, M. (ed.), *Variations on a Theme Park*. New York: Noonday Press, pp. 154–80.

—— (1992b). *City of Quartz: Excavating the Future in Los Angeles*. New York: Vintage Books.

—— (1998). *Ecology of Fear: Los Angeles and the Imagination of Disaster*. New York: Metropolitan Books.

Dean, J. (2010). Affective networks. *Media Tropes eJournal*, 2:2, 19–44.

de Cauter, L. (2004). *The Capsular Civilization: On the City in the Age of Fear*. Rotterdam: NAi Publishers.

Deleuze, G. and Guattari, F. (1987). *A Thousand Plateaus: Capitalism and Schizophrenia*. Minneapolis: University of Minnesota Press.

Della Porta, D. (2006). *Globalization From Below: Transnational Activists and Protest Networks*. Minneapolis: University of Minnesota Press.

Della Porta, D. and Diani, M. (2006). *Social Movements: An Introduction*, London: Blackwell.

Della Porta, D. and Sidney T. (eds) (2004). *Transnational Protest and Global Activism*. Lanham, MD: Rowman and Littlefield Publishers.

Doherty, B. (2000). Manufactured Vulnerability: Protest Camp Tactics. In Seel, B., Paterson, M., and Doherty, B. (eds), *Direct Action in British Environmentalism*. London: Routledge, pp. 62–78.

Dubai School of Government (2011a). Facebook Usage: Factors and Analysis. *Arab Social Media Report*, 1:1.

—— (2011b). Civil Movements: The Impact of Facebook and Twitter. *Arab Social Media Report*, 1:2.

—— (2011c). The Role of Social Media in Arab Women's Empowerment. *Arab Social Media Report*, 1:3.

Duncombe, S. (1997). *Notes from Underground: Zines and the Politics of Alternative Culture*. London: Verso.

Dunn, A. (2011). How the Internet Kill Switch Didn't Kill Egypt's Protests. Meta-Activism Project; http://www.meta-activism.org/2011/02/how-the-internet-kill-switch-didnt-kill-egypts-protests

Durkheim, E. (1912/1965). *The Elementary Forms of the Religious Life*. New York: Free Press.

Ellison, B., Lampe, C., Steinfield, C., and Vitak, J. (2011). With a Little Help From my Friends: How Social Network Sites Affect Social Capital Processes. In Papacharissi, Z. (ed.), *A Networked Self: Identity, Community and Culture on Social Network Sites*. New York: Routledge.

Ellul, J. (1964). *The Technological Society*. New York: Knopf.

Eltahawy, M. (2010). Generation Mubarak/Generation Facebook. *Huffington Post*, 25 June; http://www.huffingtonpost.com/mona-eltahawy/generationmubarakge nerat_b_625409.html

Eurostat (2011). Labour Market. *Eurostat Yearbook 2011*. Brussels: Eurostat.

Evans, S.M. and Boyte, H.C. (1986). *Free Spaces: The Sources of Democratic Change in America*. New York: Harper and Row.

Eyerman, R. (2006). Performing Opposition or, How Social movements Move. In Alexander, J.C., Giesen, B., and Mast, J.L. (eds), *Social Performance: Symbolic Action, Cultural Pragmatics, and Ritual*. Cambridge: Cambridge University Press.

Eyerman, R. and Jamison, A. (1991). *Social Movements: A Cognitive Approach*. Cambridge: Polity Press in association with Basil Blackwell.

Fanon, F. (1965). *The Wretched of the Earth*. New York: Grove Press.

—— (1967). *A Dying Colonialism*. New York: Grove Press.

Feigenbaum, A., Frenzel, F., and McCurdy, P. (forthcoming). *Protest Camps*. London: Zed.

Foster, S.L. (2003). Choreographies of Protest. *Theatre Journal*, 55:3, 395–412.

Freeman, J. (1972). The Tyranny of Structurelessness. *Berkeley Journal of Sociology*, 17: 151–64.

Fukuyama, F. (1992). *The End of History and the Last Man*. New York: Free Press.

Gamson, W.A. (1995). Constructing Social Protest. In Johnston, H. and Klandermans B. (eds), *Social Movements and Culture*. Minneapolis: University of Minnesota Press, pp. 85–106.

Gerbaudo, P. (2010). *Navigating the Rebel Archipelago: Space, Communication and Participation in the Autonomous Scene*. Unpublished doctoral dissertation. Goldsmiths College, London.

Ghonim, W. (2012). *Revolution 2.0: The Power of the People is Greater than the People in Power: A Memoir*. Boston: Houghton Mifflin Harcourt.

Gitlin, T. (1998). Public Sphere or Public Sphericules? In Curran, J. and Liebes, T. (eds), *Media, Ritual and Identity*. London: Routledge, pp. 168–75.

Gladwell, M. (2010). Small Change: Why the Revolution Will Not be Tweeted. *New Yorker*, 4 October.

Goffman, E. (1959). *The Presentation of Self in Everyday Life*. Garden City, NY: Doubleday.

—— (1974). *Frame Analysis: An Essay on the Organization of Experience*. New York: Harper and Row.

Goodwin, J., Jasper, J.M., and Polletta, F. (2001). *Passionate Politics: Emotions and Social Movements*. Chicago: University of Chicago Press.

Gordon, E., and de Souza Silva, A.S. (2011). *Net Locality: Why Location Matters in a Networked World*. Chichester, West Sussex: Wiley-Blackwell.

Graeber, D. (2002) The New Anarchists, *New Left Review*, 13 (second series), 61–74.

—— (2009). *Direct Action: An Ethnography*. Edinburgh: AK Press.

Gramsci, A., Hoare, Q., and Smith, G.N. (1971). *Selections From the Prison Notebooks*. London: Lawrence and Wishart.

Granovetter, M.S. (1974). *Getting a Job: A Study of Contacts and Careers*. Cambridge, MA: Harvard University Press.

Habermas, J. (1987). *The Theory of Communicative Action*. Cambridge: Polity Press.

—— (1996). *Between Facts and Norms: Contributions to a Discourse Theory of Law and Democracy*. Cambridge, MA: MIT Press.

Hands, J. (2011). *@ is for Activism: Dissent, Resistance and Rebellion in a Digital Culture*. London: Pluto.

Hardt, M. and Negri, A. (2000). *Empire*. Cambridge, MA: Harvard University Press.

—— (2005). *Multitude: War and Democracy in the Age of Empire*. New York: Penguin Books.

—— (2009). *Commonwealth*. Cambridge, MA: Belknap Press of Harvard University Press.

Haunss, S. and Leach, D. (2009). Scenes and Social Movements. In Johnston, H. (ed.), *Culture, Social Movements, and Protest*. Farnham: Ashgate.

Heidegger, M. (1971). *Poetry, Language, Thought*. New York: Harper and Row.

Hessel, S. (2010). *Indignez-vous!* Montpellier: Indigène éd.

Hofheinz, A. (2005). The Internet in the Arab world: Playground for Political Liberalisation. *International Politics and Society*, 3, 78–96.

International Telecommunication Union. (2010). *Monitoring the WSIS Targets: A Mid-term Review*. Geneva: ITU.

—— (2011). *World Telecommunication/ICT Indicators Database 2011* (15th Edition) [Data file]. Geneva: ITU; http://www.itu.int/ITU-D/ict/publications/world/world.html

Invisible Committee. (2009). *The Coming Insurrection*. New York: Semiotext(e).

Jansson, A. (2007). Encapsulations. *Space and Culture*, 10:4, 418–36.

Jasper, J. M. (2011). Emotions and Social Movements: Twenty Years of Theory and Research. *Annual Review of Sociology*, 37, 285–303.

Jenkins, H. (2006). *Convergence Culture: Where Old and New Media Collide*. New York: New York University Press.

Johnston, H. and Klandermans, B. (1995). *Social Movements and Culture*. Minneapolis: University of Minnesota Press.

Jordan, J. (1998). The Art of Necessity: The Subversive Imagination of Anti-Road Protest and Reclaim the Streets. In McKay, G. (ed.), *DiY culture: Party and Protest in Nineties' Britain*. London: Verso.

Jordan, T. (2002). *Activism!: Direct Action, Hac[k]tivism and the Future of Society*. London: Reaktion Books.

Jordan, T. and Taylor, P.A. (2004). *Hacktivism and Cyberwars: Rebels With a Cause?* London: Routledge.

Juris, J.S. (2005). The New Digital Media and Activist Networking within Anti-Corporate Globalisation Movements, *Annals of the AAPSS*, 597:1, 189–208.

—— (2008). *Networking Futures: The Movements Against Corporate Globalization*. Durham, NC: Duke University Press.

—— (2012). Reflections on #Occupy Everywhere: Social media, public space, and emerging logics of aggregation. *American Ethnologist*, 39:2, 259–79.

Kamalipour, Y.R. and Hamelink, C.J. (2010). *Media, Power, and Politics in the Digital Age: The 2009 Presidential election Uprising in Iran*. Lanham, MD: Rowman and Littlefield.

Kaplan, A. and Haenlein, M. (2010). Users of the World, Unite! The Challenges and Opportunities of Social Media. *Business Horizons*, 53:1, 59–68.

Kellner, D. (2012). *Media Spectacle 2011: From the Arab Uprisings to Occupy Everywhere!* London: Continuum.

Kelty, C.M. (2008). *Two Bits: The Cultural Significance of Free Software*. Durham, NC: Duke University Press.

Kirkpatrick, D. (2010). *The Facebook Effect: And How it is Changing Our Lives*. London: John Murray.

Klandermans, B. (1984). Mobilization and Participation: Social-Psychological Expansions of Resource Mobilization Theory. *American Sociological Review*, 49:5, 583–600.

—— (1985). Individuals and Collective Action. *American Sociological Review*, 50:6, 860–61.

—— (2004). The Demand and Supply of Participation: Social-Psychological Correlates of Participation in Social Movements. In Snow, D.A., Soule, S.A., and Kriesi, H. (eds), *The Blackwell Companion to Social Movements*. Malden, MA: Blackwell.

Klandermans, B. and Oegema, D. (1987). Potentials, Networks, Motivations, and Barriers: Steps Towards Participation in Social Movements. *American Sociological Review*, 52:4, 519–31.

Klein, N. (2000). *No Logo: No Space, No Choice, No Jobs*. New York: Picador.

—— (2002). Farewell to the 'End of History': Organization and Vision in Anti-Corporate Movements, *Socialist Register*, 13.

Kohn, M. (2003). *Radical Space: Building the House of the People*. Ithaca: Cornell University Press.

Konijn, E. (2008). *Mediated Interpersonal Communication*. New York: Routledge.

Kriesi, H., Koopmans, R., Duyvendak, J.W., and Giugni, M.G. (1995). *New Social Movements in Western Europe A Comparative Analysis*. London: Routledge.

Laclau, E. (1990). *New Reflections on the Revolution of our Time*. London: Verso.

—— (1996). *Emancipation(s)*. New York: Verso.

—— (2005). *On Populist Reason*. London: Verso.

Laclau, E. and Mouffe, C. (1985). *Hegemony and Socialist Strategy: Towards a Radical Democratic Politics*. London: Verso.

Latour, B. (2005). *Reassembling the Social: An Introduction to Actor-Network-Theory*. Oxford: Oxford University Press.

Lefebvre, H. (1974/1991) *The Production of Space*, Malden, MA: Blackwell.

Lenin, V.I. (1902/1969). *What is to be Done?: Burning Questions of our Movement*. New York: International Publishers.

Lichterman, P. (1996). *The Search for Political Community: American Activists Reinventing Commitment*. Cambridge: Cambridge University Press.

Lievrouw, L.A. (2011). *Alternative and Activist New Media*. Cambridge: Polity.

Ling, R.S. (2004). *The Mobile Connection: The Cell Phone's Impact on Society*. San Francisco: Morgan Kaufmann.

Ling, R.S. and Campbell, S.W. (2011). *Mobile Communication: Bringing us Together and Tearing us Apart*. New Brunswick, NJ: Transaction Publishers.

Lim, M. (2012). Clicks, Cabs, and Coffee Houses: Social Media and Oppositional Movements in Egypt, 2004–2011. *Journal of Communication*, 62, 231–48.

Livingstone, S. (2008). Taking Risky Opportunities in Youthful Content Creation: Teenagers' Use of Social Networking Sites for Intimacy, Privacy and Self-expression. *New Media and Society*, 10:3, 393–411.

Lum, C.M.K. (2006). *Perspectives on Culture, Technology and Communication: The Media Ecology Tradition*. Cresskill, NJ: Hampton Press.

McAdam, D. (1988). *Freedom Summer*. New York: Oxford University Press.

McCaughey, M. and Ayers, M.D. (2003). *Cyberactivism: Online Activism in Theory and Practice*. New York: Routledge.

McCurdy, P., (2008). Inside the Media Event: Examining the Media Practices of Dissent! at the Hori-Zone Eco-village at the 2005 G8 Gleneagles Summit. *Communications: European Journal of Communication Research*, 33: 293–311.

McDonald, K. (1999). From Solidarity to Fluidarity: Social Movements Beyond 'Collective Identity' – The Case of Globalization Conflicts. *Social Movement Studies*, 1:2, 1474–2837.

—— (2006). *Global Movements*. Oxford: Blackwell.

McKay, G. (1998). *DiY Culture: Party and Protest in Nineties' Britain*. London: Verso.

Marwell, G., Oliver, P.E., and Prahl, R. (1988). Social Networks and Collective Action: A Theory of the Critical Mass. III. *American Journal of Sociology*, 94:3, 502–34.

Mason, P. (2012). *Why it's Kicking Off Everywhere: The New Global Revolutions*. London: Verso.

Mattelart, A. (1996). *The Invention of Communication*. Minneapolis: University of Minnesota Press.

—— (2003). *The Information Society: An Introduction*. London: Sage.

Mattoni, A. (2012). *Media Practices and Protest Politics: How Precarious Workers Mobilise*. Burlington, VT: Ashgate.

Mazzarella, W. (2010). The Myth of the Multitude, or, Who's Afraid of the Crowd? *Critical Inquiry*, 36:4, 697–727.

Melucci, A. (1996a). *Challenging Codes: Collective Action in the Information Age*. Cambridge: Cambridge University Press.

—— (1996b). *The Playing Self: Person and Meaning in the Planetary Society*. Cambridge: Cambridge University Press.

—— (1996c). Individual Experience and Global Issues in a Planetary Society. *Social Science Information*, 35:3, 485.

Meyer, D.S. (2004). Protest and Political Opportunities. *Annual Review of Sociology*, 30, 125–45.

Michels, R. (1999). *Political Parties: A Sociological Study of the Oligarchical Tendencies of Modern Democracy*. New Brunswick, NJ: Transaction Publishers.

Miles, H. (2011). The Al Jazeera Effect. *Foreign Policy*, 8 February; http://www.foreignpolicy.com/articles/2011/02/08/the_al_jazeera_effect

Mitchell, D. (1995). The End of Public Space? People's Park, Definitions of the Public, and Democracy. *Annals of the Association of American Geographers*, 85:1, 108.

Morozov, E. (2011). *The Net Delusion: The Dark Side of Internet Freedom*. New York: PublicAffairs.

Negri, A. (1989). *The Politics of Subversion: A Manifesto for the Twenty-First Century*. Cambridge: Polity Press.

Nichols, B. (1994). *Blurred Boundaries: Questions of Meaning in Contemporary Culture*. Bloomington: Indiana University Press.

Novack, C.J. (1990). *Sharing the Dance: Contact Improvisation and American Culture*. University of Wisconsin Press.

Nunns, A., Idle, N. and Soueif, A. (2011). *Tweets From Tahrir: Egypt's Revolution as it Unfolded, in the Words of the People who Made it*. New York: OR Books.

Oberschall, A. (1973). *Social Conflict and Social Movements*. Englewood Cliffs, NJ: Prentice-Hall.

—— (1978). Theories of Social Conflict. *Annual Review of Sociology*, 4, 291–315.

Oegema, D. and Klandermans, B. (1994). Why Social Movement Sympathizers Don't Participate: Erosion and Nonconversion of Support. *American Sociological Review*, 59:5, 703–22.

Osman, T. (2010). *Egypt on the Brink: From Nasser to Mubarak*. New Haven: Yale University Press.

Papacharissi, Z. (2002). The Virtual Sphere: The Internet as a Public Sphere. *Communication Abstracts*, 25:5, 591–750.

—— (2010). *A Private Sphere: Democracy in a Digital Age*. Cambridge: Polity Press.

Peterson, M.A. (2011). *Connected in Cairo: Growing up Cosmopolitan in the Modern Middle East*. Bloomington: Indiana University Press.

Pickerill, J. (2003). *Cyberprotest: Environmental Activism Online*. Manchester: Manchester University Press.

—— (2006). Radical Politics on the Net, *Parliamentary Affairs*, 59:2, 266–82.

Poster, M. (2001). *What's the Matter With the Internet*. Minneapolis: University of Minnesota Press.

Putnam, R.D. (2000). *Bowling Alone: The Collapse and Revival of American Community*. New York: Simon and Schuster.

Rheingold, H. (1993). *The Virtual Community: Homesteading on the Electronic Frontier*. Reading, MA: Addison-Wesley Pub.

—— (2003). *Smart Mobs: The Next Social Revolution*. Cambridge: Perseus.

Rudé, G.F.E. (1964). *The Crowd in History: A Study of Popular Disturbances in France and England, 1730–1848*. New York: Wiley.

Sampedro Blanco, V.F. and Haro, C. (2011). Activismo politico en Red: del Movimiento por la Vivienda Digna al 15M. *Teknokultura: revista de cultura digital y movimientos sociales*; http://teknokultura.com/index.php/tk/article/download/14/pdf

Sennett, R. (1977). *The Fall of Public Man*. New York: Knopf.

Schneekloth, L.H. and Shibley, R.G. (1995). *Placemaking: The Art and Practice of Building Communities*. New York: Wiley.

Shirky, C. (2008). *Here Comes Everybody: The Power of Organizing Without Organizations*. New York: Penguin Press.

—— (2010). *Cognitive Surplus: Creativity and Generosity in a Connected Age*. New York: Penguin Press.

—— (2011). The Political Power of Social Media. *Foreign Affairs*, January/February.

Singerman, D. (2009). *Cairo Contested: Governance, Urban Space, and Global Modernity*. Cairo: American University in Cairo Press.

Singerman, D. and Amar, P. (2006). *Cairo Cosmopolitan: Politics, Culture, and Urban Space in the New Globalized Middle East*. Cairo: American University in Cairo Press.

Sloterdijk, P. and Hoban, W. (2011). *Bubbles: Microspherology*. Cambridge, MA: Semiotext(e).

Snow, S.A., Soule, S.A., and Kriesi, H. (2004). *The Blackwell Companion to Social Movements*, Oxford: Blackwell.

Taylor, A. (2011). *Occupy!: Scenes from Occupied America*. London: Verso!

Tarrow, S. (1994). *Power in Movement: Social Movements, Collective Action, and Politics*. Cambridge: Cambridge University Press.

—— (1998). Fishnets, Internets, Catnets: Globalization and Transnational Collective Action. In M. Hanagan, Page L. Moch, and W.Te Brake (eds), *Challenging Authority: The Historical Study of Contentious Politics*. Minneapolis: University of Minnesota Press, pp. 228–44.

—— (2005). *The New Transnational Activism*, Cambridge: Cambridge University Press.

Thompson, J.B. (1995). *The Media and Modernity: A Social Theory of the Media*. Stanford, CA: Stanford University Press.

Tilly, C. (1978). *From Mobilization to Revolution*. Reading, MA: Addison-Wesley Pub.

—— (2000). Spaces of Contention. *Mobilization*, 5:2, 135–59.

—— (2003). *The Politics of Collective Violence*. Cambridge: Cambridge University Press.

—— (2008). *Contentious Performances*. Cambridge: Cambridge University Press.

Tilly, L. and Tilly, C. (1981). *Class Conflict and Collective Action*. Beverly Hills: Sage.

Tufekci, Z. and Wilson, C. (2012). Social Media and the Decision to Participate in Political Protest: Observations from Tahrir Square. *Journal of Communication*, 62:2, 363–79.

Van de Donk, W., Loader, B.D., Nixon, P.G., and Rucht, D. (2004). *Cyberprotest: New Media, Citizens and Social Movements*. London: Routledge.

Vaneigem, R. and Nicholson-Smith, D. (1983). *The Revolution of Everyday Life*. Seattle: Left Bank Books.

Van Gelder, S. (2011). *This Changes Everything: Occupy Wall Street and the 99% Movement*. San Francisco: Berrett-Koehler Publishers.

Virno, P. (2004). *A Grammar of the Multitude: For an Analysis of Contemporary Forms of Life*. New York: Semiotext(e).

Weber, M., Roth, G., and Wittich, C. (1978). *Economy and Society: An Outline of Interpretive Sociology*. Berkeley: University of California Press.

Wellman, B. and Haythornthwaite, C.A. (2002). *The Internet in Everyday Life*. Malden, MA: Blackwell.

Wellman, B., Quan-Haase, A., Boase, J., Chen, W., Hampton, K., de Diaz, I.I. et al. (2003). The Social Affordances of the Internet for Networked Individualism. *Journal of Computer-Mediated Communication*, 8:3.

White, M. (2010). Clicktivism is Ruining Leftist Activism. *Guardian*, 2 August; http://www.guardian.co.uk/commentisfree/2010/aug/12/clicktivism-ruining-leftist-activism

—— (2011). To the Barricades! *Adbusters*, 4 March; http://www.adbusters.org/magazine/94/barricades.html

Wilson, C. and Dunn, A. (2011). Digital Media in the Egyptian Revolution: Descriptive Analyses From the Tahrir Data Set. *International Journal of Communication*, 5, 1248–72.

Wright, R. (2011). *Rock the Casbah: Rage and Rebellion Across the Islamic World*. New York: Simon and Schuster.

Writers for the 99%. (2012). *Occupying Wall Street: The Inside Story of an Action That Changed America*. Chicago: Haymarket Books.

Zuckerman, E. (2008). The Cute Cat Theory (blog entry); http://www.ethanzuckerman.com/blog/2008/03/08/the-cute-cat-theory-talk-at-etech

Index

6th of April Youth, Egyptian protest
group, 53–4, 60–1, 63, 142, 164
16 Beaver, activist space in New York,
112
'99%', Occupy Wall Street slogan, 10,
102–3, 116–7, 120, 149

ABC No Rio, activist space in New
York, 112
activism, 5, 19, 25, 40, 107
activist community, 72–4, 112;
impact of new media on, 20, 22;
digital, 53, 56, 65, 75, 80, 92, 96,
107, 142, 148, 159; clicktivism,
102; slacktivism, 7, 109
see also mobilisation, organisation
Adbusters, 102–4, 108–12, 113, 114,
117, 119–20, 131–2, 142
el-Ahly, football club, Egypt
ultras, 58, 72, 142
'ahwa, Egyptian coffee-shops, 51
aktivix, activist mailing list service,
124
Alexander, Jeffrey, 40
Alexandria, 46, 51, 53, 60, 61, 66, 67
Ali, Zine El Abedine Ben, president of
Tunisia, 46, 60
Al-Jazeera, 50, 69, 75
The Stream, 6, 138
American University in Cairo (AUC),
55, 72
Amin, Galal, 70
anarchism
in the anti-globalisation movement,
23; in contemporary movements,
112–13, 131, 132, 138, 143, 144,
162
Anderson, Benedict, 8
Android, 162
anti-globalisation movement, 6, 36,
99, 139, 143, 150
and counter-summit protests, 167;
and minoritarianism, 10–11, 86,

120; and networks, 23–5; and
subcultural identity, 85, 119, and
the valuing of diversity, 11, 14
Anonymous, hacker group, 107–8
Arab Spring, 4, 6, 8, 11, 26, 58, 76,
112
Arendt, Hannah
on the space of appearance, 38, 39
ashwaa'iyyat, Egyptian slums, 32
Assange, Julian, 107
assembly
as a process, 27, 38; right of, 32, 51,
79, 105, 137; general, G.A.,
94–5, 99, 112–3, 129, 131
see also gathering, public space
ATTAC, 86
Augé, Marc, 25
Aznar, José María, 83
Azzellini, Dario, 139

Bakunin, Mikhail, 143
Bambuser, 3
Barlow, John Perry, 158
Bastille, square, Paris, 156
Bauman, Zygmunt, 12, 21
on the crisis of public space, 31–2;
on individualisation, 12, 29, 30;
and the notion of 'liquidity', 13,
29, 138; on 'virtual proximity',
33
Beck, Ulrich
on individualisation, 12, 29, 30,
120
Benkler, Yochai, 143
blogs, 14, 52, 132, 149, 159
bloggers, 46, 48, 89; in Egypt, 50,
51, 52, 55, 57, 68, 73; in Spain,
80, 83, 89; in the US, 117–19
Bloomberg, Michael, Mayor of New
York, 105, 112
Bloombergville, protest camp, 112
Bologna, Anthony, NYPD officer, 117
Borgman, Albert, 155